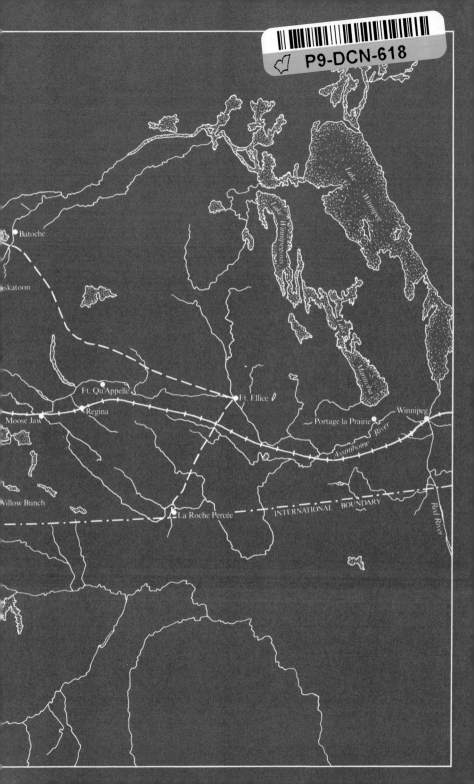

John K Smith

FEB. 1980

Sam Steele: Lion of the Frontier

Also by Robert Stewart

LABRADOR

Sam Steele:
Lion of the Frontier

Robert Stewart

Doubleday Canada Limited, Toronto, Ontario
Doubleday & Company, Inc., Garden City, New York
1979

Library of Congress Cataloging in Publication Data

Stewart, Robert.
Sam Steele, lion of the frontier.

Bibliography: p. 285
Includes index.
1. Steele, Samuel Benfield, Sir, 1849–1919.
2. Police—Canada—Biography. 3. Canada. Royal
Canadian Mounted Police.   I. Title.
HV7911.S77S73   363.2′092′4 [B]
ISBN: 0-385-13598-X
Library of Congress Catalog Card Number 77–27718

FOR RED

CONTENTS

PART THREE: Calls of Destiny

Part One

AT THE CREATION

1: A REGULAR YOUNG GENT

He was only a boy—a big, strong lad to be sure, but still floundering in adolescence. His flesh had not yet filled out his six-foot frame, and he moved with the awkwardness of a colt. So it took some self-effacement for the leading citizens of the village of Clarksburg, Ontario, to approach this sixteen-year-old store clerk to take command of the local militia company. Still, no man there was better qualified for the job than young Sam Steele.

An army officer in the 1860s had to be able to ride, and no one who had seen the Steele boy in the saddle could deny that he was a first-class horseman. An officer had to teach musketry; Steele was a crack shot who handled the heavy muzzle-loaders of the day with fluid ease. Moreover, the young man possessed all the formal qualifications for command of a small militia unit. He held a commission as an ensign and qualified on paper for the rank of major. He had topped his class in the British Army officer's courses, scoring 100 per cent in discipline and drill, and he had already seen active service in the recent Fenian campaign. Finally, Sam Steele alone had shown the initiative to organize the Clarksburg Company of the 35th Canadian Militia Regiment. He was the obvious choice to lead the unit he had formed.

But when they tried to appoint him, Steele told them he was too young for the responsibility. He said the local captain should be a prominent member of the community; there were many men thereabouts who deserved the honour more.

The elders of Clarksburg were impressed by the broad-shouldered youth's selfless gesture. It was the act of a gentleman, and in that thirtieth year of Queen Victoria's reign, gentlemanliness counted for a great deal. They were rugged men, these Canadian pioneers; but they were also civil men, adhering to the social conventions that governed behaviour in the old country. The traditional British class distinctions had been eroded somewhat by the conditions of life on this frontier, but a gentleman was still a gentleman, set apart from the rest.

It was much more than just a matter of having the right manners. A gentleman enjoyed privileges, but they had to be earned. A gentleman bore a heavy load of social responsibilities and followed an elaborate code of behaviour—at least in public. For the most part those who flouted the code were branded "black sheep," ostracized and even exiled for the grievous offence of letting down one's class.

To be a gentleman, then, was to shoulder one's duty to society. It was to be willing to serve one's country at the risk of one's life. To be a gentleman was to be a living example to the less fortunate: to be a man of one's word, a man of affairs, of justice, of religion, of learning. To be a gentleman was, in fact, to be very much like Sam's late father, Captain Elmes Steele, R.N., retired.

Elmes Steele was one of six sons of a physician in Coleford, Gloucestershire, England. Three became officers in the Navy and three in the Army. Of Elmes's sailor brothers, one was drowned in a sinking in the Baltic, and the other was assistant surgeon aboard the *Victory* at Trafalgar. The soldiers in the family campaigned throughout the Napoleonic Wars; one died of wounds sustained at Waterloo. Another was known as the tallest man in the British occupying forces in Paris after Napoleon's downfall. Elmes himself was a handsome, clean-shaven, blue-eyed man of five feet ten whose ruddy face showed the effects of many years at sea.

Sam's father joined the Royal Navy as an officer candidate on the H.M.S. *Triton* in 1798. He won distinction his first time in action. While *Triton* was attacking the Spanish frigate *Santa Brigida* off Cape Finisterre, Midshipman Steele perceived that the Spaniards had changed course in an attempt to lure the British ship onto a reef. He warned the captain and saved the ship. The *Santa Brigida* was duly captured. It yielded the richest haul of booty ever taken by the Royal Navy in a single fight up to that time.

Some years later when he was master's mate of the H.M.S. *Caroline*, Steele was ordered to sail a captured French ship called *La Bonne Mère* back to England. His crew broke into the spirits room and got drunk, enabling the French crew to recapture the ship. The French lost their reckoning, however, and called on Steele to help them navigate. He gave them false bearings, then managed to spring the hatches and release his crew. "Do not strike or hurt an unarmed man, or I will pistol the one who does it! You lost the ship by your rascality," he told the crestfallen English sailors. They recaptured the French vessel and sailed it to Cork, where Steele was awarded freedom of the city.

Steele was in action several times during the Napoleonic Wars, once leading a bold commandolike raid on a French shore station. He also had the odd distinction of firing the shot that led to a war. This was in 1807, when, as lieutenant of H.M.S. *Leopard*, he ordered his gun crew to put a shot across the bows of the U.S.S. *Chesapeake*. When the American vessel made a run for it, he commanded a broadside against her that killed three American sailors and wounded eighteen. The *Leopard* seized four sailors from the *Chesapeake*, claiming they were deserters from the Royal Navy. Searching for a pretext to invade Canada in 1812, President James Madison picked on the right of search by British vessels, singling out the *Chesapeake* incident. Although they had merely followed standing orders, the *Leopard*'s officers were blamed for dragging England into an unwanted conflict. Their promotion was blocked and their pay cut in half.

For all his swashbuckling, the elder Steele was an erudite and urbane man who led a life of cultivated leisure in the south of France after taking early retirement. By then he had married the former Elizabeth Seeley Coucher of Bath, whose family owned the property in London that is now 10 Downing Street. The Steeles fled France during the revolution of 1830. Two years later Captain Steele became one of a number of retired officers to take up an offer by Governor Sir John Colborne, a hero of the Napoleonic Wars, of land grants in Upper Canada. On the way across the Atlantic there occurred another typical Elmes Steele episode. The master of the *Blanches* panicked as the vessel threaded

its way through a foggy sea of icebergs. Steele assumed command
and saw the ship through.

He was allotted 1,000 acres in Simcoe County and went to work
clearing boulders, felling trees, and pulling up stumps like any
other pioneer farmer. He built a fine, big house of cedar logs with
broad verandas, which he named Purbrook after the birthplace of
his wife. In the wilds of the New World he set about duplicating
the life of the landed gentry in England. He donated the land for,
and financed construction of, Medonte County's first Anglican
church. He became a magistrate, a member of the Assembly, and
colonel of the county militia. In the Assembly he promoted the
building of the Trent Canal and the first highway between
Toronto and Orillia.

Captain Steele was a man of fifty-one with a family of six when
he emigrated. His wife died in 1846. Two years later he married
Anne Macdonald, daughter of Neil MacIan Macdonald of Islay,
Scotland, one of a long line of Highland Army officers. The first
of his second family was born at Purbrook on January 5, 1851.
The infant boy was christened Samuel Benfield: Samuel after his
paternal great-grandfather, Benfield after his paternal grand-
mother's family. Sam's mother died at the age of twenty-nine,
when he was nine years old.

The bereaved family moved into Orillia, which only a few years
before had been an Indian encampment. Because they came from
an isolated homestead, the Steele children had never been to
school as such. But dutiful man that he was, Captain Steele had
stocked Purbrook with school books and had personally tutored his
children from a very early age. Sam's homemade education soon
carried him to the top of his class at the private school in Orillia
run by an old English gentleman and his wife. The wife taught
Sam and his brothers to speak French.

In his spare time the boy was learning the skills of a woodsman,
building brush lean-tos, fishing, tracking and shooting game, rac-
ing down rivers in canoes, tramping the woods in winter on snowshoes. Sam swam, skated, and boxed bareknuckled. His reminiscences of boyhood give a picture of a kind of Canadian Tom
Sawyer, roaming the woods with his young cousins, building huts
and rafts, making their own powder and shot.

When Sam was eleven, his father returned to the farm. The

boy then came under the influence of another Victorian gentleman. His new mentor was his half brother, John Coucher Steele, who had taken the children into his Orillia home. More than thirty years Sam's senior, John Steele was a model old-fashioned sportsman. He was celebrated as a marksman, said to be able to shoot the heads off two partridges at a time. From him Sam learned how to keep his seat on a high-spirited horse and to clamp his big octagonal-barrelled rifle tightly to his shoulder lest the kick knock him flying. As Sam Steele gratefully wrote of his half brother fifty years later in his autobiography, *Forty Years in Canada*, "an association with him would have been an advantage to any lad."

Elmes Steele died at eighty-four in August 1865. Sam had then turned fourteen, and the scent of battle was in the air of colonial Canada. The Fenian campaign to win home rule for Ireland by raiding Canada from bases in the United States was growing dangerously active. An armed force was being raised to fight the Fenians. For a fatherless and adventurous youth from a military family the natural course was to enlist. Extraordinarily big and mature for his age, he was able to join the militia by convincing the recruiting officer that he was sixteen.

His company saw no action in the Fenian campaign, but Sam made the best of his time in uniform by taking his officer's courses in Toronto. He might have joined the regular British Army then, but being a professional officer in Victorian days was an expensive proposition, and his family was relatively poor.

Hence the year 1867 found Sam Steele employed as a clerk in Mr. Turnbull's store in the village of Clarksburg, near Orillia. Down the road in the tavern, the talk was all of the confederation of Nova Scotia, New Brunswick, Quebec, and Ontario, to be formalized July 1. Doubtless there were those who remarked over their pots of ale that Premier John A. Macdonald was taking a wild political gamble. And when the talk turned to local matters, we can imagine them agreeing, in the idiom of rural Ontario, that that young fellow Sam Steele was a "regular young gent."

2: CALL TO ARMS

Nothing better conveys the spirit of brashness with which Canada's Fathers of Confederation brought the new nation into the world than the grandiose official name they bestowed on it: the Dominion of Canada. The term *dominion* was plucked out of the Bible: "He shall have dominion also from sea to sea." It was outright presumption. Far from holding sway from sea to sea, the new nation trailed off indeterminately into the forbidding wilderness west of Lake Superior. It would be two years before an agreement could be concluded under which the British Government would purchase the immense territory of Rupert's Land from the Hudson's Bay Company with a view to turning it over to Canada. British Columbia would not be enticed into the Canadian confederation until 1871.

In the meantime there was always a danger that the sparsely inhabited reaches of western British North America might fall into the all-too-willing hands of the United States, whether by design or by default. Canada had neither the economic nor the military means to win the West, and few people in eastern Canada cared whether it was won or not. They were not especially progressive, they cared about their own plots of land first, and they hated paying taxes. The logical course for the government was to consolidate the fragile union they had formed in the East and leave the West be.

In retrospect it is next to amazing that they did not follow just this course, that as hardheaded politicians they did not quietly slide the dream of a continental nation onto the back burner. But just as Sam Steele chafed at the confinements of a Dickensian clerk's life in pioneer Ontario, the nation builders of Ottawa could hardly keep their restlessness in check. Had they been a little less impatient to burst Canada's territorial bonds, Steel might have settled down to the life of a small-town businessman, giving vent to his martial instincts by acting as a spare-time soldier in the local militia. But as it turned out, Ottawa could not wait to plunge westward, and Sam Steele could not wait to join in the plunge.

The ink was scarcely dry on the Rupert's Land agreement of March 1869 before Canadian Government surveyors were bustling about the Red River colony, still formally the property of the Hudson's Bay Company, laying out lots in the British "block" fashion against the grain of the traditional French-Canadian system of "strip" land holdings, which ran down to the front of the river. This raised fears among the inhabitants that their land and rights would be taken away. Then, in a stunning show of political insensitivity, a dim-witted Canadian politician named William McDougall was sent to install himself as governor before the ownership of Rupert's Land had been transferred from the company to the Crown, much less before any attempt had been made to explain to the Red River people where they would stand in the new scheme of things. Enter the fiery métis leader Louis Riel and an insurgency that reached its bloody climax in the execution of the bumptious Ontario Orangeman Thomas Scott on March 4, 1870.

The news that one of their own had been killed by a provisional government headed by French-speaking métis literally sent the English of Ontario up in arms. The militia was mobilized, and volunteers streamed to the colours. Among the first was young Sam Steele, who abandoned his storekeeper's job to join the 1st Ontario Rifles on their march west to bring the Red River Settlement under Canadian control.

During Steele's first few days in the Rifles at the assembly camp in Barrie, Ontario, he wilfully disobeyed an order. A parade was called to select noncommissioned officers; all men with officer's certificates were told to fall out on the right. Sam stayed in the ranks. He had made up his mind to serve as a private. "As far as experience went I was better off without chevrons and learned how to appreciate the trials of other men to an extent that I should never have been able to do had I been promoted," he explained.

It would not be long before he was experiencing trials that would have daunted any but the hardiest. Before that, though, young Steele was to become acquainted with the spectre of sudden death. The steamboat *Chicora*, which carried his battalion from Sault Ste. Marie to Thunder Bay, was churning through a dense fog on Lake Superior early one morning when the sentry spotted a big rock jutting up dead ahead and shouted for hard aport; the helmsman alertly wheeled the boat out of danger. It happened that the sentry had spent many years in the Navy. Steele soberly reflected that if a landlubber had been on duty, the ship probably would have been sunk with all hands.

Prince Arthur's Landing, now part of Thunder Bay, Ontario, was a mushroom city of tents stretched along the shore of Lake Superior. No sooner had Steele's company landed than, to the accompaniment of much grumbling, the men were put to work on the excavations for a stockade. When not thus disagreeably employed, the militiamen had a look at the country around them. It did not hold much encouragement for their trip to the Red River. Forest fires had ravaged the land, leaving thousands of acres of burnt-over desolation. Some stretches of forest were still burning when Steele's company set out on June 30 on their epic journey to Fort Garry over the Dawson Road.

The Dawson Road was a striking misnomer. It was actually a meandering string of rivers, lakes, and portages relieved by occasional bridges and corduroy roads built of logs. It had been hastily mapped out two years earlier by Simon Dawson of the Dominion Public Works Department to answer the need, at least on paper, for a colonization highway from the head of the Great Lakes to the prairies. The route traversed some six hundred miles of water, barren rock, and dense bush swarming with mosquitoes and blackflies capable of pestering men and animals to the point of madness. To make matters worse that summer, fire had destroyed some of the culverts and bridges, and torrential rainstorms had turned much of the overland track into gluelike mud.

The Red River expedition was led by a dapper, ambitious Anglo-Irish officer, Colonel Garnet Joseph Wolseley. At the age of thirty-seven Wolseley had already demonstrated a penchant for being on the scene at the high points of British military history: He had lost an eye before Sevastopol, led a charge at the relief of Lucknow, and served in the British advance into China in 1860, recording his experiences in a popular book. The future commander in chief of the British Army was now in his first independent command at the head of a force of 2,213 troops, assisted by more than 700 voyageurs from the rivers of eastern Ontario and Quebec.

Taking along his sketchbook, his diary, his Bible, the works of Shakespeare, *The Imitation of Christ,* the Book of Common Prayer and the *Meditations* of Marcus Aurelius, Wolseley was all set for a romantic adventure that would also enhance his career prospects. He was not disappointed. He reminisced about the great journey through the forests of Canada for the rest of his life.

Facing Wolseley and his men was the task of moving 140 boats, each capable of carrying eight or nine soldiers, two or three voyageurs, and supplies enough for sixty days, over some of the world's most rugged country. The voyageurs, who so impressed Wolseley that he subsequently called for their services in his famous 1884 expedition up the Nile to Khartoum, manhandled the heavy boats on skids over the portages, sometimes toiling up hills at a forty-five-degree angle. The current on the Kaministiquia River was so swift that the boats frequently had to be tracked along by towlines thrown out from the shore and kept on course in the wild rapids by sheer physical might. The tremendous thunderstorms common to the Lake Superior country at that time of year made the going all the rougher. Such crude bridges as existed were swept away by torrents raging down the hills, and the trail was in constant need of repair.

The task of fixing and refixing the road fell to parties of soldiers posted along the route. No sooner had they finished filling in one washout than they were hustled along to another, humping their rifles and burdensome full kit. According to Steele, "this road work was the hardest task in my experience in this land of severe trials and strenuous pioneering." If it was any harder than the portaging of stores, it must have been very punishing indeed.

Everything about the expedition leads to the conclusion that men in those days were a great deal stronger and tougher than the men of today, modern nutrition notwithstanding. The boats con-

tained loads of about four thousand pounds. Pork barrels and arm
chests weighing two hundred pounds each had to be packed over
every one of the forty-seven portages. The lithe young man named
Sam Steele took a pork barrel or arm chest plus his seventy-pound
pack on every trip.

As he looked around him, Steele was impressed by the officers,
who did more than their share of the heavy labour. He was particularly taken with two of them: a tall Scots-Canadian major
named Jim Macleod who was always at the head of the line for
the pork barrels, and the quartermaster, a thick-chested British
captain named Redvers Buller. Looking on, the nineteen-year-old
Private Steele was forming an idea of the kind of man he wanted
to be: a tough gentleman-soldier like Macleod or Buller. He had
come into contact with men he could admire—and men who
would play a part in his future career.

Steele found nothing to complain about in the hard work along
the trail. On the contrary, he was pleased that it put him in such
fine physical condition. The exercise made him stronger than ever
and gave him a marvellous appetite for the pork and beans and
hardtack biscuits, washed down with strong tea, that made up the
soldiers' unscientific diet. The spirits of the men were sky-high as
they tramped the portages, shot the boiling rapids, and sailed the
lonely lakes.

It was a life of action, of vigour and good fellowship heightened
by the discomfort of the unrelenting rain and frequent flashes of
danger. Steele had several brushes with death as the expedition
wound its way down the "white water hell" of the Winnipeg
River, a tumultuous torrent that dropped an average of more
than two feet a mile. It took all the men's strength to hold the
boats steady as they streaked along. Heavy oars snapped like
matchsticks in the furious current. When a boat successfully ran a
stretch of rapids, the bowsman would triumphantly throw his pad-
dle in the air, and the men would raise their voices above the roar
of the waters in hearty cheers. It was only after several near sink-
ings that Steele's party reached Fort Garry, on the Red River, on
the evening of August 29, 1870, ninety-four days after they had
landed at Thunder Bay.

By then Louis Riel had already fled across the U.S. border. The métis flag, with its fleur-de-lys and shamrocks, had been hauled down from Fort Garry's flagstaff. The Red River rebellion had been nipped in the bud, but the enmity between the métis and the Ontarians lingered on.

In the aftermath of the insurgency the hamlet of Winnipeg (population 215) was the scene of a wild orgy of drunkenness. Fights broke out constantly in the rough-and-ready grogshops as the English-Canadian militiamen and French-speaking métis clashed. Fortunately the roistering could not continue indefinitely. It was fueled by liquor, and such was the demand that little Winnipeg's supply soon ran out. Still, one particularly nasty incident occurred when a métis leader named Elzear Goulet, who was accused of participating in Thomas Scott's execution, was chased by a drunken mob and drowned trying to escape across the Red River. Because a couple of militiamen—they were bugle boys— were among the crowd, the tragedy further envenomed relations between the métis and the occupying force.

The British regulars who made up a third of Wolseley's force were soon withdrawn, leaving a small garrison of Canadian militiamen to keep the peace and guard against threatened Fenian invasion from Minnesota. Snugly quartered with his unit in the old Hudson's Bay post of Fort Garry, Simcoe Sam, as Steele had been nicknamed, was happy enough to be among those who remained. He liked the life in the Army, liked the dash of his green rifleman's jacket, the pride that shines through spit and polish, the parades in the Rifle Corps's quickstep. Moreover, he was beginning to sense the lure of the western frontier. He remarked on the sharp differences between the colourful life on the Red River and the drab existence he had known in Ontario. He admired the clothes the local folk wore: the dark blue Hudson's Bay coats with bright brass buttons, the cozy fur hats, the moccasins gaily decorated with dyed porcupine quills and beads.

He got to know the people and talked to them about the ways of the Indians, taking careful notes that he was to preserve for a lifetime. He was intrigued by all he heard about the exotic, savage life out there on the plains. He liked the idea of the West being so big and free and open; it appealed to his sense of individuality. This, he mused, was a land where, as long as a man had health

and strength, it was his own fault if he failed. And there he was—
a young man with health and strength in abundance. We can picture him sitting on the edge of his cot on those long prairie evenings, thinking about the land where circumstances had placed
him, his fascination with the West slowly, solidly taking root.

3: SINGLE MEN IN BARRACKS

On the whole, Rudyard Kipling has left us with a reasonably balanced picture of life in the ranks of Queen Victoria's armies. Unfortunately, the portions of his work that have stuck most firmly in the public mind give the impression that it was mainly a matter of dallying with dusky nymphs and roguish fun and games. It did not take long for Sam Steele to encounter some of the harsher facts of army life that lurk in the forgotten passages of Kipling's writings. In his first few months in the Red River garrison, Steele's boyish illusions about the joys of soldiering were rudely chased away.

His hero worship of officers was dashed when the commanding officer of his unit, the Ontario Rifles, paraded the troops to deliver a scathing reprimand after Elzear Goulet's drowning. Without having bothered to ascertain that the militia's representation in the mob amounted to two buglers, the colonel accused his men en masse of being bloodthirsty fanatics who had hounded the métis leader to death. It was a sample of the injustice that abounds in the military, of the unwillingness of some officers to stand by their men, and of the helplessness of the lower ranks to do anything about it. It also showed how the Army could be used as a political whipping boy. Steele was convinced that the rumours of the soldiers' culpability in Goulet's death came from people trying to make political capital out of the affair.

The indignation in the ranks at the colonel's unwarranted attack reached the boiling point when word of the dressing down leaked to the press, which further exaggerated the militia's part in the tragedy. Picking up long-awaited eastern newspapers for news from home, the men were faced with headlines virtually calling them murderers. It was a bitter taste of civilian ambivalence towards the soldiery. In the public eye the militiamen had been heros on their glamorous march over the Dawson Road, when it looked as if they were going to do battle with Riel's rebels. Now that the campaign was over, they were regarded as a gang of thugs.

And in fact, as in any armed force, there were some thugs among them. No one knew better than Sam Steele, who, in yet another blow to his illusions, was thrown among them in the most inauspicious way. He had been promoted to corporal (primarily, it seems, because he was one of the few eligible men who could read and write) and transferred to another company, which incorporated most of the battalion's rowdy element. When he reported to the senior sergeant, one of the mavericks was on hand, obviously rather drunk. He called Steele an interloper who should not have been promoted over the heads of the men already in the company.

For a well-brought-up young fellow of refined good looks, the next few weeks must have been exceedingly trying. The toughs in the squad did everything they could to trip him up and get him stripped of his rank. They knew all the tricks: dumb insolence, deliberately misinterpreting orders, creating confusion about whose turn it was for duty. He tried to laugh it off.

Then came the night they learned not to trifle with Sam Steele. It began with a warming little tableau of barracks room domesticity. Some men had been cleaning their sheath knives and had put them aside on a long table in the corner of the room. The cook was chatting with a big, amiable private named Jack Kerr, who was cleaning the stove with grate polish. Steele was sprawled on his cot after coming off guard.

A private, one of the rough crowd quartered downstairs, was lounging around before going on duty; he was all dressed up in full review order. The cook started clowning with Jack Kerr, who took a swipe at him with the stove brush, leaving a black streak across his nose.

"You could not do that to me," the man in review kit challenged.

"Oh yes I could," said Kerr. He made a playful lunge at him with the stove brush.

Steele was watching with detached amusement when the man seized a sheath knife from the table and plunged it into Kerr's thigh. Before Steele could get up, the man made another rush with the knife. Kerr dodged him, grabbed the iron stove tongs, and smashed them down on his head. The man crashed to the floor with such force that the building shook, bringing his friends from the room below rushing up an outdoor stairway. As they flung the door open, they were confronted by the sight of Kerr sitting on a cot, holding his bleeding thigh, and their friend lying unconscious at his feet.

They charged furiously at Kerr, but Steele snatched up a rifle and barred their way. There was a momentary standoff as they cursed at him. Then he started swinging the rifle, driving them back. He swung and clubbed at them until they backed out the door and went tumbling down the stairway. It was an electrifying glimpse of the Sam Steele of later years, who, as one former Mounted Policeman put it, "was feared and respected by men who as a usual thing feared neither God nor man."

"This scrimmage seemed to clear the air, and we had no more trouble in barracks," Steele's memoirs record laconically. Both Kerr and his assailant spent some time in hospital while a chastened battalion settled down.

Meanwhile the citizens of the fledgling Province of Manitoba, totalling 11,963, were getting ready for the election of their first legislative assembly. The campaign was replete with the chicanery, boozing, and brawling that characterized nineteenth-century Canadian politics. Each candidate had his own personal bully who accompanied him everywhere. Drink buying, fisticuffs, and blatant promises of patronage were part of the political routine in those days, but this campaign had an extra overlay of bitterness. Neither Riel's opponents nor his sympathizers were in the mood to forgive and forget, and some of the politicians had no compunctions about opening old wounds.

Steele found himself remarking on the way the newly formed mounted police force under Captain Villiers of the Quebec Rifles comported themselves during this touchy interlude. He noted that in their dealings with the rival parties, they showed cool, impartial

judgment that gained the confidence of all sides. Resolute and
tactful, he thought, just what a police force in a frontier society
should be. He could not know then that he was looking at the
precursors of the North-West Mounted Police.

But level-headed police work could go only so far in the
supercharged atmosphere of racial and partisan hostility that surrounded the election. When polling day finally came on November 29, 1871, rioting inevitably broke out. As he hurried from his
hut to join his company when the fighting began, Steele was challenged by three rioters. He routed them with his rifle butt. He
had just fallen in when the order rang out to load with live ammunition as the shouting mob, armed with axe handles and
wagon wheel spokes, advanced on the soldiers. It had all the makings of a slaughter, but the officers kept their heads, and the
crowd was fenced back with rifle butts.

There were numerous minor injuries, but good sense and steady
nerves had averted a bloody tragedy that could have twisted the
whole course of Canadian history. The pattern of substituting
moral force for violence in resolving the problems of western Canada was being set.

The lesson in restraint was not lost on Steele; little was, it
seems. He took in everything around him, particularly whatever
he could learn about the life of the Indians and métis buffalo
hunters on the plains. He acquired a detailed knowledge of how
the natives found it possible to live almost entirely off the vast
herds of buffalo, how this single natural resource yielded not only
money and trade goods but food from the meat, clothing and
shelter from the skins, candles from the fat, and heat from burning the dung. He also learned that the number of buffalo was on
the wane and that for several months past a smallpox epidemic
had been taking an enormous toll among the Indians. And Lieutenant William Francis Butler had lately returned from his marathon nine-hundred-mile reconnaissance mission across the prairies
—the journey that resulted in the writing of the classic *The Great
Lone Land*—with news of another deadly scourge of the Indians:
the American whiskey traders.

As a famous British Army general in later years, the sensitive
Butler would come to have his doubts about imperialism, but in
the 1870s he believed wholeheartedly that the British Empire

had a sacred duty to lead the march of civilization. He recommended that an armed force be sent west to prevent the whiskey traders from despoiling the Indian way of life and to stop the internecine tribal wars. The ultimate aim, of course, was to pacify the Indians so that the West could be made safe for settlement by white men. Still, Butler did not take the attitude, then prevalent in the United States, that the natives should be eradicated to make way for the whites.

Sam Steele listened, learned, and agreed. He, too, had been brought up to believe in the civilizing role of imperialism. He could see a place for himself alongside Butler and Wolseley in the Queen's legions as they spread the red ink marking British possessions across the map of the world. He had easily come to terms with the difficulties and drawbacks of being in uniform. The soldiers felt more comfortable in the settlement now; the local folk took them into their homes and invited them to their dances, wild affairs that made the wooden houses rock in the frigid night to the thump of the Scotch reel and Red River jig. Steele spent much of his spare time skating on the river with the local girls. This was the happy side of the service, this and endless yarning sessions in the barracks that formed such a large part of a nineteenth-century soldier's recreation. Steele was an avid listener to the old campaigners' tales of the Crimea, India, and Africa, which lost nothing in the telling around the big, warm stove.

The lure of the military life stayed in his mind when his unit was disbanded in the spring of 1871, after the new Canadian Province of Manitoba had been formed and the threat of a Fenian invasion had receded. Before long he was back on the parade square, this time at Fort Henry in Kingston as a member of the artillery school in the first Canadian Permanent Force, which was being formed to take over from the departing British regular troops. Sam Steele was the twenty-third man ever to join the modern Canadian Army; his younger brother Dick was the twenty-second. The commandant of the new force was a peppery ex-trooper of the Royal Irish Constabulary in his early thirties, Lieutenant Colonel George A. French.

4: THE RED COAT

Steele's diligence and ability brought him regular commendations from his superiors at Kingston. He quickly passed the artillery course and was promoted to sergeant in A Battery. His sergeant major and chief mentor was a grand old British Army man named John Mortimer. When a young new acting sergeant major named Jim Mitchell arrived a few months later, Mortimer offered some words of advice: "You must expect that the sergeants will naturally try to put things over on you as you will be acting in a senior position. . . . There is one sergeant, however, whom you may fully trust, whom you will always find the same, and anything he tells you may be relied upon to the letter. If you have any doubt at any time and it is not convenient to refer to me, you will be quite safe in asking Sergeant Sam Steele, and the information you get will be as reliable as if given by myself." Mitchell, later to rise to the rank of lieutenant colonel, went to the sergeant's mess to meet the man who had been given such a high recommendation. Thus began a friendship that lasted all their lives.

Steele was made an instructor, assigned, because of the command of French he had acquired at school in Orillia, to a French-speaking troop from Quebec. He was happy in the service. The Army suited him, amused him with its vivid characters and funny vignettes. In later life he liked to tell about how one sergeant at Kingston reported a chronic malingerer to his officer: "I do not know what to make of this man, sir! He goes out when he likes, comes in when he likes, gets drunk when he likes—in fact he might be an officer, sir!"

In the spring of 1873 he caught wind of exciting news: A mounted force was being raised to establish a permanent armed presence in western Canada. Later he learned that Major James Morrow Walsh, a noted Fenian fighter and former commander of the Prescott Cavalry Troop, was in Ottawa recruiting men for the new force. It was to be known as the North-West Mounted Police, its name having been changed by a stroke of John A. Macdonald's pen from the North-West Mounted Rifles when the first-chosen name provoked alarmist newspaper reports in the United States that Canada was arming along the border. Steele happened to be on a brief tour of duty in Ottawa with his battery. He hastened to see Major Walsh.

Bub Walsh turned out to be Steele's kind of man. He was thirty-one, compact, and handsome, one of Canada's leading lacrosse players. As they talked in the major's temporary office, Steele found himself being offered the job of sergeant major of A Troop of the North-West Mounted Police. The offer was conditional on his getting a discharge from the artillery. Steele learned that his commanding officer, Colonel French, was also in Ottawa. He hurried off to see the colonel in his room at the Russell House Hotel. He took with him four other members of his battery: his brothers Dick and Godfrey, Sergeant Major Jim Mitchell, and Sergeant Percy Neale. With a twinkle in his eye, the colonel gave them permission to leave the Army and join the Mounted Police. He knew full well that they would soon be under his command again; he had already accepted an appointment as the first commissioner (commanding officer) of the new force.

The North-West Mounted Police Act received royal assent on May 23, 1873, but it was not until August 21 that year that the final details were approved by order-in-council. Broadly, the legislation called for the formation of a body of not more than three hundred healthy men of good character between the ages of eighteen and forty, able to ride and to read and write English or French.

In his dual capacity as prime minister and minister of justice, Sir John A. viewed the dispatch of the force west as a matter of urgency. Though an inveterate reader of penny Westerns, the prime minister was well aware of the dark side of the American Wild West. He was determined that the settlement of the Cana-

dian frontier should not be marred by the scorn for law and life
that had taken hold across the American border. It might be
diverting to read about shoot-outs outside of a saloon, but Macdonald had no intention of presiding over a land of gunfights,
vigilantes, and lynchings. Nor would he condone the appalling
slaughter of Indians that accompanied the progress of white settlement to the south.

As it broke one treaty after another in the interests of winning
the West for the whites, the U. S. Government had provoked the
Plains Indians into wars that could only lead to their destruction.
Encouraged by the official campaign of repression, the white civilians of the Wild West made little distinction between the lives of
the Indians and those of other wild creatures of the plains. There
are recorded instances of bounties being offered in the United
States for the scalps of Indians. On the other hand, the natives
served the purposes of the crooked Indian agents and traders, who
exploited them unmercifully. The traders were hardly more than
robbers, taking much and giving very little in return.

The manifest horrors of American practices towards the Indians
were bound to spread north in the absence of anyone to maintain
law and order on the Canadian side of what the natives called the
Medicine Line (because to be on the north side of it was "good
medicine"). Traders from Montana had gradually built up a lucrative business taking in buffalo hides in return for their "whiskey"
(made of a combination of raw spirits, chewing tobacco, molasses,
black pepper, vinegar, laudanum, muddy slough water, and red
ink). It was literally liquid murder, especially because some
traders also dealt in firearms. When Colonel P. Robertson-Ross of
the British Army returned from his fact-finding mission across the
prairies in 1871, he reported that drunken brawls had taken the
lives of more than a hundred Indians in the past few months.

Robertson-Ross recommended the establishment of a mobile
armed force (with a strength, he suggested, of 550) to police the
prairies. Perhaps the colonel's most memorable contribution was
to note: "During my inspection of the North-West, I ascertained
that some prejudice existed amongst the Indians against the
[green] colour of the uniform worn by the men of the Rifles,
for many of the Indians said, 'Who are these soldiers at Red

River wearing dark clothes? Our brothers who formerly lived here (meaning H.M. 6th Regiment) wore red coats,' adding, 'We know that the soldiers of our great mother wear red coats and are our friends.'"

Recognising that the red coat represented the British tradition of fair dealing to the Indians, Macdonald adopted a scarlet uniform for the N.W.M.P. based on that of the British dragoons, although, in his words, with as "little gold lace, fuss and feathers as possible." As the birds began to fly south in 1873, however, the men of the new police force had little time to bother about how they would be dressed. Public opinion in Canada had been grimly aroused by reports of the massacre of at least sixteen Assiniboine Indian men, women, and children in the Cypress Hills area of the Saskatchewan country by American traders and wolfers (pelt hunters who trapped and poisoned wolves for a living). Concluding that the time was overdue to plant law and order in the West, Macdonald ordered the first draft of the Mounted Police, under Major Walsh, to start for the Red River right away.

Without uniforms or equipment, that first body of recruits could not have been a prepossessing sight as their new sergeant major stood on the station platform at Prescott Junction and watched them detrain from Ottawa on October 2. Steele himself had come by boat down the river from Kingston with his two brothers, Dick and Godfrey, and four other recruits from A Battery. That night, in an intimation of things to come, the force lost its first man: Trumpeter T. O'Neil "was discharged and sent back to Ottawa for being drunk and riotous." The next day brought further exasperations for Sam Steele as he herded the motley crowd onto the train for Toronto. One of the recruits was missing, and they had to leave without him. The group proceeded to Collingwood on Lake Huron to catch the steamship that was to take them to Prince Arthur's Landing. At Collingwood a recruit went down to the lakeshore for some revolver practice and shot himself in the arm.

As he issued a haversack, straps, a greatcoat, two blankets, a knife, a fork, a spoon, a tin plate, a tin cup, soap, and a towel to each man, Steele must have wondered what on earth he had got himself into. The men—some in lumberjack's outfits, others in

their bowler-hatted Sunday best—can scarcely have seemed like
the future guardians of the great Northwest. Some smelled of
strong drink, and Steele got together with Walsh to frame an
order: "While he (the C.O.) is no advocate of wholly abstaining,
still it will be his duty to report to the Commissioner on his arrival at the Fort any cases of drunkenness. . . . The C.O. wishes
it to be distinctly understood that this is intended more as a
request than a warning." The tone of tolerance reflects the fact
that both Walsh and his sergeant major liked a drink themselves.

The advance party of forty-one left Collingwood October 6
aboard the side-wheeler *Cumberland*, arriving at Prince Arthur's
Landing two days later. Drawing an issue of tents, camp kettles,
frying pans, and axes from the government stores, the party went
under canvas beside Lake Superior to await the arrival of another
group of two officers and sixty-two men. As soon as the second
contingent disembarked, it was off on the Dawson Road again,
covering the first fifty miles by horse-drawn wagon. The route had
been improved somewhat since Steele was there last but was still,
as Manitoba historian R. G. MacBeth phrased it, "more suitable
for aquatic animals than for human beings."

The men reverted to the spartan life of the trail, the kind of life
that many of them would lead intermittently for years to come on
the prairies. The journey to the Red River was a race against the
onset of winter, the men putting in fourteen-hour days on the portages, rivers, and lakes. The year's first snowstorm struck as they
were leaving the Lake of the Woods. The party had with it the
last group of settlers to travel west that year, a family with a couple of teams of horses. According to MacBeth, the settlers "would
probably never have got through without the help of these kindly
giants."

The troop reached Lower Fort Garry, some twenty miles north
of the present Winnipeg, on October 22. Within days the temperature dropped to —40° F. as the men settled in to face the
winter ahead. Then on November 3 the acting commissioner,
Lieutenant Colonel W. Osborne Smith, had the men assemble to
take the enlistment oath. They swore to "well and faithfully,
diligently and impartially execute and perform such duties as may
from time to time be allotted to us." The first three to sign the

roll were Arthur H. Griesbach, Percy R. Neale, and Samuel Benfield Steele. Steele witnessed Griesbach's signature, and Griesbach witnessed the others'. The North-West Mounted Police had officially come into being.

5: THE ORIGINALS

"Drill, drill, drill," wrote a young recruit from Lower Fort Garry in the winter of 1874. "Foot drill, rifle practice, guard mount, horseback, all the fatigues. Breaking in my new mount isn't my idea of fun. Especially with Steele drilling. The man has no feelings. He drills four rides a day."

Sam Steele had fitted easily into the role of the hard-driving sergeant major, one of those bellowing tyrants who, since Wellington's time, had formed the backbone of the British Army. His performance as a taskmaster at the force's inception became legendary, recalled in years to come in cotside bull sessions and around campfires. The story was told of how a bronco threw its rider in the Lower Fort Garry corral, then proceeded to stamp on him: "Someone catch and look after that poor horse," Steele is supposed to have shouted. "And a couple of you carry that awkward lout off the square!" The awkward lout in question was one of Steele's brothers. Apocryphal though this tale may be, the fact that it became part of the force's oral history signifies what a holy terror Troop Sergeant Major Steele must have been.

It is not the job of sergeants major to curry popularity among their men, and Steele's uncompromising ways aroused deep dislike among some of the troopers. Men complained to each other about how demanding he was. Barracks gossip had it that he wound a sash around his waist inside his tunic to lend his slim figure the bulk to match his booming parade-square voice. The recruits gave him a nickname that reflected both his artillery background and his hardness: Smoothbore Steele.

But what seemed like gratuitous bullying was all to a purpose. The sojourn at the draughty old former Hudson's Bay fort was designed to temper the recruits for service that would seek out the physical and emotional cracks in the toughest human beings. The prospect of policing, with the barest equipment and supplies, a vast, wild, unmapped country full of hazards meant that these men had to be as fit as physical constitution and character permitted. In a few short months of bitter Manitoba winter they had to be forged, as a plain matter of survival, into some of the world's most resourceful troops.

As chief equitation instructor Steele had been told that the Mounted Police could not hope to do their job unless they could ride as well as the Indians. This gave him the task of turning a mixed bag of former clerks, lumberjacks, university students, teachers, farmers, and a bartender into some of the finest horsemen in the world. And, to put the best possible face on it, many of the men had "rated their abilities in this line too highly," as their commanding officer reported. For Steele this presented a dilemma of untrained riders and untamed mounts. Most of the horses initially purchased for the force in Manitoba were rugged broomtail broncos that had never been ridden. In charge of breaking these wild creatures, Steele formed a special squad of the best riders in the party. They conducted a daily round of bronc-busting while the recruits looked on from the corral fences with admiration mixed with trepidation. Drawing on the horsemanship he had learned as a boy from his half brother, Steele broke the most difficult broncos himself.

Once the horses had been gentled, they were handed over to the recruits for mutual training. Even then the mustangs were prone to furious bucking spells. The men were pitched violently to the frozen ground again and again, only to have Steele order them to get up and get back in the saddle. Determined that the Mounted Police should be able to ride "anything with hair on it," he kept the troopers at it all that cruel winter, rubbing salt on their saddle sores to prevent infection. The orders were that as long as the temperature was higher than −36° F., the breaking and riding were to proceed.

It was obviously not a life for men unable to surmount their weaknesses. The recruits slept on raw wooden pallets in ice-cold

rooms, to be rudely aroused—"Show a leg, boys! On the jump!"
—by Sam Steele and the other NCOs at 6:30 A.M. Their buffalo
coats, mitts, and moccasins were comfortable enough, but the
food was bad, and the terrible weather took its toll on the less robust individuals. None who had joined knew the full extent of
what they were getting into, but those who had done it for a lark
began to slip away quietly. Several were released for physical
unfitness. A number of incorrigible drunkards were dismissed.

By the time the spring floods broke, the unit had been honed to
a fine cutting edge. The farm boys and city slickers of a few
months before were now disciplined soldiers and accomplished
riders. They were fit to face the challenge of the prairies. Like
many a sergeant major before and since, Sam Steele was owed
much of the credit for the future achievements of his men.

The honing down had left 120 of them, with a few more recruits to come. In November of 1873 the new commissioner—
Steele's old chief, Colonel French—arrived at the fort. French
quickly recognized the absurdity of trying to police an area the
size of Western Europe with a rump company of 300. Steele
reckoned from what he had gathered in his renewed contact with
the people of the prairies that, to be on the safe side, the force
should number at least 1,000 men.

Colonel French returned to Ottawa in February with an urgent
plea to double the strength of the force. The Pacific Scandal had
swept Macdonald's Conservative Government out of office, but
the Liberals, under Prime Minister Alexander Mackenzie, grudg-
ingly acceded to his request. The colonel spent the rest of the
winter in eastern Canada raising the fresh contingent and pur-
chasing horses, the best Ontario had to offer. On June 6 cheering
crowds gathered in Toronto to see 217 officers and men and 244
horses off to the West in two special railway trains.

A diplomatic arrangement had been made to permit this second
wave to travel to Dakota unarmed and in civilian dress via U.S.
railroads. From there they were to proceed to Dufferin, Manitoba
(near the present Emerson, Manitoba), by horse and wagon. A
few days earlier Sam Steele had been called before the assistant
commissioner of the force, Major Macleod, the same James
Macleod who had so impressed him on the Wolseley expedition.

"You'll arrange all our camps on the march to Dufferin," Macleod said.

A ramshackle collection of huts and grogshops near the American border, Dufferin was the staging point for the force's march across the plains to the Rocky Mountains. The plan was to take all the provisions and equipment needed to establish posts on the prairies with them, including livestock to set up food-producing farms.

Steele organized the transport, equipment, and provisions for the eighty-mile move to Dufferin. On June 7 he rode with the column down the wide, muddy main street of the village of Winnipeg. Resplendent in scarlet Norfolk jackets, rakishly cocked pillbox caps, and gleaming brass and leather, the first Mounties must have seemed a bit incongruous to those who assembled to see them leave. They looked more like a snobbish British cavalry regiment prancing down Pall Mall than a body of men equipped to deal with warlike Indians and gunslinging outlaws. No doubt they presented a far less formidable spectacle than the dusty veteran Indian fighters of the U. S. Cavalry.

The night the second contingent arrived brought intimations of disaster. As Sam Steele told it in a speech delivered in 1910, "A corral was formed, composed of all the wagons—about eighty—and about fifteen Red River carts, and on of the severe thunderstorms of the Red River Valley came on. The horses were inside the corral and tied up with the usual picket lines. A thunderbolt struck inside the corral. The horses broke everything and rushed to one side. They upset the loaded wagons and went through the gates five or six deep."

Steele was riding near the corral at around ten o'clock when all this happened. He watched from fifty yards away as the hysterical horses trampled over the six men on duty who tried to stop them; one man was critically injured in the rush. The frenzied mass of animals smashed the compound gate, overturned big wagons, and charged through a row of tents as the men who had been inside them scampered to safety. Then the horses were off across the prairie, about 250 of them, galloping madly in the direction of the United States.

It was no time for lone men to be out looking for strays. Sioux Indian war parties were on the move just across the border, and these fearsome "tigers of the plains" could not be expected to give up a captured horse without a fight. Luckily the police still had plenty of horses, because the western broncos obtained in Manitoba and Dakota were conditioned not to be spooked by thunderstorms. In the next twenty-four hours Steele covered 112 miles on his western horse, splashing through flooded streams, avoiding gopher holes that could break a horse's leg, and keeping a constant eye out for the Sioux, who could have pounced on the scattered riders at any moment. By the end of the next day all but one of the runaway animals had been safely rounded up from as far as fifty miles away.

All the horses were exhausted; so were the men. Commissioner French decided to put off the start of the march for two or three days. In the meantime the Sioux struck at the village of St. Joseph, thirty miles away across the U.S. border, slaughtering several métis families. The commissioner turned out his troops, and they rode to the assistance of the survivors; but after they had gone a few miles, they learned that the Sioux had decamped.

The Indians were not the only decampers. Coming on top of the other trials the troopers had to endure, the stampede and the danger of a clash with the Sioux caused a wave of desertions among the men. By the time the force pulled out for the West on July 8, 1874, thirty-one would-be Mounted Policemen had fled. Combined with reinforcements, the entire force now numbered 486 men.

The first two days of the journey were what would now be called a shakedown phase designed to determine what was missing and what could be dispensed with. Besides, the métis ox drivers were on a binge; it was not until they were "mostly sobered," in the words of Commissioner French, that the 2½-mile-long column made its real start, on July 10.

That day has left us with one of the most unforgettable spectacles in Canadian history. In their full dress of red coats, white helmets and gauntlets, brass buttons and fittings, on their trim, well-curried mounts festooned with polished leather, the Mounted Police were a magnificent sight. Steele's A Troop, on their fine dark bay horses, led the column over the rolling prairie in the dazzling sunlight. After them came the other troops, some bearing upright lances, escorting ammunition wagons and polished brass guns. And then, as French's elegant Victorian pen recorded it, came "a motley string of ox carts, ox wagons, cattle for slaughter, cows, calves, &c., mowing machines, &c., &c.

"To a stranger it would appear an astonishing cavalcade," wrote French. "Armed men and guns looked as if fighting was to be done; what could the ploughs, harrows, mowing machines, cows, calves, &c., be for? But that little force had a double duty to perform: to fight, if necessary, but in any case to establish posts in the far west."

6: THE HARDEST MARCH

The land into which the Mounted Policemen rode that day was alive with danger. Sam Steele knew better than most what they were up against. Few people had any idea of the extent of the bloodletting that occurred in this seemingly empty country. "There was no white man dared to travel through the Blackfoot country and the Assiniboine country," he related in a lecture many years later. "If a large party out looking for buffalo got into the plains and found Indians, they killed every one they met, for if any Indian escaped they were destroyed themselves."

Steele was aware that even the experienced frontiersmen of the Hudson's Bay Company were frightened of the southern Plains Indians. The company once established a post on the Saskatchewan that cost ten thousand pounds, only to have the Indians destroy it within a matter of weeks. Its Little Bow Fort, above what is now Calgary, Alberta, was destroyed twice by Indians who wanted nothing to do with white men.

The killing among the Indians went on right up to the Mounted Police's arrival. In 1870 a huge battle had taken place near the present site of Lethbridge, Alberta, between the Piegans, led by the great métis scout Jerry Potts, and a mixed band of Crees and Assiniboines under Chief Piapot. Piapot's braves had killed and scalped a group of defenceless Piegan and métis women, children, and old people. In retaliation the Piegans, according to an eyewitness, killed no fewer than 480 Assiniboines and Crees.

The lawless American whiskey traders led an embattled but lucrative life. According to Steele the famous Fort Whoop-Up "was quite a strong place. It mounted a couple of guns and had strong gates, with large rooms in the square, and chimneys all barred so that the Indians could not clamber down and get in; and the whiskey was traded through a hole in the wall. A buffalo robe was pushed in and a drink of whiskey handed out—a buffalo robe for a drink of whiskey. A pony could be bought for a quart of whiskey, and it was poor whiskey, too."

Steele had heard about a place called Dead Man's Lake, where the Indians went to drink their "whoop-up bug juice." It apparently owed its name to the fact that drunken orgies there regularly resulted in sudden death. He also knew that legitimate traders had been driven out of the territory by an armed band of whiskey peddlers. When they were not killing their trading rivals and Indians, the whiskey traders were killing each other. They engaged in frequent gun fights while under the influence of their own stock-in-trade.

But the bloodthirsty inhabitants of the Northwest were only a part of its hazards. The Mounted Policemen were introduced to some of the other unpleasant facts of life on the plains early on in the march. Always there were mosquitoes, buzzing in clouds as they rode along, leaving their faces streaming with blood, tormenting the livestock. There were violent thunderstorms that could suddenly turn into hailstorms, dealing out a painful battering to a man astride a horse. Once when they had camped at the end of a day, they were chased into their tents by heavy rain that turned to hail. With typical prairie capriciousness, the sun then came up brightly, but the drumming on the canvas went on. When he peered out curiously, Steele realized that the tent was covered with locusts. In fact everything was covered with them: the grass, the trees, the flowers. They were eating the tents, the paint and woodwork on the wagons, even the stocks of the carbines. The men had to scramble among the swarms of these pests to pack the tents away safely and to beat them off the equipment. When the horde finally passed, the air was full of them, their wings flashing in the sun for hundreds of yards up in the sky.

For a day or two the column travelled the path of this plague, where the land had been stripped bare of vegetation. With no natural forage the animals had to be fed from the scarce grain

supplies. The heat was scorching, telling heavily on the horses and
oxen. The condition of the eastern horses especially ran down as
their ill-fitting harnesses chafed open sores on their hides.

The pitiless sun dried up most of the water holes, leaving only
black, saline mud. Steele applied a trick he had learned as a boy
to get clear water: sawing barrels in half and drilling holes in the
bottoms, then sinking them into the springs. But conditions did
not often permit this, and there were times, according to Commissioner French, when the force was "obliged to drink liquid
which when passed through a filter was still the colour of ink."

As they made their dusty way through this burnt-up desert
strewn with buffalo bones, the animals began to sicken and the
men to contract dysentery. The thermometer frequently hit
100° F. in the shade. Still the column pushed on at a pace of up
to twenty-five miles a day.

La Roche Percée was a crossing on the Souris River about one
third of the way to the foothills of the Rockies, so called for a
nearby pierced rock with a hole in it big enough for a man to
crawl through. There French brought his weary party to a halt.
He had decided they could not make it to the mountains and
back in time to establish posts for the winter while weighed down
with an entourage of sick men and animals. Also, he had belatedly
received orders to send a detachment to Fort Edmonton, 875
miles by trail to the northwest.

"Monday, 29th July," French's diary records. "Finished with
the stores, paraded all the horses, and told off 55 of the weakest
for Fort Ellice under Inspector Jarvis, took the horses of A Troop
(Jarvis') and divided them amongst the others. I have broken up
the train and feel relieved. . . ."

The new plan was for the remnants of A Troop to proceed to
Fort Edmonton, dropping off some of the animals and supplies en
route at the Hudson's Bay post of Fort Ellice, a hundred miles
away. It was a blow to Steele, whose troop, now commanded by
Inspector W. O. Jarvis, was reduced from forty to a dozen able
men. A Troop was to proceed northwest, taking with it everything
that might impede the main column. This included six sick men,
another seven of the youngest and weakest recruits from the other
troops, fifty-five sick and almost played-out horses, twenty-four
wagons, fifty-five oxcarts with twelve métis drivers, sixty-two oxen,

fifty cows and their fifty calves, and a huge load of surplus
supplies. After the reshuffle of men, horses, and supplies, the main
body left La Roche Percée for the Rockies on July 29, leaving A
Troop with the dirty work.

"We were a disconsolate lot when we saw the force depart on
their long trek," wrote Steele, "but we had a much harder time
before us than any were to experience that year." The distance to
Fort Edmonton was almost double the distance to the Rockies,
and it had to be covered on an unpredictable trail with failing
horses and no grain to feed them, horses that had never been fed
on grass alone before.

They started out on August 3 after a brief rest to store up energy. At the very outset they ran into swarms of grasshoppers as
thick as snow. Then came heavy rainstorms, turning the track to
gumbo. The harness horses were so weak that they had to be
changed twice a day. The cows and calves became footsore and
started lying down every few yards. The cattle were constantly
straying, making it necessary for the men to backtrack in order
to keep the herd on the trail. It was a risky occupation because
a party of none too friendly Sioux was travelling parallel with
them. Jarvis ordered a double guard as a precaution against attack by the Indians, and so the men got very little sleep.

It took eleven days to reach Fort Ellice. Here the animals got
better feed, but they had to be continually hauled out of quicksand bogs. It was here that Sam Steele proved himself as strong as
an ox. Veterans of the march remembered him grasping oxen by
the horns and heaving them out of the morass. It was here, too,
that Steele nearly became a victim of the quicksands himself.

One day he jumped his horse over a small creek to a grassy
bank that looked solid enough but concealed a bog of quicksand.
Within seconds the horse sank up to its neck. As he started to
sink, Steele threw himself face downwards in the mud to distrib-
ute his weight and struggled as if he was swimming until he
caught hold of the reins. He pulled and called the horse, which
heaved forward. Then he wriggled gingerly back to safety. With
another heave the horse was free.

The small trading post at Fort Ellice served as a camping
ground for parties of Crees, Salteaux, and Sioux, who followed the
redcoats everywhere, such was their curiosity. Subinspector Sévrère

Gagnon, who kept a colourful diary of the march, noted that "some of the women are almost pretty." Apart from that, the stop offered little consolation. Three of the horses died.

They left half the animals and the sick men behind at Fort Ellice and entered into a country where, in Jarvis's words, "I found the water so bad that I had great difficulty procuring enough to keep life in the horses and oxen." The horses were reduced to shambling skeletons that were constantly collapsing on the trail. Steele's immense strength and energy were taxed to the fullest in keeping the animals moving. "I lifted horses forty times a day," he once said in recollecting the march.

Despite some long stops at good resting places the hardships of the trail were unremitting. Rain and hail combined with intense heat and blinding dust storms to make conditions as miserable as could be. Most of the lakes were saline, so that there was only a scarce supply of rainwater to drink for long stretches. The cattle were in the maddening habit of straying back to the last camp. The horses, evidently recalling the storm at Dufferin, were ready to stampede at the first clap of thunder. Autumn began to set in; and as the weather turned colder, the animals grew weaker. On September 8, when the column crossed the South Saskatchewan River in a terrible hailstorm, it took all day to get the cattle across.

It sounds utterly grim, and it would have been but for the out-doorsman's instinct for making the best of things. What spare time they had the men spent shooting and fishing, then cooking up feasts of prairie chicken, ducks, geese, and trout. They clowned and told stories around the campfire. Inspector Jarvis, a Canadian who had been in the British Army, was a likeable man who amused them with his tales of campaigning in Africa. "The half breed drivers had great fun after supper," Steele wrote. "One of them had a violin, and to its music the remainder in turn danced a Red River jig on a door which they carried in their carts for the purpose. Tired of ducks, geese, prairie chicken and pemmican, these strange fellows caught skunks, boiled them in three waters and then roasted them, thinking them preferable to any other food!"

But by September 11, when the column reached the Hudson's Bay Company's Fort Carlton in the teeth of a terrible windstorm, the métis drivers had had enough. There were rumours that the Crees and Blackfeet were on the warpath and that Commissioner French's force had lost nearly all its horses, leaving it defenceless against Indian attack. The drivers wanted to turn back, and it took all the arguments that Jarvis, Gagnon, and Steele could muster to dissuade them. They went on a three-day strike that at least offered a chance to rest the horses and feed them up on wheat.

The party spent a week in Carlton; despite their labour problem the rest lifted the policemen's spirits. Just as they were leaving, however, word came confirming that the Crees and Blackfeet were making threatening moves. The weather was turning colder by the day, and their hopes of a better trail were dashed by the driving chill rain that made the track a morass. The worn-out horses suffered pitifully from the cold, even though the men used their own blankets to keep them warm. When they slumped down from exhaustion, the animals were so stiff that they could not rise up again. Several times Steele had to keep his men up most of the night lifting horses to their feet and massaging them, knowing that they would never recover if they were left to lie. As it was, one horse and one ox had to be shot.

Often the only way to keep a fallen horse going was to put a long pole under it and lift and walk it along, with Steele at one end of the pole and Corporal Ted Carr at the other. Carr, a witty Irishman who was a graduate of Trinity College and a great favourite of Steele's, once cracked while engaged in this labour, "I thought I'd have an easy ride to the Rockies, with a fine horse carrying me. Instead I'm having a tough walk to Edmonton with me carrying the horse."

It was true enough. With so much of their time needed to bring up the rear of the column, prod cattle, chase strays, and lift horses, Steele and his little party (including his brother Dick) had long since given up riding. Strung out for miles, the column often had to halt at bad spots on the trail, some of them covered with water for hundreds of yards. At these spots, the men would have to use their axes and spades to build corduroy roads of logs. The ceaseless labour in the mud and cold and rain left them exhausted. They were close to collapse when they took a short rest at the Hudson's Bay Company settlement of Victoria, where they palavered with some not unfriendly Crees, one with the mar-

vellous name of Sky Blue Horn Sitting Down Turning on a
Chair.

When they set out again, the going got even worse. On this last
leg of the trip Steele, Carr, and blacksmith Tom Labelle spent
practically all their time lifting fallen horses. One animal, a beautiful Ontario thoroughbred, had to be jacked up at least a dozen
times a day. Some could not go on at all, and Steele pitched a
marquee tent to shelter them and left them. He was now in sole
command; Jarvis had ridden ahead to Fort Edmonton, and Gagnon had gone on with the ox teams.

They pressed on through the roughest country yet. The trail
was knee-deep in mud and crossed by sloughs every few hundred
yards. At each slough the wagons had to be unloaded and dragged
through by hand, then reloaded. They came to several ponds covered with a thin coating of ice; there the thirst-maddened animals
rushed to the ponds to drink while the men were unloading the
wagons. The horses broke through the ice into the water and had
to be dragged out with ropes.

By nightfall of October 31 the party had struggled to a point
twelve miles from Fort Edmonton. Steele's orders had been to get
to the fort that afternoon. He believed that orders were made to
be obeyed, so he kept the men toiling until 5 A.M. the next day.
At that time they caught up with Gagnon and his oxen teams five
miles from the fort. Steele told the officer it was useless to continue. The men and horses had been on the move for at least
twenty-one hours; all were about to collapse. Gagnon consented
to a halt, and they washed and rubbed down the horses, then set
them out to graze while the men had a hot meal.

They were ready for bed when a man called out that a horse
had broken through the ice of the creek. Steele rushed to the spot
with a rope and found the animal partly through the ice in a hole
with high edges. He threw one end of the rope to the men while
he tied the horse around the neck and hindquarters. He had just
let the rope slacken and clambered to the surface of the ice when
it broke and the horse sank, pulling him and the rest of the men
into ten feet of water. Luckily they still had hold of the rope.
Dick Steele, on the bank, grabbed it and pulled out the man
nearest him. After a few heaves they were all back on dry land.

It was then 6 A.M., and incredibly, Steele was still not tired.

While the men slept, he took an axe and cut poles to make a bridge across the creek. Inspector Jarvis found him laying the poles when he rode in from Fort Edmonton to say that he had arranged for winter quarters there.

The column immediately re-formed and travelled over fairly dry ground to the fort. The poor horses made a feeble attempt to trot when they sighted the rooftops. Steele was the last man into the stockade, holding one end of a pole supporting the hind end of a thoroughbred horse. Inspector Jarvis later reported that the sergeant major had "done the manual labour of at least two men" on the journey. Steele had earned his wage of $1.20 a day.

7: SHOWING THE FLAG

Fort Edmonton, where the future capital city of Alberta was to rise, was a key Hudson's Bay Company post on the North Saskatchewan River. In the early days it had been the scene of skirmishes between traders and hostile Indians; now most of the natives had become reconciled to its presence, passing in and out of its heavy log gates to exchange the wild produce of the North Saskatchewan country for trade goods such as the distinctive striped blankets which, draped over the shoulders, were almost a uniform for the western Canadian tribes. To the twenty-four ragged Mounted Policemen who trudged into it at the beginning of November in 1874, the fort must have seemed a mecca of luxury. Warm, dry quarters, hot food, comfortable chairs and beds, sheltered privies—all were like godsends after the hardships of the Edmonton trail.

They spent their first few days at the fort in comparative leisure, nursing their sickly livestock and settling down in cramped but snug billets. They could look back on their journey with satisfaction: Inspector Jarvis's odometer showed they had covered nearly 1,300 miles in the 114 days since they left Fort Dufferin and nearly 900 miles in eighty-eight days out of La Roche Percée. The reassuring word reached them that the main force had arrived at the foothills of the Rocky Mountains 350 miles to the south without clashing with the Indians. A fort was being built on the Oldman River in the southern foothills under the supervision of Assistant Commissioner Macleod, after whom it would be named.

Commissioner French meanwhile had doubled back east, leaving one troop at a desolate spot called Swan River and taking another with him all the way back to Fort Dufferin. The party that made the round trip set a record for a mounted military expedition living off its own supplies: 1,959 miles at an average of more than 19 miles a day.

The heroic tradition of the force was already taking shape. The discipline and determination shown on the march west set a monumental standard. Moreover, the force immediately began to show the dashing style that enabled this handful of men to carry off one of history's greatest bluffs. With staggering dispatch Macleod's men swooped down on the whiskey traders of the foothills area, confiscating their stocks of "forty rod" whiskey (said to be capable of knocking a man down from that distance) and relieving them of working capital by imposing heavy fines.

Even more important than suppressing the whiskey outlaws, the Mounted Police were winning the confidence of the Indians. That winter the chief of the Blackfoot confederacy, Crowfoot, came to call on Macleod to smoke the peace pipe and to deliver a characteristically eloquent speech welcoming the Mounties—and with them, the rule of law—to the West.

In Fort Edmonton, meanwhile, all was agreeably quiet. Steele helped to organize a Christmas ball to entertain the white and métis settlers of the region, who were mostly engaged in trading furs. The menu included buffalo tongues and humps, venison, prairie chicken, wild goose, plum pudding, and mince pie. The Queen's health was drunk in tea because the policemen were expected to set an example of abstinence. The fiddles sang out, and they danced jigs and reels all night long, the ladies lifting the hems of their long skirts to allow their feet to swing freely. The party ended with a huge breakfast before the guests went jingling off home in their sleighs.

The Fort Edmonton detachment's first whiskey raid turned into a harmless fiasco. Early in January, Inspector Jarvis, with Sam Steele, his brother Dick, Ted Carr, and ten others, set out for the big hunting camp at Buffalo Lake, where bootleggers were reported to be selling whiskey to the métis and Crees. During the two-week journey, the temperature ranged between −42° F. and −56° F. Anybody who has ever experienced the anguish of —40° F. and —50° F. weather will be struck with how Steele and his companions took it in stride. "We had no tents," he recorded, "as we were better off without them, and we had no stoves, such luxuries being then unknown in the West. Our halts for the night were made about an hour before dark, so that the ponies could be made snug and a large fire built, buffalo robes laid down, and after a supper of buffalo steak, bread and tea, we lay in front of the fire like herrings in a barrel and slept well."

It was the first prolonged winter excursion the North-West Mounted ever made, the forerunner of many thousands of arduous patrols from the American border to the high Arctic. When they reached their destination, the men found themselves caught up in a marathon frontier wedding celebration with their prime suspect as their host. There was no evidence that he was selling liquor. The policemen were, however, able to round up and fine several genuine whiskey traders in a hundred-mile sweep of the area before they returned to Fort Edmonton. From then on the detachment's main job was vigilant patrolling. Psychologically (and though the force's early officers might never have heard the word, they were masters of psychology) it was up to them to convince the outlaws and Indians that, as Inspector Jarvis kept saying, "we're here to stay."

Already the inspector was working on a plan to give the force a permanent presence: construction of a N.W.M.P. post at Fort Saskatchewan. That winter they had a visit from a survey party, headed by Jarvis's cousin, that had crossed the Rockies from west to east in search of a suitable route for the proposed Canadian Pacific Railway. The policemen were aware that one reason they were there was to clear the way for this adventurous project. Inspector Jarvis had the railway in mind when—over the objections of the people of Fort Edmonton, who thought the police post should be built close by—he chose a site nineteen miles to the northeast at the confluence of the Saskatchewan and Sturgeon Creek, where he predicted the tracks would run.

Steele was put in charge of laying out the fort and organizing the construction. It was to be built along classic Wild West lines, with hewn pickets loopholed for rifles, bastions at the corners, and a heavy log gate greased for quick closing in case of attack. As soon as spring came, he had the broad axes swinging, whipsaws whining, and hammers banging until nightfall as the men, fed on pemmican and mountain trout weighing up to twelve pounds, erected one stout log building after another. By early summer the new Fort Saskatchewan was nearly complete.

The Hudson's Bay steamboat *Northcote* arrived at Edmonton from Lake Winnipeg for the first time in July. The mail it brought carried welcome news for Steele. He had been appointed regimental sergeant major of the force, succeeding his old friend Art Griesbach, who had been commissioned subinspector. A pay raise of five cents a day accompanied the promotion. The new RSM was ordered to report to the headquarters of the force at Swan River at once.

Steele boarded the *Northcote* for its return voyage. Crewed by colourful American rivermen who had once sailed the Mississippi and Missouri, the big side-wheeler wound its tortuous way through the 1,100-mile Saskatchewan River system to the Grand Rapids connecting the river with Lake Winnipeg. But the smaller steamboat that was to relay passengers down the lake to Lower Fort Garry failed to arrive on schedule, and the *Northcote*'s passengers found themselves stranded with nothing to eat but sturgeon out of the lake.

Eager to get going, Steele managed to join a party of Indians on their way south in a York boat, the traditional sail-and-oar craft used by the Hudson's Bay traders. Before long a violent storm arose, forcing them to take shelter up a creek. They lived for several days on unpalatable seagull meat. Then the wind died, and they sailed on, stopping only for meals and prayers. The big, red-coated white man felt a strong sense of kinship as he knelt beside the devout Christian natives. "I parted with my Indian friends with much regret," he wrote. "I should have liked to sail, fish or hunt with them all summer long."

When the new RSM arrived at the Swan River headquarters, he found it a shambles. The parade square was strewn with huge boulders that made it impossible for troops to form up. Masses of garter snakes, harmless but annoying, were everywhere, the beds included. The siting of the buildings guaranteed a maximum of discomfort both in the summer's heat and the winter's cold.

Steele was more pleased by the new recruits to the force, a mixed lot of young gentlemen adventurers and resourceful ex-farm

boys intent on taking advantage of the government's offer of free
land in the West when their three-year terms of enlistment
ended. He settled down to the work of training these young men
into a crack corps of mounted rifles, breaking with British military
tradition by employing drills adapted from the mounted infantry
tactics of Generals Stuart and Sheridan in the American Civil
War. In the meantime mounted patrols kept the peace among
the Indians as surveyors mapped the course of the coming railway. Geologists came to look for coal, safe in the knowledge that
the police had things under control.

Psychologists always, they let the Indians know that they were
determined to bring the Cypress Hills killers to justice. Although
more than two years had elapsed since the massacre, Lieutenant
Colonel Acheson Gosford Irvine, a former commandant at Fort
Garry, was specially commissioned as a superintendent in the
force to bring the murderers to trial. After an undercover mission
across the border, Irvine caught up with seven suspects in the
wide-open town of Fort Benton, Montana Territory. Two escaped, but Irvine, now joined by Assistant Commissioner Macleod, launched extradition proceedings against the remaining five.

No admirers of things British, the Montana frontiersmen were
incensed by this attempt to force their countrymen to face trial—
and possibly the hangman's noose—in Canada. Under public pressure, the extradition court promptly ruled against the Canadian
accusers. Three other suspects were subsequently arrested on Canadian soil and tried in Winnipeg. They were acquitted, but not
before it was clear to all concerned that the Mounties meant
business and that they would enforce the law among Indians and
whites alike.

The determination shown by the N.W.M.P. over the Cypress
Hills affair helped to establish a climate of trust among the Canadian Indians that was soon to be of crucial importance. On June
25, 1876, the long trail of broken promises by the U. S. Government to the Sioux nation came to a bloody halt at the Little Big
Horn River with the annihilation of Lieutenant Colonel George
Custer's (he was not, as is commonly supposed, a general)
225-man 7th Cavalry force.

Prior to the battle the Sioux had made an offer to their old
enemies the Blackfeet to help wipe out the white men in Canada

if the Blackfeet would first help them to destroy the whites on the American side of the border. The Blackfoot Chief Crowfoot refused to smoke the Sioux peace offering of tobacco. He told the Sioux envoy that the Mounted Police had proved to be friends and that the Blackfeet would not fight them.

The threat that U.S. forces avenging the Little Big Horn defeat would drive the warring Sioux onto Canadian soil lent urgency to the need to pacify the Indians in Canada. They had grown more susceptible to agitation for a blood war against the whites since the coming of the railway surveyors, which led many of them to fear they would be driven from their land. Thus at six o'clock on the morning of August 6, 1876, Sam Steele was roused from his bed at Swan River by Commissioner Macleod. Macleod had just been appointed to head the Mounted Police, succeeding Commissioner French, who had conducted a running war with Ottawa over various issues and who had resigned to resume his army career in England. The new chief of the force had ridden in overnight from Winnipeg.

He told Steele that they were abandoning Swan River as headquarters and that all headquarters personnel plus most of D Troop were to march at 9:30 for Fort Carlton, where government representatives were about to open negotiations for a treaty with the Cree Indians. By this time Steele had worked his men up to such a pitch of efficiency that they had the horses reshod and everything else ready for this 1,150-mile trek northwest with half an hour to spare.

At Fort Carlton Steele was glad he had helped to form the first N.W.M.P. band while at Swan River; the glittering brass instruments and the martial music delighted the Indians. Although the Mounted Policemen were nominally present to escort the treaty commissioners, impressing the natives was a prime consideration. The Indians loved pageantry and were quite willing to contribute a lot of colour of their own.

It was a stirring time, that summer of 1876. When he came to write his memoirs almost half a century later, Steele recalled the scenes at Fort Carlton: "The council tent was pitched on an eminence about a quarter of a mile from the Indian camp which contained upwards of 2,000 redskins. These assembled soon after the arrival of the commissioners, firing rifles, beating their tom-toms, dancing and yelling, the whole band chanting to the accompaniment of their drums.

"When quite ready they advanced in a semi-circle, preceded by a large number of mounted warriors giving an exhibition of their magnificent horsemanship. These braves had been painted by their squaws in the most approved Indian style, some like zebras, some like leopards, each according to the skill and fancy of the painters. It was a fine show, well worth coming many hundred of miles to see."

Resplendent in cocked hat, gold braid, and lace, Lieutenant Governor Alexander Morris smoked the peace pipe under the Union Jack with the Cree chieftains. He told them that the White Mother (Queen Victoria) did not want to interfere with the Indian way of life. She wanted Indian families to live in comfort on their own chosen land, and it was important to arrange this before the white settlers came to the country. The White Mother wanted every Indian family of five to have one square mile of land reserved for themselves. Schools would be built, and agricultural tools, oxen, cows, and seeds would be provided so that the Indians could feed themselves after the buffalo disappeared.

"Three years ago," he reminded them in a reference to the Cypress Hills incident, "some Americans killed some Indians. When the White Mother's councillors heard of it they said, 'We will send men there to protect the Indians; the White Mother's children shall not be shot down by the Americans.' Now you understand why the police are in this country and you should rejoice."

The Crees negotiated warily. Their great fear, which was to prove to be all too valid, was that with the buffalo gone, they might face starvation in the transition to the agricultural life.

The chiefs signed the treaty after five days of parleying. Besides money (the first annual payment of twenty-five dollars for a chief, fifteen dollars for a band councillor, and twelve dollars for everyone else in the tribe) the leaders were given a British flag, a medal and a gold-laced uniform, and top hats to identify them as officers of the Queen.

After the ceremonies Steele marched the police party north to Fort Pitt, where there was the same show of pageantry as at Carlton, followed by the same sort of powwows. Here a prominent chief was absent from the scene. This was Big Bear, who rode in after the other chiefs had signed the treaty. He had not wanted to negotiate, he explained, because he had not yet fully consulted his people. But he wanted Morris to agree in advance to one condition: that Indians convicted of murder would not be hanged.

"You ask what cannot be granted," the governor said. "Why are you so concerned about that? The law of the White Mother punishes murder with death, and your request cannot be granted."

Looking on, Steele realized what the chief was getting at. Indians were terrified of hanging because they believed that the rope choked off their soul's progress to the happy hunting ground. Big Bear parted with Morris with a handshake, saying that he was not against the treaty but could not sign it in the absence of his followers. He would sign it the following year, he said. Something about Big Bear's attitude made Steele doubt that he would ever sign at all.

8: THE INDIAN MENACE

Steele arrived at Fort Macleod, the new headquarters of the force, late in October of 1876. He reckoned that he had travelled exactly 1,149 miles since his party had left Swan River in August. For much of that rambling excursion over the plains not another human being was seen. The policemen had, however, encountered immense herds of buffalo, enough to cast doubt on the theory that the buffalo population was waning. Once they had nearly been trampled to death when a band of Indian hunters drove the main herd into their path. Amid the deafening thunder of hooves the Mounties stood their ground, shooting so many animals at point-blank range that they built a protective wall of carcasses around them. The herd parted and galloped past them. When the dust and smoke cleared, they speculated over whether it had been an accident, or whether the Indians had tried to use the buffalo herd as a weapon to wipe them out.

One day on the trail Commissioner Macleod took Steele aside for a talk about his future in view of the fact that his three-year term of enlistment was nearly over. Macleod promised to promote him to commissioned rank at the first opportunity if he stayed in the force. It was not a difficult decision for Steele to make; he had become a Mounted Policeman first and anything else after. He was willing to bide his time as RSM until the chance of a commission came up.

Macleod also explained why they were headed for the fort that bore his name. The battle of the Little Big Horn that June posed a serious new challenge for the N.W.M.P. Custer's stunning defeat, depicted in the American press as a bloody massacre of U.S. soldiers, had provoked an outcry throughout the United States for a conclusive victory over the Sioux Indians. As a result heavy reinforcements had been sent to the American Army in the West to seek and destroy the Sioux. Each skirmish in this determined campaign of harassment had driven the hostile Indians closer to the Canadian border. To prepare for the threat raised by their eventual crossing, the N.W.M.P. was well advised to mass its strength in southwestern Canada, and Fort Macleod was the logical base.

The approach of thousands of Sioux warriors raised a number of frightening possibilities. The Sioux might use Canadian soil as a refuge from which to launch raids into the United States, in which case the Americans could be expected to retaliate. There was ample sympathy in the U. S. Congress for a forcible takeover of western Canada; the Sioux might provide the excuse. Short of a planned invasion, there was always the possibility of border incidents that might precipitate armed conflict between Canada and the United States, with Great Britain weighing in on its self-governing colony's side.

Then, too, there was the threat of a full-scale Indian war if the Sioux decided to take on the Mounted Police, whom they overwhelmingly outnumbered. Though for the most part the Canadian Indians were traditional enemies of the Sioux, the chance remained that all the Indians and métis might band together to wipe out the whites on both sides of the line. Louis Riel, in exile in Montana, was thought to be advocating this, and the Sioux had already proposed it to the Blackfeet. A more immediate prospect was that of bloodshed among Indian tribes fighting over the dwindling supply of buffalo. If the Sioux began hunting the animals on the Canadian side of the border, it would put heavy pressure on the food supply. The Canadian Indians would be quite willing to do battle with the interlopers for their ancestral hunting grounds.

The N.W.M.P. was hopelessly short of the men, horses, and ammunition needed to cope with any kind of armed conflict. By 1876 an apathetic government in Ottawa had allowed its strength to drop through attrition to a total of 335 officers and men. An unspecified number of recruits from the East were due to arrive in the spring; in the meantime mounts had to be made ready for them. At Fort Macleod Steele soon found himself back at his old task of supervising bronc-busting in winter weather, in addition to his many other duties as regimental sergeant major of the North-West Mounted Police.

Several ranches, including one run by an ex-whiskey trader, had been established in the Fort Macleod area by the time Steele arrived, but ranching was difficult because the Indians were so adept at cattle rustling. The chief commerce of the white civilian community that had grown up around the police fort was trading in buffalo hides. Gambling ran a close second. Faro games flourished in a string of sod hovels along the main street. Gambling was still legal in the Northwest Territories, but not trading in liquor. Nevertheless the rawest sort of whiskey could be purchased and consumed in numerous blind pigs, which often doubled as gambling dens. Liquor was probably the cheapest commodity available. Prices for other produce from the outside were appalling. People paid six dollars for a dozen eggs.

The wild and woolly nature of the white civilian population kept the Mounted Police on the go breaking up drunken brawls and chasing whiskey traders, horse thieves, and cattle rustlers. Steele participated in his share of these activities along with his other duties, such as preparing police cases for the local court, which was presided over by N.W.M.P. officers who were also justices of the peace. The courtroom was usually crowded with colourful offenders and witnesses bearing such illustrative nicknames as "Wagon Box Julie," "Mormon Mike," and "Liver-Eating J." (the latter was said to have once eaten the liver of an Indian brave he had killed to ingest extra courage). Those convicted were locked up in the fort's guardroom. At Christmas the prisoners, including two U. S. Army deserters and an Indian horse thief, shared in the Mounties' feast of roast antelope, buffalo, wild goose, and turkey and, by way of a special permit, a spirituous milk punch.

As they celebrated the holiday with a concert featuring recitations, storytelling, and a bagpipe recital, the Mounties were unaware that the Sioux menace had already begun to materialize. The first party of Sioux refugees—about 500 men, 1,000 women, and 1,400 children with 3,500 horses and 30 U. S. Army mules—

had crossed the border a few days before, camping at Wood Mountain in what is now southwestern Saskatchewan.

The officer in charge of the district, Steele's old commander, Inspector Walsh, rode out to meet them. Making a point of displaying his scarlet coat, the inspector explained the laws to the Sioux chiefs. The American Indians eagerly volunteered to submit to the Queen's law if they were allowed to stay in Canada. Walsh reported: "They had been told by their grandfathers that they would find peace in the land of the British. . . . They had not slept sound in years and were anxious to find a place where they could feel safe."

Walsh warned them that "the Queen would never allow them to go from her country and make war on the Americans and return to her protection." He later wrote to Macleod that he believed more Sioux were on the way. His report arrived at Fort Macleod just after Christmas; shortly after the New Year the commissioner called a meeting, which Steele attended, to discuss how the police should react. They agreed on the urgency of ensuring the neutrality, if not the support, of the Canadian Indians by negotiating a treaty as soon as possible with the Blackfoot confederacy (embracing the Blackfoot, Blood, Piegan, and Sarcee tribes) and factions of other tribes on the western part of the prairies. The officers believed that although treaties were of no great value in controlling "bad Indians," the majority would be willing to stick to their agreement and resist joining the Sioux in any anti-white campaign.

During the early months of 1877 thousands more refugee Sioux drifted across the border in the Wood Mountain area. Then, towards the end of May, came the event the Canadian Government had been dreading: Sitting Bull came across. The victor of the Little Big Horn and generalissimo of the Sioux armies exercised tremendous influence over his people. As far as anyone then knew, he was still determined to drive the white man from Indian territory, at least in the United States. His presence in Canada would undoubtedly cause masses of hostile Sioux still on the American side of the line to cross over and rally to him in the hope that he would lead them in the reconquest of their homeland. When American newspapers wrote of Sitting Bull as the most dangerous man in North America, they were not far wrong.

The intrepid Walsh lost no time in riding out to meet Sitting Bull and his party and laying down the law to them. The chief was remarkably docile. Like the Sioux who had come before him, he claimed to be an ancestral British Indian who had "buried his arms on the American side of the line before crossing into the country of the White Mother." He declared that "his heart was always good, with the exception of such times as he saw an American." Walsh was highly impressed by the handsome, dignified chief, though no less so than the chief was impressed by the Mounted Police officer. Still, Walsh concluded that "Sitting Bull is of a revengeful disposition. . . . If he could get the necessary support he would recross the line and make war on the Americans."

Over the next few months, as party after party of Sioux crossed the border following Sitting Bull's lead, the Mounted Police were virtually defenceless except for their prestige. The total strength of Fort Walsh (named after Inspector Walsh) and the newly established Wood Mountain Post was 106 officers and men and only seventy horses, compared with an estimated 1,000 full-fledged Sioux warriors in the vicinity. The force was alarmingly short of ammunition as well.

That summer Commissioner Macleod embarked on the sensitive task of preparing the way for the Blackfoot treaty, which he saw as essential to the maintenance of the peace. Macleod himself was to be one of the government commissioners at the treaty negotiations; the other was David Laird, lieutenant governor of the Northwest Territories. The police commissioner was respected above all men by the Blackfeet and other Indians of the region to be covered by the treaty. Throughout these many thousands of square miles Macleod, whom the Indians called Bull's Head, was a living symbol of integrity.

Macleod had sounded out the Indian attitude towards the treaty and explained the government's position. The treaty would extinguish the Indians' rights to the territory and formally make them subject to the law administered by the Mounted Police. In return they would be given land reserves, money, farm implements, cattle, and schools for their children as insurance against the day when they could no longer rely on the buffalo. The way Macleod put the proposition, the Indians had a choice of starving

or becoming self-supporting with government help on reserved
land to which they had undisputed legal rights.

The site of the treaty negotiations was to be the Blackfoot
Crossing on the Bow River east of Fort Calgary. This was a traditional Blackfoot camping and burial ground where the Blackfeet
had won many battles against invading tribal enemies in the past.
It took weeks of negotiations to settle on this location. As a result
the gathering had to be postponed until September 1877.

On the twelfth of that month Sam Steele set out from Fort
Macleod with about eighty men. When they arrived that night at
the Blackfoot Crossing, the place was already bustling. Indians of
all tribes were streaming in and pitching thousands of teepees decorated with colourful picture writings on the outside walls. A
buffalo herd was passing nearby, and in the next few days the
place took on the look of a permanent encampment, with the
women tanning hides and cooking and drying the meat their men-
folk brought back from the hunt. In the meantime the Mounties,
with Steele in charge, raised their own impeccable camp, which
contrasted with the disorderly lean-tos erected by the free-lance
traders attracted thither by the treaty money the Indians would
soon have to spend. The big trading companies—the Hudson's
Bay, I. G. Baker, and W. T. Power—built large stores covered
with canvas and stocked with a large variety of merchandise.
Métis, missionaries, and Indians already covered by treaties arrived on the scene. At length it seemed as if everybody in the
Northwest Territories was there. When the negotiations opened
on September 17, someone meticulously counted 4,392 Indians.
No fewer than 15,000 horses grazed on the surrounding hills.

The powwow at the Blackfoot Crossing was by all accounts a
brilliant spectacle. The chiefs and tribal councillors were in all
their splendid finery, from their intricately beaded moccasins to
their feather warbonnets, with not a few scalps attached to their
persons in between. They sat in the warm sunlight in front of the
gleaming white council marquee tent to hear the opening address
of Lieutenant Governor Laird. It was obvious that the smart, red-
coated men flanking him were central to the issue when he declared: "When bad white men brought you whiskey, robbed you
and made you poor, and through whiskey made you quarrel
among yourselves, [the Queen] sent the Mounted Police to put

an end to it. You know they have stopped this and punished the offenders, and how much good has been done. I have to tell you how much pleased the Queen is that you have taken the Mounted Police by the hand and helped them and obeyed the laws since their arrival. She hopes you will continue to do so, and you will always find the police on your side if you obey the Queen's law."

The next day Chief Crowfoot replied in kind: "If the police had not come to this country, where should we all be now? Bad men and whiskey were indeed killing us so fast that very few of us indeed would have been left today. The Mounted Police have protected us as the feathers of the bird protect it from the frosts of winter. I wish them all good, and I trust that all our hearts will increase in goodness from this time forward. I am satisfied. I will sign the treaty."

Over the next few days forty-nine other chiefs and councillors followed suit, making X's beside their names, names like Bull Fat Back, Eagle Shoe, and Weasel Calf. A celebratory atmosphere prevailed, with much drumming, dancing, and feasting. By September 21 all the chiefs had signed, and the police staged a thirteen-gun salute. Over the next three days the police paid out the treaty money, about $1,500 in total. As he assisted in this task, Steele noted some odd requests, such as premiums for babies yet to arrive and payments for a surprisingly large number of infirm and blind relatives who could not attend.

In his official report on the negotiations the lieutenant governor wrote: "I would urge that the Mounted Police be entrusted to make the annual payments to the Indians under this treaty. The chiefs themselves requested this, and I said I believed the Government would gladly consent to the arrangement. The Indians have confidence in the Police, and it might be some time before they acquire the same respect for strangers." It was hard to believe that they had been in the West for only four years.

9: A TIME OF TENSION

When all the Blackfoot treaty money had been paid, Steele was ordered to break camp as soon as possible. On the morning of September 28, 1877, he paraded twenty-eight enlisted men and NCOs and rode out with Commissioner Macleod and Inspector Lief Crozier, bound east for Fort Walsh. In the past month a meeting had been arranged between Sitting Bull and the other fugitive Sioux chiefs and a U. S. Government commission headed by the well-known Civil War general, Alfred H. Terry. The Americans were to try to persuade the Sioux to agree to peace terms and return to the United States to take up reservations there.

It was a fine morning when the police party, guided by the great métis scout Jerry Potts, left the Blackfoot Crossing. But when they reached the junction of the Bow and South Saskatchewan rivers, near the present site of Medicine Hat, a violent snowstorm began to sweep across the plains. Potts had never been this way before, but he led the party unerringly. "We could see him riding ahead like a centaur amid the blinding snow," the commissioner later recalled. "No one dared to ride beside him for fear of distracting him from his task."

The storm raged for four days before the party finally arrived at Fort Walsh. Inspector Walsh himself was away, having gone to Sitting Bull's camp to try to talk him into meeting the American delegates. A strange relationship had grown up between the dapper Mountie and the Indian leader. Sitting Bull could be exasperating, and Walsh had an Irish temper, so they frequently engaged in shouting matches. During one of these rows Walsh

kicked Sitting Bull in the pants in front of all his followers. Yet
an enduring friendship had formed between these two rock-hard
men. The Sioux camp was seething with violent emotions over
the investment of the Nez Percé Indians, then besieged by a U. S.
Army force in the Bear Paw Mountains of Montana. Only the
great respect Sitting Bull held for Walsh induced him to meet
General Terry. Until the last minute Sitting Bull had half a mind
to lead his powerful army against the Americans in the Bear Paw
Mountains instead.

Steele found considerable tension at Fort Walsh. The presence
of the Nez Percé in Montana, where they were making a valiant
stand, had so exercised local white settlers that the American dispatch riders carrying messages in connection with the conference
demanded five hundred dollars for making the trip of 160 miles
between Forts Walsh and Benton, on the U.S. side. The morning
after their arrival Steele and his men rode out to meet Walsh, Sitting Bull, and the other Sioux chiefs and escort them back to the
fort. Steele was impressed by the appearance of these Indians, not-
ing the black, piercing eyes peculiar to the Sioux. There were
about twenty in all, including one tall woman in the prime of life.

The Indians jogged along beside the mounted white men and
talked familiarly. From what they said, it was obvious to Steele
that none had the slightest intention of accepting the American
offer to return to the States. Late in the afternoon one of the
Sioux peeled off towards a passing buffalo herd and killed a fat
cow. Then they all made camp beside a lake while the woman
deftly dressed the carcass and cut the meat into thin strips that
the Indians broiled on a fire of buffalo droppings (known idio-
matically as *chips*). As usual the Mounties had plenty of tea with
them, which satisfied an Indian passion. The whole group feasted
well into the night, "with each [Indian] stowing away at least
twenty pounds of the well-cooked meat," as Steele recalled. "This
gastronomic feat may seem incredible to those who do not know
the capacity of the North American Indian to eat large quantities
of food when favourable opportunity presents itself. He has to be
ready for the morrow, and it should be borne in mind that the
flesh of the buffalo is much easier to digest than beef."

The next day the police rode out to meet General Terry's party
at the border. The American commissioners were decidedly edgy

about their proximity to the Sioux despite their escort of Mounted Policemen and a large party of U.S. infantrymen riding in wagons drawn by mules. General Terry personally set the pace, riding at a lively trot. When they camped that night some forty miles south of Fort Walsh, the Americans posted piquets who nervously called out "all's well" every few minutes. They were so anxious to reach the safety of the fort that several mules collapsed of exhaustion on the way.

Steele could not help observing the differences between the Americans and Canadians in their attitudes and methods. He talked to a scout with the U.S. party who carried on vocally about his contempt for Indians. The U.S. troops were lavishly equipped in comparison with the Mounties. They had tents and stoves to heat them; whereas the Canadians had to make do with their blankets and a campfire even in the dead of winter on the plains.

The conference convened in the Fort Walsh mess hall in the midafternoon of October 14. Steele posted several Mounted Policemen at the doors and joined the officers inside the room. Sitting Bull entered in a wolfskin hat and a tattered shawl. He pointedly ignored the American commissioners and just as pointedly pumped Commissioner Macleod's hand. Then he sat down on a buffalo robe, coolly turned his back on the Americans, and lit his pipe.

The woman Steele had met on the trail entered with the chiefs. Because, according to custom, females never took part in Indian councils, the policemen construed this as a calculated slight to the Americans. When the time came for her to speak, she proved to be eloquent in her own tongue, but, as Steele reported, the translation was atrocious. She said that harassment by the Americans gave the Sioux women no opportunity to raise a family in peace. In the mouth of the translator this emerged as, "She say you never gave her time to breed."

It was clear from the outset that none of the chiefs would be moved in any way by the American commission's arguments. When they spoke at all, it was to reiterate their grievances; they kept repeating that they never wanted to see an American again. Finally General Terry asked Sitting Bull, "Are we to tell the President that you all refuse the offers made to you?"

The Sioux leader replied, "I have told you all I have to tell.

This country does not belong to you; all on this side belongs to these people," referring to the policemen. He stood and shook hands with Macleod and Walsh. The other chiefs rose, and there was a general round of handshaking and embracing of the other Mounted Policemen in the room.

After the conference had broken up, Macleod went to Sitting Bull's tent. He summoned the other chiefs to gather around him and announced, "The answer you have given the United States Commissioners today prevents you ever going back to the United States with arms and ammunition in your possession. It is our duty to prevent you from doing this. I wish to tell you that if any of you or your young men cross the line with arms in your hands that then we become your enemies as well as the Americans. . . . As long as you behave yourselves the Queen's Government will not drive you out."

Macleod again made it clear that the food supply in Canada could not support them and that they could never expect to be given reserves and provisions as Indians belonging to Canada. Like it or not, they belonged to the United States. The chiefs were adamant. "It's no good," the commissioner later told Steele. "I used all the old arguments. But the Sioux won't go. So I warned them that we'll give them nothing but protection and not even that if they make trouble. In the meantime, see to it that they get rations, tobacco, ammunition, and one blanket for everybody in Sitting Bull's party." This order led Steele to conclude that in a minimal fashion, the Sioux were to be bought off to avert bloodshed on Canadian soil.

After escorting the Sitting Bull Commission back to the border, Steele's party returned to Fort Macleod. With each passing month more people arrived in the area, and that meant more crime. The force was worked to the limit. Although he rose at six in the morning, Steele was seldom in bed before midnight. For the Mounted Police, life at Fort Macleod that winter was a time of ceaseless patrolling on horseback, snap raids on Indian camps to recover stolen horses and cattle, lying quiet in lonely coulees to intercept outlaws headed for the border with their loot or trying to escape arrest warrants, and riding out to cut off whiskey smugglers on their way north.

All this time more serious trouble was looming in the background. Big Bear, the temperamental Cree chief who had refused to sign the Carlton-Pitt Treaty the year before, disrupted the treaty payment sessions for some other Crees. Chief Beardy of the Duck Lake Crees also agitated for more money and attempted to invade a trading post at the head of a large party of heavily armed braves in war paint. Inspector James Walker met him on the stairs of the post with three armed Mounties and made him back off by threatening to shoot the first Indian to take another forward step.

Driven from their normal migratory pattern by prairie fires, many of the buffalo veered south over the American border. Only emergency issues of food supplies by the N.W.M.P. prevented starvation among the Blackfoot tribe. At Wood Mountain Inspector Walsh got word that Louis Riel had sent emissaries to attempt to capitalize on the situation, urging Chiefs Sitting Bull and Crowfoot to form a Sioux-Blackfoot-métis alliance to wipe the white men out.

In his annual report for 1877 Commissioner Macleod nevertheless was able to state: "Happily the year has passed over without any signs of the rumoured alliance of the Indians against the whites, and there has been no sign of disaffection on the part of our own Indians. They have visited and mixed with the Sioux, and the Sioux with them, and I have no reason to think that those visits have meant anything more than a desire to make peace with one another, as they have been enemies for years before." As Macleod noted, Crowfoot and Sitting Bull had met and parleyed cordially, agreeing that to obviate possible causes of friction, it would be advisable for the Blackfoot and Sioux not to camp too close to each other. Sitting Bull was so taken with the Canadian chief that he renamed his favourite son after him.

The buffalo did not return to the far western end of the prairies. Instead they tended to concentrate in the Fort Walsh area, and so did Indians from all over the territory who depended on the animals for a livelihood. Having so many Indians from so many different tribes in the same locality raised the prospect of serious tribal clashes. To add to this threat, Canada was faced with another influx of strange Indians, members of the Cheyenne tribe who were being driven towards the border in a running battle with U.S. troops; there was little doubt that they would cross over

if the Americans did not catch up with them first. Tight control
of the potentially explosive situation around Fort Walsh was
called for. As a result the headquarters of the North-West
Mounted was transferred from Fort Macleod to Fort Walsh in
May 1878.

The reinforcements the force so badly needed arrived shortly afterwards. Regimental Sergeant Major Steele had to train this
batch of recruits up to the high standards of the N.W.M.P. in a
drastically short time. Steele placed strong emphasis in his training syllabus on shooting: pistol practice on horseback with the
force's old, awkward, and often defective revolvers and target
practice with carbines. After years of being outgunned by the Indians and outlaws (practically everyone in the Northwest had repeating rifles, but the Mounties carried single-shot Snider-
Enfields), the force was slowly catching up. The first shipment
of the new Model 1873 Winchester carbines had arrived, but
there were only fifty of them. Practice with the repeaters had to
be curtailed because ammunition was scarce.

Inevitably there were many outbreaks of violence among the Indians in and around Fort Walsh. But in the words of the official
N.W.M.P. historian, John Peter Turner, "Unwavering justice and
tolerance by the Mounted Police had achieved almost unbe-
lievable results. Each flare-up that threatened to become serious
was promptly suppressed, the chief offenders arrested, tried, convicted, and punished with less tumult than the same procedure
would have caused in a Canadian city." It was nevertheless hard
and time-consuming work; and Steele was relieved to be assigned
in the fall to a long patrol to Edmonton.

Where once there had been a Hudson's Bay fort and nothing
else, a thriving little town was growing. Here was a tangible tribute to the work of the Mounted Police. And when Steele rode
back to Fort Walsh, he found that his own personal contribution
to the pacification of the Canadian West had not gone unno-
ticed. Sergeant Major Tom Lake greeted him with an exaggerated
salute. "Welcome back, Subinspector Steele," he said. "You've
been an officer, sir, for the past six weeks!"

10: WINTER ON THE PLAINS

His first command as an officer was very nearly his last. In January
1879 the Mounted Police were assigned to do a census of the
métis population, and Steele was detailed to cover the region between Calgary and Fort Macleod. He took with him two constables, named Holtorf and Mills, and an old métis hunter named
Tom Foley as a guide and interpreter. They set out on an extremely cold morning. The policemen were dressed in the force's
regulation winter outdoor uniform of buffalo coats and black
bearskin hats, woollen scarves around their necks and waists, and
moccasins covering several pairs of socks.

They brought along an eight-day supply of food and forage,
which should have been ample to carry them to their first stop at
Fort Macleod, about 150 miles away. Steele and Foley were on
horseback; each constable drove a light sleigh, called a *jumper*,
drawn by a pony. As they moved out into the treeless, undulating
landscape, Steele sensed a storm in the air. He reflected that the
winter thus far had been unusually severe, with frequent howling
blizzards and temperatures far below zero. The snow was very
deep; they had covered only a few miles when the jumpers started
getting bogged down and had to be shovelled free.

A blizzard struck savagely on their second day out, making
travel impossible. They dug a shelter in the side of snowbank and
huddled around a fire. They holed up in this way for the next two
days while the storm raged relentlessly. When the sky finally
cleared, the temperature plummetted. The storm had left behind

vast snowdrifts. The jumpers were constantly getting stuck, and the ponies pulling them were beginning to grow weak.

They trudged on for days through a maze of coulees choked with snow, moving cautiously and having to backtrack frequently to find clear passages. All this time they were steadily using up their supplies; on the ninth day out they ran out of food. Fort Macleod was still forty miles off. For the next three days they travelled on empty stomachs. Weakened by hunger and the excruciating cold, they moved at a meagre pace, stopping frequently to rest. The supply of feed for the horses was also exhausted. On the twelfth day it was clear that the ponies were too weak with hunger and stiff with cold to pull the sleighs.

Steele decided to leave the sleighs and baggage on the trail and have Holtorf and Mills ride the ponies. Foley had lost track of the route by now, so Steele led the way, navigating by the dim winter sun. Another blizzard struck at nightfall of that day. Still Steele "pushed on"—his favourite expression—until his horse stopped suddenly. It stood stock still despite his urgings forward. Finally he dismounted in disgust, only to find that the animal had halted within a yard of the precipitous bank of the Belly River. One more step and Steele probably would have been killed by plunging a hundred feet or more to the riverbed.

They camped nearby and woke the next morning to find themselves completely buried in a snowdrift. The blizzard still blew fiercely. The starving ponies could no longer carry the constables, so Steele decided to leave the animals behind.

The snow was too deep for men on foot. Steele told Holtorf, a tall, burly German-Canadian, to get on his horse behind him. The smaller Mills, one of the many Irishmen in the force, was mounted behind Foley. Steele knew they were close to Fort Kipp, the old whiskey-trading post. In the teeth of the snowstorm they rode up a valley to find the fort, where they thought they could at least find shelter and build a fire. When they reached the abandoned building, they found not a scrap of fuel. There was no choice but to strike out in the blizzard once again for Fort Macleod, seventeen miles away.

The snow was blowing worse than ever when the little party left the fort. The trail had long since been obliterated by the snow, but Steele had a good idea of the right direction. He set a course westward with Foley following. His horse plodded on slowly until Foley drew level with him and called, "The man behind you is freezing to death!"

Steele jumped off his horse and looked at his passenger. Sure enough, Holtorf was in the death sleep of exposure. Steele dragged the man off the horse's back and threw him roughly to the ground. He smacked his cheeks and shook and pummelled him, roaring, "A nice fellow you are, trying to steal off in this way! You must wait a while, you are too young to die yet. Wait a while!" In this way he roused the man out of his deadly slumber and got him back on the horse.

They rode into the storm at a slow walk for some time until Steele looked over at Foley and shouted, "The man behind *you* is freezing to death!"

It was Mills's turn to be manhandled back into consciousness. Later Holtorf had to be revived again, then Mills. Every few minutes one or the other would relapse into a death sleep. Luckily Foley was as robust as his leader. Both he and Steele had their wits about them, even though they had not eaten in four days.

Then Holtorf passed out one last time. Steele had him on the ground, beating him and shouting at him, when he noticed smoke in the wind. It was from Joe Macfarland's Pioneer Ranch, which he knew to be four miles east of Fort Macleod. Steele managed to get the constable on his feet and support him through the snow to the ranch house door, his horse instinctively following.

Mrs. Macfarland was alone in the house; a pot of soup was simmering on the stove. They wrapped the half-dead constables in blankets, fed them some soup, and put them to bed. Steele and Foley ate a hot meal, tended to their horses, and had a brief rest, then rode in to Fort Macleod to arrange for an ambulance for the men and a rescue party to recover the ponies they had left behind.

The remainder of the census went off without notable mishap. Steele covered some five hundred miles of territory in bitter winter weather before he returned to Fort Walsh early in the new year. He had scarcely settled back in his quarters when Assistant Commissioner A. G. Irvine summoned him with orders to hit the trail again. His mission concerned an Indian named Wandering

Spirit, the head soldier (second in command) of Big Bear's band of Crees.

Wandering Spirit was a bitter, foul-tempered, dangerous man who never passed up an occasion to show his defiance of the white authorities. In this case he and a party of followers had attacked a group of Cree people, not of their own band, who were out on a buffalo hunt. They assaulted the hunters and their women, cut up their harnesses, and made off with their horses. A métis hunter had found them wandering on the plains and had taken them to Fort Walsh. After hearing their story, the assistant commissioner ordered Steele to form a strong party to arrest Wandering Spirit and his gang.

Steele's party took three days to cover the hundred miles to the forks of the Red Deer and South Saskatchewan rivers. There the aggrieved Crees, who had ridden along, showed them the wrecked camp where they had been attacked. Steele had a hunch that the culprits were still in the vicinity. He rode ahead by himself to search the south branch of the Red Deer River. Soon he discovered the tracks of Indian ponies under a coating of fresh snow.

By the time he rejoined the party, it was too dark to follow a trail. They made camp in a grove of trees, prudently posting a guard. In the morning they picked up the Indians' tracks. A little farther on they sighted crows circling in the distance, indicating an encampment in the river valley. They split up into sections to surround the place and grab any Indian sentries who might be lurking about. When all were in place, Steele led the main body stealthily towards the camp. They reached the top of a bluff, formed up quietly, and then swooped into the camp at a gallop. This action drew a few wild shots from Indians who happened to be outside, but most of the Indians were still in their teepees when the Mounties burst in.

Only a handful of Indians were in this camp; Wandering Spirit was not among them. Steele ascertained, however, that they were Wandering Spirit's men and had participated in the attack on the other Crees. They were whisked off, escorted by the entire patrol in the direction of Fort Walsh. Towards evening Steele and fourteen men slipped away from the main body, fading into the woods while the prisoners and most of the policemen proceeded

11: THE LAST OF THE BUFFALO

In 1879, with devastating suddenness, the age of the buffalo in the Canadian West ended. Of the large herd that had migrated south the previous autumn, only a relative trickle returned northward across the border that spring. The steady toll taken on their numbers by hunting in Canada had been accelerated over the past few years by a relentless mass slaughter by Indian and white commercial hunters south of the border. In 1879 most of the animals that survived the winter stayed on the American side, partly because widespread prairie fires on the Canadian side had destroyed much of the grass on which they normally fed.

The long-expected food crisis in the Northwest thus arrived much sooner than anyone had predicted. It came after a terrible winter when deep snow and blizzards often precluded hunting the remnants of the herd that had wintered in Canada. This meant that the Indians and métis had mostly exhausted their usual stocks of buffalo meat.

Only the barest start had been made by the authorities to equip the natives to feed themselves by farming and ranching. Unlike the Indians of the woods, they were not skilled at fishing or hunting other game. They had never needed to look beyond the buffalo for sustenance. And now it had almost disappeared.

The crisis could not have happened at a worse time, with almost 5,000 Sioux and other American Indians living in Canada. As food became scarcer, the prospect of bloodletting between the refugees and the Canadian Indians grew. The Blackfeet bitterly blamed excessive hunting by the Sioux for the shortage of buffalo;

across the open plains to deceive any of Wandering Spirit's scouts who might be watching.

Steele and his party rode as inconspicuously as possible down the South Saskatchewan River, where he speculated Wandering Spirit might have camped. Well after dark that chilly evening they spotted fires glowing in a clearing in the woods along the riverside. They dismounted and surrounded the spot, then crept towards the teepees. Steele's sharp call to come out with their hands up took the Indians totally by surprise. This time Wandering Spirit was present. He was placed, muttering, under arrest.

On the trail back to Fort Walsh a minor incident occurred which so touched Steele that he was to remember it more than thirty years later. At one point the Mounties stopped for some provisions they had cached on the way out. A few hardtack biscuits were missing from a box that had been broken open. There were moccasin tracks around the spot.

"When we returned to the fort," Steele wrote in his memoirs, "an Indian came to offer payment for the biscuit which he had taken 'because he was hungry and knew they had enough.' Such was the Indian before he came into contact with the low white. It was perfectly safe to leave anything out of doors, neither Indian nor white man would touch it. The former, and sometimes the latter, would steal the horses of their enemies, but the Indians looked upon that as war and an honourable act."

Still, much as he respected most red men, he had no use for Wandering Spirit or his chief, Big Bear. He wrote, "Our prisoners were tried . . . the day after our return, and were given several months' imprisonment, which might appear to be sufficient punishment, but after events proved that the longest term that could be given to the wretches who composed Big Bear's soldier lodge would be none too much for them." Steele was never one to waste personal animosity on his adversaries. But Big Bear and his henchmen were a special case.

the Sioux blamed it on the Blackfeet for deliberately setting prairie fires in a self-defeating attempt to confine the buffalo within their own hunting grounds.

In the spring hungry Indians from all parts of the territory came drifting into the Cypress Hills area, first to await the migrating buffalo, then to draw emergency rations from the police when the migration failed to materialize. Steele was assigned to the heartrending work of doling out scant supplies of flour and beef in the Indian camps that had sprung up around Fort Walsh. The government's food supplies were severely limited; the rations were only sufficient to keep the Indians from outright starvation. To supplement them the Indians ate whatever they could lay their hands on: gophers, mice, small birds, and stolen cattle, which they persisted in regarding as fair game.

Steele was able to escape temporarily from the depressing scene around Fort Walsh in June, when he was ordered to a place called the Coal Banks on the Missouri River to pick up a much-needed draft of eighty reinforcements for the N.W.M.P. who had travelled from eastern Canada through the United States via rail and riverboat. While awaiting the recruits, he passed a pleasant interlude as guest of a U. S. Infantry detachment stationed there. Heavy rainstorms delayed his party's return journey. He arrived back at Fort Walsh to find that orders had arrived from Ottawa for a reclassification of ranks that raised him one notch. Henceforth he would be an inspector.

In the summer Steele's main duty became protecting the Fort Walsh corrals against horse thieves. Horse stealing by the Indians who were concentrated in the area had become so prevalent that the corrals were crammed with recovered horses waiting to be claimed by their owners, in addition to the force's own mounts. One night the whole herd stampeded. Steele had with him only one constable possessing the riding and roping skills required to recover the horses. The two rode out into the darkness, rounding up batches of horses here and there.

In the course of this Steele was loping along in a ravine when his horse put a hoof through a gopher hole, turned a somersault, and crashed down on top of him. It is a measure of his ruggedness that he was not hurt so badly as the horse, which regained its feet with blood streaming from its nostrils and had to be taken temporarily off duty. In the meantime its badly bruised master continued to do his rounds on a substitute mount.

But if injuries could not get him down, illness could. When Fort Walsh was struck late in the summer by an epidemic of the typhomalarial disease known as *mountain fever*, he was one of the first to catch it. He stayed in bed for several days, then characteristically got up too soon. He immediately went to visit a friend, Fred Clarke, who was suffering from the same disease. Clarke, who was the local agent for the I. G. Baker Trading Company, lay in a dark corner of a stifling log cabin. A group of Indians lined up against a wall kept a silent watch; the stinking air was loud with the buzzing of flies. Steele tried to cheer up his friend, but obviously he had lost his will to live. As he sat by Clarke's bedside, Steele reflected on the hardships of the western pioneers, who had left their comfortable homes in the East to live such a lonely life —and in this case to die such a lonely and squalid death. The most Steele could do was chase the Indians out of the place, retaining only one small boy whom he persuaded to fan the flies off the dying man's face.

He had just got back to his room when he collapsed. He was soon deep in delirium. Over the next few days the post surgeon, Dr. Kittson, gave him large doses of quinine, the only medicine that seemed to help. Then the doctor himself came down with the disease. When Dr. Kennedy arrived from Fort Macleod to replace him early in September, he found seventeen policemen and a number of civilians suffering from the fever. Several people had already died from it, including Steele's friend Fred Clarke.

By this time Steele had virtually been given up for dead. The man famed in the force for his ability to carry a load of three hundred pounds on his shoulders had shrunk to a pitiable living skeleton, too weak to stand by himself. Dr. Kennedy did what he could for his patient, but it was not long before he came around to ask Steele if he had any last messages to send to his family. With no apparent justification Steele replied that he hadn't because he intended to survive.

There were no nurses in that distant outpost, so the able-bodied policemen looked after their bedridden comrades in their off-hours. Young Constable Holtorf volunteered to nurse the man who had recently saved his life. The big lad devoted himself wholeheartedly to making Steele comfortable. Every day he rode several miles up into the hills to fetch a bucket of cool spring water for Steele to drink. Like the doctor and everyone else who had seen Steele's condition, Holtorf was convinced that his hero was on the brink of death.

When at last there seemed to be no hope left, Holtorf crept into Steele's room on his hands and knees, dragging a blanket behind him. He intended to settle down at the foot of the bed so that he could be with Steele when he died. Steele awoke as the constable came in and feebly asked what he was doing. Holtorf's explanation amused him greatly. He somehow found the strength to guffaw and order the constable to get out of the room and let him get back to sleep. That moment of mirth marked a turning-point; the fever broke the next morning. He was soon back on his feet, although for some time he could not get around without a walking stick and in the next few weeks he occasionally lost his memory while commanding parades.

When the treaty payments on the reserves had all been made in the fall, masses of Indians again converged on the Cypress Hills area. They had come to hunt buffalo, but, as in the spring, the animals did not pass that way that year. Those that had not been killed in Canada in the summer had been turned back into the United States by the Sioux, who hunted the north flank of the main herd along the Canadian side of the border. It seemed as if the migratory pattern of the animals had been altered for good.

The Indians and métis who ventured across the border to the United States to hunt the buffalo (and sometimes steal horses) were unceremoniously ejected whenever the U. S. Army could locate them. Indeed Sitting Bull himself had been forced back over the border in July in a running battle between a party of his Sioux followers and a far superior U. S. Army force.

As another winter set in, more and more of Steele's time was spent distributing rations to the Indians who clustered around Fort Walsh. At least five hundred of these people had no other source of food. As he rode around their camps, placing meagre portions of meat into the trembling hands of once-proud braves, he felt a surge of indignation that they should be in such a position. Although it was true that the Indians had been very improvident while the buffalo were still plentiful, sometimes killing animals only to eat their tongues and abandoning the rest, he also blamed the "ruthless white hunters who had been sent by the merchants of the United States, who were in the robe trade, to slaughter the noble animals for their hides alone. This resulted in the wretched Indians, once the wealthiest and happiest of primitive races, being forced to loiter about frontier posts and villages, to live on garbage or the contents of swill barrels not fit for hogs to eat."

The constant begging of the Indians for food in addition to rations got on the nerves of the policemen. The men of a detachment living at a horse-herding camp about three miles from Fort Walsh had a particular problem with a party of Bloods who camped beside them and continually pestered them for extra food. At length one of the constables, a recent recruit named Marmaduke Graburn, lost his temper with the boldest and most persistent of the beggars, a diminutive, pinch-faced young man named Star Child. Exasperated by Star Child's wheedling, Graburn called him a "dirty dog" and chased him out of the camp.

At daybreak of November 18, 1879, Steele was ordered out to lead a patrol to search for Graburn. The previous evening the young Constable had ridden off from the herding camp to recover some gear he had forgotten at a nearby cabbage patch; he had not returned. With Jerry Potts scouting ahead, Steele's patrol spent all day scouring the vicinity of the herding camp. They were just able to make out the prints of one shod police horse and two unshod Indian ponies. Later they found some Indian pony tracks leading south.

Darkness halted the search, and snow fell during the night, making their task that much more difficult. They started again at daybreak, but it was some time before Jerry Potts reined up and called out to Steele. The scout had been riding through a patch of snow, and his horse's hooves had churned up blood on the ground underneath. Everybody dismounted to search the bushes close to Pott's discovery. Within a few minutes Potts found Graburn's pillbox cap hanging from a limb.

After hours of further searching scout Louis Leveille uncovered Graburn's body at the bottom of a brush-choked ravine. It had a gaping bullet hole through the neck.

Steele formed a mental picture of what had happened: The

murdered man had been joined on his way to the cabbage patch by two Indians who had ridden along beside him, talking to him. Then one of the Indians had halted suddenly and shot him in the back of the neck. His body had pitched forward into the ravine where it was found. His horse had been led into the woods nearby, tied to a tree, and shot. One of the Indians, presumably the murderer, had then ridden off in the direction of the United States.

They tried to track the fugitive across the open prairie, but a warm chinook wind had blown up and melted the snow. They went through the routine of searching every fold in the terrain, although by then it was fairly clear that he had fled safely across the border. Steele was mystified about the motive. Graburn had been an agreeable young man who had quickly picked up the Blackfoot language and was known to be popular with the Indians. It was not until a sunny day early the next spring that a clue to the murder emerged.

It was then that a couple of Blood Indians awaiting trial for horse stealing at Fort Walsh decided to make a run for it. They darted out of an open gate in the stockade during their exercise period, picking up their Winchesters and ammunition belts from their wives, who were waiting outside the gate for them as they sped past. Steele, who happened to be nearby, saw that the Indians in their moccasins were leaving their riding-booted jailers far behind. He bawled out for a mounted muster and sent the first men who saddled up after the Indians. The policemen caught up with the escapers about a mile away, riding straight into the mouths of their levelled rifles. The Indians threw down their arms and surrendered. Once they were back in their cells, Steele busied himself in the search for another suspected horse thief, a Blackfoot, who had taken advantage of the commotion to light out in another direction.

Late that evening a guard told him that the Bloods were asking to see an officer. Steele arranged for them to talk to his superior, Superintendent Lief Crozier, in his quarters at around midnight. The Indians insisted that Crozier's windows be covered with blankets so that they could not be seen. They then told him that they knew who murdered Graburn. They gave him the name and description of Star Child.

Meanwhile the third escaper was still missing. Eventually Steele halted the search for him, assuming that by then he was far away. But a few days after the jailbreak, a constable who lived in the married quarters next to the fort reported that he thought he had heard someone groaning in the backyard. It turned out to be the young Blackfoot, who had been lightly dressed on the warm day he escaped, and who had been hiding out in the backyard when the weather again turned stormy and cold. He died shortly after they got him into the hospital. The police had to show his body to his Blackfoot relatives, who had the idea that they had hanged him. Even Dr. Kennedy had difficulty convincing them he had died a natural death.

Star Child was not brought to trial for another two years, after he returned to Canada from his hideout in the Bear Paw Mountains of Montana. He was acquitted on the evidence, and, Steele believed, on the strength of the jury's fear of reprisals at a time when white-Indian relations were particularly tense.

The spring of 1880 was a time of constant alarms for the Mounted Police at Fort Walsh because of an outbreak of horse stealing among the Indians. There were now an estimated five thousand of them in the area, belonging to at least seven different full-scale tribes. All the tribes stole horses from each other, and raiding parties from the United States stole horses in Canada and vice versa. The altercations that arose from this round robin of thievery threatened an outbreak of bloodshed that could spread and spread. On one occasion the Assiniboines fired shots into a Sarcee camp. The Sarcees did not retaliate. The Assiniboines evidently thought better of their action, repairing to Fort Walsh to complain about the Sarcees stealing their horses. Superintendent Crozier sent Steele to bring in the Sarcee thieves.

He waited for nightfall, then rode out with his troop and a couple of scouts to a coulee near the Sarcee camp. He sent the scouts up a hillside overlooking the camp while he led the troop noiselessly up a ravine. After the scouts had reported all quiet, he ordered his men to encircle the camp. This done, he took several men with him and walked into the inner circle of teepees. He had assumed the Indians were sleeping, but they apparently had been expecting a visit from the police and were sitting in a circle with their rifles in their hands. They recognized the big redcoat, calling out "How, Manistokos," using the Blackfoot name (meaning "Protector") by which Steele was known throughout the Cypress Hills. He shook hands with them and told them why he was there. Despite their friendliness, he knew that they would do everything they could to cover up for the horse thieves among them. He told them to assemble all their braves in the middle of the camp while his men carried out a search.

They looked into teepee after teepee; each was empty. But realizing that he might be involved in a cat-and-mouse game, Steele had stationed men to watch the gaps between the tents. Sure enough, the horse thieves were darting back behind the line of teepees from the ones the police were about to search to the ones they had already found empty. Steele's lookouts spotted one of the thieves doubling back and tackled him. Two more were caught later in the same fashion. Then Steele had the stolen horses rounded up and galloped off to the fort with them and the thieves.

Inspector Crozier cited the incident of the Assiniboines firing on the Sarcees in his 1880 annual report as an example of the inflammatory nature of the horse-stealing situation. He commented: "Perhaps no better proof can be adduced of the authority and influence of the force, and the respect in which it is held, than the fact of detachments being able, when the Indians were greatly excited, to enter their camps and recover stolen property. Certainly I can say that it was only by the constant and prompt action, as well as mediation of the police, that much serious trouble between the tribes was averted."

12: FORT QU'APPELLE

There was no relief from the near famine in the Canadian West in 1880. Buffalo were scarce even across the U.S. border; on the Canadian side they became very rare indeed. Steele heard that the refugee Sioux had been making themselves sick in their desperation by eating the flesh of horses that had died in a mange epidemic. Some Sioux chiefs were bowing to pressure from the authorities on both sides of the border to return to reservations in the United States, where they at least were guaranteed an adequate diet.

By April 1,200 Sioux had followed their chiefs back across the border. On July 3 the chiefs of all the Ogalala Sioux surrendered to Superintendent Walsh, specifying conditions which the U. S. Government subsequently met. Walsh was about to leave his post at Wood Mountain, having been relieved of command because Sir John A. Macdonald thought that he was too friendly with Sitting Bull. The superintendent rode off on an old white U. S. Army horse captured at the Little Big Horn, which he had acquired from the Sioux and had named Custer. As a parting gift, Sitting Bull gave him his magnificent feathered warbonnet, saying, "Take it, my friend, and keep it. I hope never to have to use it again."*

The official excuse for Walsh's departure was that he was on his way back east on an indefinite sick leave; he had been suffering from recurring spells of a skin disease. He was also on a personal mission on behalf of his great Sioux friend. Sitting Bull had asked him to attempt to see U. S. President Rutherford B. Hayes to

* The bonnet is now on display in the Royal Ontario Museum in Toronto.

secure a guarantee that he could return to the United States safely if he so decided. The Sioux war chief understandably feared that as the man who had wiped out Custer's troops, he might be killed in vengeance if he recrossed the border. Walsh promised to do his best to arrange to talk to the President, subject to permission from Prime Minister Sir John A. Macdonald. Macdonald, who was furious with Walsh because he thought that Walsh had encouraged Sitting Bull to remain in Canada, rudely turned down this request.

Steele was assigned to command B Division while Walsh was absent. Man for man it was probably the most experienced unit in the force. For several years it had kept the peace among Sitting Bull's Sioux and all the other Indians at Fort Walsh and Wood Mountain. Now Steele was to move it en masse to the tiny trading settlement of Qu'Appelle, three hundred miles to the northeast. Up to then Qu'Appelle had been a small N.W.M.P. outpost. Steele was ordered to turn it quickly into a full-scale fort.

Preliminary surveys of the route of the Canadian Pacific Railway indicated that it would run northwest through the Qu'Appelle Valley, which had the makings of a good agricultural area. By establishing the new fort with its various outposts, the force was getting ready for the advent of the railway and the white settlement that would come in its wake. At that time, though, the nearest white homesteaders were still about 140 miles to the east at Rapid City, which boasted all of twelve houses. A more immediate task was to assist in the settlement of the Indians on reserves in this easterly part of the Northwest Territories. Abandoning their futile search for buffalo, the Indians were streaming into the reserves, and the police were needed to escort them and issue rations on the way.

The reserves themselves would have to be patrolled, and liquor smuggling presented another problem. For illicit liquor traders supplying the Indians and métis, the Qu'Appelle Valley was a profitable sieve. There were numerous ways to skirt the police outposts at the main points of entry. Steele's orders were to tighten up surveillance of the liquor traffic. He was afforded a total of thirty-eight men to police a territory of roughly four hundred square miles.

He arrived at Qu'Appelle after a fast nine-day trek with eight four-horse wagons heavily laden with supplies and equipment. The government Indian agent, Colonel Allen McDonald, was just about to depart on an inspection trip, so Steele had to take temporary charge of the Indian agency along with everything else. An old Cree chief named Pasqua immediately approached him for rations to take a party of young braves across the U.S. border on a hunting expedition. Steele had been present earlier when the Indian agent had refused this request, but Pasqua did not recognize him and was taking advantage of McDonald's absence to give it another try. Steele knew the reason for McDonald's decision: that Pasqua and his men were a particularly wild bunch who were likely to make trouble with the U.S. Indians. When Steele turned him down a second time, the chief went off muttering angrily and formed a small party to go across the border nevertheless.

The Indian agent's fears proved all too valid. Near the Missouri River the Crees raided a Mandan Indian camp, killing and scalping several old people and women and children left behind while the able-bodied men were out on a hunt. Pasqua's party then turned back for Canada, but they had not gone far before the Mandan hunters returned to the grisly scene at their camp and galloped off after them. The Mandans took the wrong trail. On it, at a point within Canada, they came across a party of Assiniboines whom they mistook for Pasqua's Crees. The Mandans attacked and were driven off with some losses. It was the last battle between Indians to be fought on Canadian soil.

Steele was not aware of what had happened for some time; he heard about it only after Pasqua had succeeded in holing up in a well-guarded hideaway on the Qu'Appelle Lakes. At any rate, there was little he could do about the Cree chief's part in the incident because the authorities in the United States, where the Mandan massacre occurred, typically failed to follow up the case.

Meanwhile he got on with the job of building Fort Qu'Appelle. He was under instructions to salvage all the sawn lumber necessary to erect the barracks at the new fort from Swan River, the onetime headquarters of the force, which was to revert to an outpost staffed by four men. Swan River and Qu'Appelle were 128 miles apart, connected by trails that were frequently flooded with knee-deep water. In between were two swift streams at which the lumber had to be laboriously unloaded and floated across. Besides dismantling the Swan River buildings and hauling the lumber, the men felled logs for building the stables in the woods seven miles from the construction site. It says much for Steele's leadership and powers of organization that the entire fort was complete by early autumn. All the work had been done by the policemen, apart from the specialized jobs of building chimneys and thatching roofs.

This was accomplished while they also maintained wide-ranging patrols, escorted Indians to their reserves, kept a sharp eye on the liquor trade, and put the post on a nearly self-supporting basis. Steele acquired a small herd of cattle, which the men tended and slaughtered for meat. They cut and hauled their own hay and firewood. They had even built dog sleds for winter travel before the snow flew that year.

Few outbreaks of crime occurred to disrupt the routine. Those that did were handled in Steele's usual decisive manner. In July an Indian informed him that Little Fisher, a Salteaux wanted for horse theft, was hiding out in a camp nearby. Steele led a party which surrounded the camp before dawn. By first light he had his informer point out the teepee in which Little Fisher was staying. He told his sergeant to wait for him and marched straight in.

His entry awoke eight Indians, including Little Fisher, who somehow produced a knife and sprang to his feet brandishing it. Steele seized his wrist and twisted it sharply, sending the knife to the floor. The policemen hustled Little Fisher out of the camp before his excited kinsmen had time to think about retrieving him. He was subsequently sentenced to six months' hard labour at Stony Mountain Penitentiary near Winnipeg.

During the winter Steele lived in a log house with a thatched roof heated by a narrow mud-cake fireplace. He slept on a pallet of round poplar poles covered with rough boards, with straw filling the cracks in between. The fire in the little box stove in his sleeping quarters always died during the night, and he would wake to find the bucket of water frozen solid to the bottom. Yet he slept well, even though the temperature inside the room once sank to more than $-30°$ F.

A few days into the new year of 1881 a Cree Indian came to the post with the news that the "great sickness" had come again: smallpox. Steele rode out to the Cree camp a few miles away to see for himself. He took with him the post's sick bay orderly, an ex-medical student named Holme, who was the nearest thing to a doctor in a hundred miles. Cree men, women, and children lay miserably in teepees bundled in buffalo robes in a state of high fever while native medicine men chanted and rattled charms over them. Doc Holme, as he was called in the force, confirmed that they were suffering from smallpox.

Steele realized that he had a crisis on his hands. North American Indians were especially vulnerable to this disease, which they rightly regarded as one of the scourges brought by the white man. If it caught hold among the thousands of Indians in the reserves scattered throughout the Qu'Appelle region, it would bring not only tragedy but a dangerous new groundswell of enmity towards the whites. He had to stop it from spreading—if indeed it had not already begun to spread.

He rushed back to the fort and summoned Indian Agent McDonald and the Hudson's Bay Company trader, W. J. McLean, to an urgent meeting. There and then they formed themselves into a duly constituted board of health with full emergency powers under the North-West Territories Act. Doc Holme arrived back from ministering to the sick Crees to find himself appointed the official medical health officer. Steele sent him back to place the affected Cree camp under quarantine and then to start vaccinating all the Indians and métis in the area.

He then dispatched squads of fast riders to post notices at every important point and fork on every trail warning travellers not to enter houses or teepees in the Qu'Appelle Valley. Over the next few weeks Doc Holme rode several hundred miles in sub-zero weather, vaccinating a multitude of highly reluctant people and choking off localized outbreaks of the disease with treatment and quarantines. The Mounties won their battle; they not only stopped an epidemic but saved those who were stricken. The outbreak did not take a single life.

The winter of 1881 had been a bad one for the Sioux in Canada. Despairing of ever finding a permanent home on Canadian soil, more than 3,500 surrendered to the U.S. authorities and moved back south. But Sitting Bull was unimpressed by evidence that those who had gone to live on the American reservations were being well treated. His ever dwindling band of followers hung around the police and trading posts at Wood Mountain, scrounging food and resisting all attempts by the police and other well-wishers to persuade them to return to the United States.

Then one day in May he arrived on Steele's doorstep. Camping just outside Fort Qu'Appelle, he sent word that he wanted to talk. Steele promptly obliged, smoking a peace pipe with Sitting Bull in front of his teepee. Sitting Bull explained that he had come to see his friend Superintendent Walsh on the assumption that Walsh had returned from the east to his division at Qu'Appelle. Steele said that he had no idea when Walsh would return. Sitting Bull expressed a belief that Walsh would obtain a reserve for him and his band in the Qu'Appelle Valley. Steele discouraged this notion, responding that it was not at all likely that the government would change its official position that the Sioux belonged back in the United States.

Steele says in his memoirs that Sitting Bull had 1,200 followers with him at the time. This was evidently a mistake, as most historians reckon that his party could have numbered no more than 100 when they left Wood Mountain to look for Walsh. At any rate Sitting Bull set out to play on Steele's sympathies. He declared that Canada was his country and that the *Shaga Lasha* (the Mounted Police) were his friends. The *Mela Hoska* (Long Knives: i.e., U.S. soldiers) had no claim on him because the Sioux had never agreed to be governed by the Americans.

Steele contradicted this last statement, reminding Sitting Bull that the Sioux had once accepted a U. S. Government reservation. They were American Indians no matter what Sitting Bull might claim. He urged the chief to return to the United States, where food and schooling would be provided to ease the transition to the new way of life that was inevitably coming. It was no use waiting for Walsh, Steele said.

Sitting Bull insisted that he had been given to understand there would be no difficulty in arranging for a reserve for the Sioux in the Qu'Appelle area. Steele reiterated that it would be useless to apply for one but added that he had no authority to deal with a question of that kind. It happened that the Indian commissioner for the Northwest Territories, Edgar Dewdney, was at Shoal Lake at the time; Steele offered to send for him to meet with Sitting Bull. When the powwow ended, Steele sent a rider to fetch the

Indian commissioner. Then he ordered rations of flour and bacon
to be issued to the Sioux—as he said, for old time's sake.

He also sent other riders around to the métis and Indians in the
area with a request that they do nothing to encourage the Sioux
to remain there. Over the next few days, however, Sitting Bull
managed to procure a supply of fish from a friendly métis and a
large stock of flour from the mission priest. Commissioner Dewdney came and told Sitting Bull that as far as the government was
concerned, the Sioux were American Indians who could not be
assisted in settling in Canada. "You go back to Wood Mountain," he advised, "and if you're wise you'll get your people together and head straight for Fort Buford." (This was the nearest
U. S. Army post.)

"I know the reason why you all want me to go back, my carcass
is nothing but gold, they would give a good deal for my carcass,"
Sitting Bull protested. But he began to see that he had no choice.

Dewdney offered him sufficient food supplies to take his party
back to Wood Mountain. Steele told the chief firmly that he
would issue rations for that purpose and that purpose alone. Finally Sitting Bull gave in. With great relief Steele detailed an escort to go with the Sioux and issue the food as required. The
supplies had all been consumed when the party reached Wood
Mountain on July 2.

There Sitting Bull went to see Inspector Alex Macdonell, who
was in charge of the local N.W.M.P. post. The chief demanded
more rations, threatening to take them by force.

"I'll ration you with bullet," Macdonell told him.

"I am thrown away!" Sitting Bull exclaimed.

"No, you are not thrown away," said the inspector. "You are
given good advice, which is that if you require food you must return to your reservation in the United States, where you will be
well treated."

After receiving assurances of good treatment in a message from
Walsh and dickering with trader Jean-Louis Legaré over supplies
for the trip, Sitting Bull at last agreed to leave for the United
States with 235 of his followers on July 10, 1881.

A convoy led by Legaré took the party across the line, and on
July 19 Sitting Bull surrendered his rifle to a U. S. Army officer.
Shortly afterwards he arrived on the Standing Rock Reservation

in North Dakota, where many of the Sioux who had returned from Canada had been sent. After a tour with Buffalo Bill Cody's Wild West Show in the mid-1880s, Sitting Bull went back to the reservation. He died there in December 1890, shot in a fracas with the reservation's native Indian police force.

Part Two

THE BUILDING YEARS

13: THE FIRE WAGON TRAIL

The charter for the Canadian Pacific Railway Company to build a rail line between eastern Canada and the Pacific Coast in return for enormous government land concession was granted by the Dominion Parliament in February 1881. It had been nearly ten years since British Columbia had been persuaded to join the Canadian confederation by the promise that a railway to link it with the rest of the country would be in place within ten years. The time originally allotted for the construction had been eaten up by political scandal, procrastination, and parliamentary wrangling. The belated completion of this stupendous engineering undertaking offered one last chance for the young nation. Otherwise it was next to certain that British Columbia would secede, and Canada, as then constituted, would collapse.

The shock waves of this historic venture were felt in Fort Qu'Appelle that autumn. Anticipating the prosperous settlement that would come in the railway's wake, land speculators and aspiring homesteaders began to pour into the Qu'Appelle Valley while the nearest track was still two hundred miles to the east. They reasoned that with the coming of the railway, the valley would blossom into a populous area; Fort Qu'Appelle itself was being touted as the future capital of the Northwest Territories. The richest pickings would go to those who were on the spot first.

Winter struck the valley, but the would-be settlers kept coming. Many had no conception of the perils of travel in the wilderness or the severity of the climate in the Canadian West. To make matters worse, some proceeded on the assumption that there was nothing special to know about such things, ignoring the advice offered by Indians, plainsmen, traders, and Mounted Policemen. On they came, in overloaded wagons drawn by horses worked to the point of exhaustion, with pathetically inadequate clothing and footwear, often with no compasses or tents.

Steele and his men were kept continually on the move aiding and rescuing these ill-prepared travellers. The newcomers got lost; they got stuck in the snow; their horses died. At least one man died of exposure. Appalled at their improvidence, Steele watched them learn about the hardships of the wild country by bitter experience while he personally learned that the recklessness of people in search of a quick financial killing could not be underestimated.

It would be remarkable if, while they were shovelling wagons out of snowdrifts and treating cases of frostbite, the policemen did not reflect ruefully on the part they had played in making such a conspicuous success of the marquis of Lorne's tour of the Northwest the previous summer. The marquis was Queen Victoria's son-in-law and governor-general of Canada, and his viceregal progress across the Great Plains had been covered extensively and enthusiastically in the Canadian and British press. The publicity that thus emanated from "the Golden West" encouraged many people to come looking for a new and richer life there. But ranging over the prairie in the glory of summer in the manner of the marquis and his entourage, with a large escort of Mounted Police to see to their every need, was a far cry from striking out into the inhospitable Qu'Appelle Valley in the winter. As it turned out, the hardships of these adventurers and the efforts of the Mounted Police to succour them were mainly in vain because the C.P.R. line was subsequently rerouted to bypass Fort Qu'Appelle.

Steele was more than ready for a rest when he rode out of the fort in February 1882 on a long-awaited home leave. A few days later he reached Brandon, Manitoba, then the end-of-track of the C.P.R. construction job. There, a locomotive chugging along a formerly empty stretch of prairie reminded him of how long he had been away from civilization; it had been nine years since he had seen one. He took a train to Winnipeg, stopping off to visit some old friends from Simcoe County who had settled on the huge spreads of land available near Portage la Prairie.

Winnipeg, that hamlet of sod huts which Steele had first seen as a young soldier, had grown into a bustling fledgling city of more than twelve thousand inhabitants. However, despite its multistorey stone houses, its gas street lamps, its shops and hotels, the capital of the new Province of Manitoba was not a physically attractive place. But as the London *Times* correspondent who had accompanied the marquis of Lorne on his tour remarked of it, it was too much to ask that a fabulously wealthy heiress should have good looks, too. Winnipeg's material prospects made it alluring enough.

Steele arrived in the midst of a feverish speculative land boom set off by the coming of the railway. Lots in Winnipeg and smaller places on the C.P.R. track were selling for fantastic sums; one lot on Main Street went for just short of two thousand dollars per front foot. Fortunes were being made and lost within hours of frenzied trading in property. The town was jammed with free-spending speculators, and the bars were doing a literally roaring trade. Steele found that the supply of beds in Winnipeg was all but exhausted. A place to sleep in a chair or on the stairs of a house cost a dollar a night.

He was able to get a suite of rooms in the Grand Union Hotel on the strength of his position. The day after he arrived, he received an unexpected telegram from Ottawa ordering him to open a recruiting office in Winnipeg. It had been decided to increase the established strength of the force from three hundred to five hundred in order to police the construction of the C.P.R. and the resulting surge in population. He set up the office in his hotel rooms and went to work interviewing candidates. But the kind of men who had rushed west in the grip of Manitoba fever were not the kind who made good Mounted Policemen, at least not according to his standards. Settling for none but the best, he had signed on only a handful of recruits before a new officer named Aylesworth Bowen Perry arrived to replace him in the spring.

The railway-policing problem dogged his tracks back to central Canada. No sooner had he checked in for the customary interview of vacationing N.W.M.P. officers by officials in Ottawa (a century later it would be called a *debriefing*) than he was ordered to stand by to command a party of reinforcements on their journey west. If Steele was aggrieved by this second imposition that year on his personal time after going for almost a decade without home leave, he showed no sign of it. In any case he managed to squeeze in a couple of weeks of visiting relatives in Simcoe County, who greeted him like the prodigal son.

We can imagine the impression he must have made on, say, a young female cousin as he sat down at the family feasts in his honour. He was thirty-one years old, tall, erect, thick-chested, and broad-shouldered, very much the handsome man of his day, with his military handlebar moustache and slicked-down hair. Years of outdoor living had given him a permanent suntan. He was a good-natured fellow who loved to tell colourful tales about the West, and he knew exactly what he was talking about. Yet he was also a contemplative man who liked to slip outside alone and smoke his pipe after supper. The youngster who had left those parts to go west for the first time twelve years before had developed into a very prepossessing figure indeed.

On his return by steamboat from Sarnia, Ontario, to Duluth, Minnesota, Steele and the thirteen recruits he commanded formed the centre of attention for their fellow passengers. All the recruits had come from Great Britain or Canada's Maritime Provinces for the express purpose of joining the Mounted Police; none was under six feet tall. When a passenger expressed surprise at how well educated they were for policemen, Steele replied proudly that the North-West Mounted Police would accept no other kind. He was convinced that much of the success of the tactful handling of the Indians by the force was due to the high level of education within the ranks. The fact was that the force was able to attract good men because it had already become a legend. Thanks to the ministrations of newspaper correspondents over the years, the N.W.M.P.'s fame had spread worldwide.

Walsh was back in command of B Division at Fort Qu'Appelle when Steele returned. There he was told that he had been appointed acting adjutant of the division in command of the detachments on the line of construction of the railway. It is doubtful that he realized what a tremendous responsibility this was. He could hardly have known that the C.P.R. would be built on a financial shoestring stretched so taut that only a few days' delay in the construction timetable could have meant bankruptcy. As it went on, the colossal task of building almost two thousand miles

Chief Constable Sam Steele in 1873. (*Glenbow-Alberta Institute*)

An artist's conception of Fort Edmonton at the time of Canadian confederation. (*National Photography Collection, Public Archives, Canada, C-8205*)

A Blackfoot Indian camp on the prairies, around 1874. (*Glenbow-Alberta Institute*)

Fort Macleod in the 1880s. (*Glenbow-Alberta Institute*)

James Farquar Macleod, commissioner of the force from 1876 to 1880. (*National Photography Collection, Public Archives, Canada, C-17494*)

Inspector James M. Walsh. (*National Photography Collection, Public Archives, Canada, C-17038*)

Men at Fort Walsh in the 1870s. (*Glenbow-Alberta Institute*)

Sitting Bull. (*National Photography Collection, Public Archives, Canada, C-20038*)

Inspector Zachary Taylor Wood. (*National Photography Collection, Public Archives, Canada*, PA-42152)

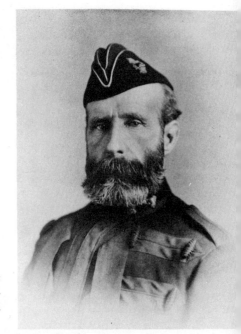

A. G. Irvine, commissioner of the force from 1880 to 1886. (*National Photography Collection, Public Archives, Canada*, PA-42139)

A card game. (*R.C.M.P. Museum, Regina*)

Interior of an officer's quarters at Fort Macleod, circa 1880. (*Glenbow-Alberta Institute*)

Superintendant Sam Steele in 188
(*Glenbow-Alberta Institute*)

Robert Belcher. (*Glenbow-Alberta In-stitute*)

of trunk line in three principal stages would strain the solvency of the entire Canadian nation; it might take years to get the construction resumed if the company failed. And if it failed, so would the bold dream of a Dominion of Canada reaching "from sea to sea," as Canada's national motto had it. If the railway was not finished on time, British Columbians were quite prepared—some were even eager—to revert to self-governing colonial status or join the United States.

Steele's job was to ensure that the railway was built across nine hundred miles of prairie by a work force of more than four thousand men without illegal disturbance. The precedents were anything but salutary; the construction of the Union Pacific in the western United States had been plagued by robberies, drunken riots, and an ever-present fear of Indian raids that kept thousands of U.S. soldiers on the alert. Frontier railway projects attracted swarms of the most disreputable members of society: outcasts, thieves, professional gamblers, confidence men, bootleggers, prostitutes, and their pimps. Most railway navvies (labourers) were the kind of men who were prone to get roaring drunk at any given opportunity. The Indians and métis would resent the railway, as well they might. It would cut a swath through land that had once been theirs and let loose a flood of white settlers to displace them. They knew that it would deal the final blow to their traditional way of life.

The march of the track westward presented a whole new challenge to the Mounted Police, one possibly greater than their original mission of subduing the whiskey traders and ending the strife among the Indians. Friction between the natives and the rambunctious whites on the construction job could well spark a native war. The natives were in a disgruntled mood already; famine still haunted the prairies, and the authorities were having difficulty persuading some of the Indians to settle on reserves, particularly the restless Crees led by Chiefs Piapot and Big Bear. This was partly because government Indian agents, going by the book, were making no extra allowances for the Indians' sensibilities and the wretched life they had been living since the buffalo had gone.

The Mounted Police sympathized with most of the Indians (though not with Piapot and Big Bear) while at the same time supporting the government campaign to encourage them to stay

on the reserves. Commissioner Irvine, who had succeeded Macleod as the head of the force in November (Macleod had become
a stipendiary magistrate), appealed to his superiors in Ottawa for
especially kind treatment of the newly settled Indians and hinted
that government insensitivity of their plight could destroy the
fragile peace the police had achieved.

This, then, was the situation in the West as Sam Steele took on
his railway assignment, pitching a tent at the track-laying headquarters. He decided that first of all it was crucial to control the
flow of liquor into the Northwest Territories, where prohibition
was in force. Much of the wildness of the American Wild West—
the lynchings, the gunfights, the Indian-baiting, and the rest—was
a product of mass inebriation. Steele was to see to it that the same
sort of occurrences did not break out on the Canadian side of the
border now that white men had arrived in force.

It was an immense undertaking; the thousands of men employed directly on the construction job would have little opportunity to spend their relatively high wages other than on liquor. It
was available in abundance just across the eastern boundary of the
Northwest Territories in Manitoba and in the bordering states.
Shantytowns replete with gambling dens, brothels, and blind pigs
had sprung up behind the freshly laid track as if by magic. As he
established his detachments at the end-of-track and along the line,
Steele recognized the impossibility of totally suppressing the liquor traffic. Instead he sensibly set himself a feasible minimum objective: to make sure that there was never enough liquor at any
one place at any one time for the navvies to go on a spree.

Thus began a prolonged battle of wits between Steele's
Mounted Police and the liquor smugglers. The ingenuity of the
bootleggers seemed limitless: Eggshells were blown out like Easter
eggs and filled with alcohol; metal kegs of alcohol were sunk inside barrels of kerosene; tins of peas and corn were found to con-
tain, not what it said on the labels, but whiskey; mincemeat and
peaches soaked in an excess of brandy suddenly became popular
staple foods to the men working along the line.

Among the more imaginative smuggling devices were the Bibles
sold on trains and in the camps; on close inspection the Mounties
found that they were made of tin and gurgled. The bare prairie
offered few convenient hiding places for caches of liquor, so bot-

tles were stashed in the many carcasses of pack horses that had died along the line. Liquor was stored in buried tanks and pumped up, as it were, from the bowels of the earth. It was put into forbidding nitroglycerin containers. It all sold for a fantastic price—five dollars a bottle—even though it was often one part whiskey to nine parts water, flavoured with a medicine called oil of smoke and coloured with tea.

Liquor, of course, was not Steele's only policing problem. Well-armed citizens of the western states who appeared on the scene often had to be parted from their guns. The Indians welcomed at least one aspect of the "fire wagon trail"; the construction employed up to 1,700 teams of horses, and huge numbers of cattle were driven in to feed the work force. They stole with abandon from this bonanza of livestock, keeping the Mounties busy tracking them down. Cattle rustlers from the badlands across the border were quick to realize that their own activities would probably be imputed to the Indians, so they took to helping themselves. Whiskey smuggling and livestock theft formed a two-way street, with smugglers from the south collecting a bounty on the hoof for their return trip.

It called for all the Mounties' vaunted firmness and tact to prevent the Indians from interfering with the construction. The navvies regarded the Indians with a volatile mixture of contempt and fear. They were constantly imagining threats from the Indians, which sent them running to the police. For their part the Indians adopted extortion tactics to get food and tobacco from the construction camps. But there was also more serious resistance from Indians who saw the railway as a threat to their birthright. On one occasion a party under Chief Piapot pulled up forty miles of surveyor's stakes ahead of the track.

Steele and his men also had a recurring problem with prairie fires. Construction crews are naturally careless, and the navvies from the East had no appreciation of how deadly wildfire on the prairies can be. The police not only organized the fighting of fires and fought them themselves, but Steele made a point of coming down hard on those who caused them. "Setting fire to prairie" was a charge he heard frequently in his capacity as a magistrate.

Uninterrupted by fire, Indian trouble, violence, drunkenness, or anything else, the rail was pushed relentlessly across the prairies.

The celebrated American railroad builder W. C. Van Horne, who
had been appointed general manager of the C.P.R., had fashioned
a masterpiece of organization. First the survey gangs drove out on
the empty plains, charting and staking the right-of-way for many
miles ahead. Then came the grading crews, with their horse-drawn
ploughs and scrapers, carving out the ever lengthening road. Then
it was the turn of the tracklayers with their sledge hammers and
crowbars, sweating and cursing as they drove the steel forward.
Behind them all came the huffing locomotives hauling trainloads
of track and ties and the wagons carrying all the paraphernalia of
a mobile camp. Gangs worked by gaslight all night, building
bridges ahead of the steel so that it might be thrown across creeks
and rivers the following morning. Under this system the steel leapt
forward at a pace as high as five miles a day.

Van Horne wanted to complete 500 miles of track in the 1882
building season, smashing every record for railway construction.
Mainly because of floods in Manitoba that delayed the arrival of
materials from the United States, the tracklaying that year was
limited to 417 miles, although the grading was completed far
ahead of the steel to what is now the city of Medicine Hat. Not a
mile had been lost to lawlessness, thanks to Sam Steele and his little band of thirty Mounted Policemen. As Commissioner Irvine
proudly reported, not a single serious crime had been committed
along the line of work.

14: A MAN OF STATURE

Steele spent the latter part of 1882 in Regina, the newly chosen capital of the Northwest Territories. At the end of July he accompanied Commissioner Irvine and Lieutenant Governor Edgar Dewdney to Pile O' Bones, as the little settlement was then called, to look over the site for the new headquarters of the Mounted Police. The commissioner showed Steele where the headquarters buildings should be placed; because of the shortage of timber on the prairies these were being prefabricated in eastern Canada and would be shipped by rail to the new western capital. Steele moved his own headquarters to Pile O' Bones in September, when the C.P.R. rail had reached that point.

He had a triple responsibility. He was still in charge of policing the C.P.R. construction. He was to oversee the laying out and erection of the new headquarters in advance of a transfer of staff from the former headquarters at Fort Walsh. He was to function as the only magistrate for Regina and the uncivilized shantytowns nearby which had sprouted up along the freshly laid rail line. It was a tall order even for Sam Steele, who had gained a reputation as the great workhorse of the force.

He was not pleased with the proposed site for the headquarters for practical reasons. He found a better one where an artificial lake could be created by damming to ensure an adequate water supply. When the comptroller of the force, Fred White, came on tour, Steele drove him by buckboard to this spot and pointed out its advantages. But the powers that be rejected his recommendation, and the site that he preferred became the grounds where the legislative and public buildings of the Province of Saskatchewan stand in splendour today.

The police were stuck with their awkward original location on Pile O' Bones Creek, so called because the Indians had dumped a huge pile of buffalo bones on its banks in the belief, it was said, that the buffalo would never desert a place containing the remains of their ancestors. People who visited the site while Steele was laying it out remarked on the ugliness of the name. Steele recalled that the Sioux word for Pile O' Bones was *Wascana*. He satisfied himself on the accuracy of the translation and named the creek Wascana, as it is called today.

The prefabricated buildings did not arrive until well into the winter. In the meantime the police lived under canvas; Steele installed himself in a sixteen-by-fourteen-foot marquee tent that served as his courtroom, office, bedroom, and mess. He decided to establish a strong post at Regina (as it had by then been named) because the town had filled up with rough characters who had settled in for the winter suspension in tracklaying. He issued orders for a show of force to let this itinerant riffraff know that the Mounties were determined to suppress lawbreaking of any kind.

Steele routinely spent a full day coming and going on police duties, then the night, until the small hours of the morning, hearing cases in his canvas courtroom. He came down hard on bootlegging, imposing fines of two hundred dollars for selling intoxicating liquor, a small fortune at the time. He usually played the part of an arbiter rather than a judge in the numerous minor assault cases that inevitably arose in a frontier town. He would have the adversaries shake hands and promise to keep the peace and would let the accused off with the cost of the court. Gambling flourished in the shanties clustered around the railway track. It was not unusual for him to try half a dozen gambling cases a night.

One of his favourites among the anecdotes he liked to tell in later years came from this period. The senior partner of a construction firm building the C.P.R. employed two nephews, the younger of whom could never pass up a poker game. One night the brothers were in Regina waiting to join their uncle on his private train going westward. At around midnight the younger brother burst into Steele's tent with an N.W.M.P. corporal close behind. "For God's sake, Cap, how much is it?" he exclaimed. "The corporal has just caught me in a poker game and has the pot. Do try me now! The old man is on the train, and is expected any minute, and I shall lose my job! Do try me, Cap!"

His brother, who had slipped into the tent behind him, explained to Steele that their uncle objected violently to gambling and would fire the lad if he knew he had been in a poker game. Steele instantly convicted him, levelled the usual fine of fifty dollars and costs, and confiscated the pot. The brothers ran frantically off to the station and caught their uncle's train in time. When the young man met Steele later on, he would say, "By Jove, Cap, you did me a good turn then!"

It was an extremely cold and stormy winter even for Regina. Inkwells had to be kept on the tops of stoves or their contents would freeze. As Steele had feared, the water supply at the headquarters site failed, and snow had to be melted to meet the needs of some fifty men and horses. Blizzards were so frequent and fierce that the policemen had to take special precautions to prevent getting lost when they had to go into the town centre a couple of miles away. They could have perished on the open prairie that has since become a network of city streets.

In March of that year Steele was relieved of his heavy work load to go on a tour of recruiting duty in Winnipeg. His instructions were to enlist as many satisfactory men as possible and send them to Regina for training posthaste. The strength of the force was well below its full complement of five hundred, which in any case was ludicrously low for its mission. At full strength it fielded one man per two hundred square miles of territory, and that figure included everyone from the commissioner to the cooks. The demands on the force were about to grow enormously. An intensified construction drive on the railway in the coming summer would employ an additional one thousand workers, for a total of five thousand men.

The line of construction would swing close to the Montana border, where the well-organized whiskey traders could be expected to launch a smuggling campaign that would dwarf all their previous efforts. The country was filling up with white settlers who would offer lush new temptations to livestock thieves, apart from any crimes they might commit among themselves. And overshadowing it all was the growing menace of Indian violence. As Commissioner Irvine told Prime Minister Sir John A. Macdonald in his 1882 annual report: "I do not wish to produce any unnecessary disquiet, but I would call your attention to the fact that the railway will next summer enter the Indian country proper, passing close to the Blackfoot Reserve.

"The Blackfoot, Bloods and Piegans form the Blackfoot nation. This powerful tribe, as you know, has but recently come in contact with white men, and their experience of them is almost altogether of the Police Force. They are as yet perfect savages, able to mount at least 1,000 warriors, exceptionally well armed and equipped. These Indians are entirely unused to large bodies of white men, and know nothing of a railway or its use. The Indian mind being very easily influenced, and very suspicious, it may be that they will consider their rights encroached upon, and their country about to be taken from them. Immediately south of them across the line is the United States Piegan Reserve. These Indians are connected with the Blackfoot, and would no doubt join them should any serious collision with the white men take place."

The tracklaying resumed in April, and before long Steele was back on the line. In June he was urgently dispatched to Maple Creek with all the reinforcements the Regina establishment could spare. A wildcat strike had broken out in this village behind the end-of-track. The C.P.R. had fired the striking employees, about 130 of them. The strikers were threatening to go on a rampage. To add to the tension, the assistant Indian commissioner on the spot reported that the Indians at the large camp nearby were in a very unsettled state.

Steele was met by irate strikers when he detrained at Maple Creek at the head of a party of twenty-seven men. He relied on his personal prestige to calm them down; many of them knew and respected him from his work on the line the previous year. He told them that the N.W.M.P. did not take sides in such disputes but that they had better keep within the law if they knew what was good for them. He posted a heavy guard on C.P.R. property in case his warning was ignored.

A strike leader who assaulted a construction foreman was briskly hustled off to Regina for a seven-day jail term. Steele announced that anyone contemplating further violence would be treated similarly.

The clampdown worked. Within a few days, Steele reported, "the strike ended in a satisfactory way for both parties." Leaving behind a strong detachment at Maple Creek, he took up duties as chief policeman and magistrate along the railway line from Moose Jaw to Medicine Hat.*

In this role Steele became one of the best-known figures on the construction of the C.P.R. The big red-coated man seemed to be everywhere: in cabooses, boarding cars, and section huts; in the cookhouses of the contractors; in the tents of the N.W.M.P. detachments spotted along the line. Most of the cases he dealt with centered on liquor or assault. Hard pressed as they were, the Mounted Police managed to establish a regime of strict law and order. Only one murder occurred in the whole of the territories that year, and it had nothing to do with the railway. There were no serious robberies except for horse thieving by the Indians and American gangs. One reason for this remarkable record was the simple expedient of having the Mounties on detachment duty keep an eye out for American gunslingers hanging around the settlements and charging them with vagrancy. Faced with this inhospitality, the desperadoes tended to drift back across the American line.

As he went about his work along the track, Steele watched the C.P.R. forge swiftly forward. He could tell how much track was being laid by the number of supply trains that chugged past. Each held sufficient track and wooden ties to build a mile of road. Never were there fewer than four a day; more often there were five or six. "Van Horne's Army" was shattering all known records for tracklaying. In one memorable three-day period they drove twenty miles of steel.

But clashes with the Indians remained a constant peril. It was at about this time that Chief Piapot played a leading role in the making of one of the most enduring legends of the Mounted

* The names of these two present-day cities, which never fail to amuse non-Canadians, are taken from Indian lore. Moose Jaw is, roughly, "the place where the white man mended the cart with the jaw of a moose." Medicine Hat is, again roughly, "the place where the medicine hat [plumed headdress] rose out of the water."

Police. Apparently in an attempt to extort food and other supplies from the railway stores, he pitched his camp of scores of teepees in the middle of the right-of-way. A train pulled up, and Piapot refused to move. The railway contractors on board called for help; presently Corporal William Brock Wilde and an unidentified constable rode up from the Maple Creek detachment. With hundreds of armed Indians milling around him and shouting threats, Wilde rode directly up to Piapot's lodge and ordered him to get his camp off the track. When Piapot disdainfully turned his back on Wilde, the corporal pulled out his pocket watch. He told the chief he would give him exactly fifteen minutes to move.

The minutes ticked by while Wilde sat solidly on his horse, ignoring the Indians who slapped at the animal and bumped their own horses against it. He was even impassive when they fired their rifles in the air next to his face. Finally he snapped his watch shut and announced that time was up. He dismounted, throwing the reins to the constable, and strode wordlessly through the tumult to Piapot's teepee. With great deliberation, he kicked over the lodge pole, sending the tent crashing down on the chief. As the Indians shrieked and brandished their rifles at him, he kicked out the pole of another teepee, then another. Piapot realized that he either had to kill the corporal or get moving. He chose to move.

In the summer trouble broke out on another part of the C.P.R. line in what is now northwestern Ontario, east of Winnipeg. The governments of Ontario and Manitoba both claimed ownership of the territory between the present interprovincial boundary and the head of the Great Lakes. Each province had appointed a magistrate in Rat Portage (now Kenora), and each magistrate claimed that the other's presence there was illegal. Each attempted to arrest the other, and each had a crowd of partisans willing to fight for their province's presumed rights.

The situation would have been comic but for the hazard it presented to the rickety Canadian union. Sir John A. Macdonald had the dispute referred to the Privy Council in London and then called by name for Sam Steele. Steele was to take a party of Mounted Policemen to Rat Portage to keep the peace at least until the council brought in its decision. It can be said that this was the conception of the present-day Royal Canadian Mounted Police. Never before had the idea been broached of employing the

Mounted Police on a national basis outside of its recognized territory in the West.

As it turned out Steele and his party got no farther than Fort Osborne barracks in Winnipeg; their very presence was a deterrent to further trouble. John Peter Turner records in his history, *The North-West Mounted Police, 1873–1893*, that "when word reached Rat Portage that the widely-known officer accompanied by picked men was at Winnipeg on his way eastward, the magisterial war subsided, and nothing more was heard of it." The disputed territory subsequently was awarded to Ontario.

Steele remained under orders to stand by in case of a renewal of the trouble. He was ordered to open another recruiting office while in Winnipeg. To his great satisfaction, "large numbers of good men came forward, attracted by the smart bearing, gay uniforms and pleasant manners of my party." If his own growing fame was instrumental in attracting volunteers, he does not say so in his memoirs. It seems likely, however, that Steele was employed as a recruiter because of his growing stature and popularity in the West, stemming from his work on the C.P.R. line.

15: SUSPICIONS CONFIRMED

He did not return to routine duty until November 1883, when he was placed in temporary command of the Calgary District. The rail line had been driven through the future Alberta city in August; the tracklaying season ended on November 28, high in the Rocky Mountains near the famous beauty spot of Lake Louise. The railway had traversed the Blackfoot country but had nearly sparked an armed conflict in the process. Only through the quick-witted intercession of the great missionary Father Lacombe had the Blackfeet been dissuaded from attacking the construction gangs. The government had done nothing to prepare or compensate the tribes of the Blackfoot nation for this intrusion into their ancestral territory. In an emergency parley with Chief Crowfoot, Father Lacombe took it upon himself to offer generous new land concessions to the Blackfeet if they would allow the railway to pass through their land. His promise was subsequently honoured by a government seemingly still ignorant of how nearly its negligence had come to provoking a bloodbath in the West.

Steele had great respect for the Blackfeet, but unlike some western white men, he did not confuse their inherent nobility with innocence. When he came to Calgary, they were busily stealing cattle from the newly established ranches in the area, particularly from a large spread called the Military Colonization Company Ranch, managed by an eccentric, black-bearded retired Royal Artillery officer with a monocle, Major General T. Bland Strange. In his old style Steele took a party of men to the ranch by night, stayed in Strange's house till dawn, then swooped into the Blackfoot rustlers' camp to capture them. He repeated this performance several times at ranches in the vicinity. Once he and Strange called the Blackfoot Chief Old Sun and his headmen together and urged them to make greater efforts to keep their people honest. He noted that such harangues did some good, but a nocturnal visit from the redcoats did more.

If Steele's name fitted his personality and Strange's his, they were in good company with Steele's new sergeant, Bill Fury. One day in January 1884, this bulldog of a man came to him in a sorry state. Fury, accompanied by a constable and an interpreter, had arrested a Blackfoot for stealing horses from Strange's ranch at a camp near the Blackfoot Crossing. He had just managed to get his captive onto his buckboard when he found himself in the midst of an angry mob.

About eighty Indians swarmed around the buckboard, demanding that Fury release the prisoner. The war chief of the Blackfoot tribe, Whitecap, had seized the horse by the bridle and defied Fury to move. Whitecap relinquished his grip when Fury smacked his face with a buggy whip. The determined sergeant then drove through the crowd while the constable and interpreter held on to the prisoner. Fury headed hell-for-leather for Calgary.

The next morning Steele rode out to the camp at the crossing with twenty-five men and demanded to know the whereabouts of Whitecap and the other ringleaders in the incident. On being told that they had gone into Calgary, Steele lectured the assembled braves about the gravity of the offence of obstructing the police. Whitecap and another Indian were later arrested and sent to Fort Macleod to be tried by stipendiary magistrate James Macleod, the retired N.W.M.P. commissioner. They were freed after a severe reprimand.

One evening in February a civilian came to him to report that Jim Adams, the young shopkeeper down the road from the police barracks, had apparently committed suicide. He had found Adams behind the counter of his shop with his throat cut; the place was spattered with blood. Steele sent his second-in-command, Inspector Tom Dowling, and Dr. Kennedy, the police surgeon who had once treated him in Fort Walsh, to examine the body. They returned to say that Adams must have been murdered.

In the meantime Steele questioned the man who had found the

body. From him he learned that the cook at a neighbouring restaurant, a black man named Jesse Williams, had argued violently with Adams over a bill that day. Steele ordered Williams's arrest.

Word of the murder spread swiftly through the little community, and soon a noisy crowd appeared at the barracks demanding to know what Steele was going to do about it. There was talk in the mob about lynching the murderer. Steele raised his strong voice above the noise: "You lads are all tenderfeet, and have visions before you of taking part in a Neck-Tie Social. There has never been a lynching in Canada, nor will there be as long as our force has duties to perform, so go away like sensible men, and remember that any attempt at lynching will be bad for those who try it!" The crowd dispersed.

Jesse Williams was duly picked up and brought to the police guardroom, where Steele and Dr. Kennedy looked him over. They found a dark stain in his right trouser pocket and traces of blood under one of his fingernails. Steele noticed that the right leg of his trousers, which was lower than the other, was frozen at the bottom from dragging in the snow. He had been wearing overshoes without boots inside, and his socks were very damp.

Williams claimed that the blood had come from some beef he had been carrying earlier in the day. But the meat was found frozen solid in the shack where he lived. Steele took a party of policemen to the scene of the crime. The snow around the shop had been trampled down to the extent that it seemed impossible to make out individual footprints. But away from the rest, almost flush with the front of the building, were the marks of the toes of a pair of overshoes, as if the wearer had stood on tiptoes to peer into the window.

The policemen traced the overshoe prints through the mess of other footmarks for about an hour, until they found that they reappeared distinctly near the back of the store. There it looked as if the overshoes had been taken off and left standing. And from there another strange set of prints were evident, those of socks. The sock prints were traced as far as the inside of the back door.

An inspection of the inside indicated that Adams's throat had been slit from behind. A twenty-five cent shinplaster with blood on it was found on the floor, confirming that the cash till had been robbed.

The sock prints were traced back to where the overshoes had been taken off. With great difficulty the police followed the overshoe tracks through all the other footprints to a haystack where a leather glove stuffed with bloodstained bills was found. As they traced the tracks from there to the shack where Williams lived, they noticed a crescent in the snow behind each right footprint. Steele had Williams brought out and led over the trail. His frozen trouser leg made the same mark. The Indians he lived with identified the glove as his; its mate later turned up at the same spot as a razor coated with blood.

Steele charged Williams with murder and assisted magistrate Macleod at his trial. Calgary's first lawyer, James A. Lougheed, conducted a spirited defence for the accused. Williams confessed only after he had been convicted. He was hanged on the N.W.M.P. barracks square in Calgary on March 29. When he had mounted the gallows, he turned to Steele and Dr. Kennedy, who were acting as the official witnesses, and calmly blamed his fate on heavy drinking. He was only the second person to be executed in the Northwest Territories since the Mounted Police had arrived in 1873.

The case was cited in official reports as an example of the change for the worse that had come over western Canada that year. The rapid growth in population had pushed up the crime rate throughout the territories. Horse and cattle theft by gangs of outlaws operating out of the United States had become epidemic; in every other type of offence the police noted a growing willingness to break the law. Certainly this was the case with the prohibition law; it was flouted everywhere. As he grappled with this problem in Calgary, Sam Steele came to the conclusion that the dry laws defeated themselves when applied to white people who had come to the West to stay.

Although prohibition had worked to keep the Indians from deterioration and had preserved the peace on the unfinished railway line, it was worse than useless among the white community in Calgary. The consumption of bootleg booze was a way of life. The powers of the police under the law were such that they could enter or search any place at any hour of day. "The officers and men hated this detestable duty, which gave them much trouble and gleams of unpopularity," Steele wrote. "We soon learned that compulsion will not make people sober; it must be brought about by the example of the best people. The prohibitory law made more drunkards than if there had been an open bar and free drinks on every street corner."

Calgary was growing at a reckless pace into a full-scale frontier boomtown. Gambling and prostitution flourished accordingly. On the latter score, we find in the records that on March 8, 1884, one Nina Dow appeared before Inspector S. B. Steele, justice of the peace, on a charge of keeping a "house of ill fame." The sentence: "6 months with hard labour unless she left Calgary by the first train, which she did."

At around this time he got word that an extensive distilling and liquor distribution system was being set up in the Rocky Mountains to supply the railway work camps. He passed the information on to headquarters in Regina with a request for reinforcements. He could foresee much greater disorder than ever when the railway construction resumed. The end-of-track was nearing the British Columbia border. The camps on the other side of the mountains, where a section of the railway was being built to join the track being pushed through from the East, were notorious for their riotous atmosphere. A new and tougher element was moving north from the United States now that construction of the Northern Pacific Railroad was complete.

But the policing problems among the whites were eclipsed by the restiveness of the natives. Requests by the métis for special government assistance in adapting to an agricultural way of life had been coldly ignored. Having learned nothing, it seems, from the causes of the Red River rebellion fourteen years earlier, the government was once again sending surveyors into métis country on the Saskatchewan River to lay out land according to the British block system instead of the French-Canadian strip system favoured by the métis. Once again the local inhabitants viewed this intrusion as the thin edge of the wedge that would displace them from their landholdings. Their persistent appeals to Ottawa for clear title to their property fell on deaf ears.

The Indians were obviously unhappy at being placed on the reserves, the more so since the government appeared intent on reneging on the agreements contained in the treaties. Many of the Indians were chronically hungry on the rations given to them on the reserves, yet Ottawa reduced the rations budget as part of a general economy drive. Angered by this, Superintendent Lief Crozier wrote from his post at Battleford to the comptroller of the force: "It is poor, yes false economy to cut down the expenditure so closely in connection with the feeding of the Indians that it would seem as if it were a wish to see upon how little a man can work and exist. . . . My firm conviction is, if some [more liberal] policy as I have outlined is not carried out, there is only one other way and that is to fight them."

To rub salt in the wounds, Indian Affairs Department officials recommended that Indians not be allowed to leave their reserves without permits. Commissioner Irvine warned that such a system would be tantamount to a breach of trust with the Indians because their treaties stated clearly that they had the unhindered right to leave the reserves to hunt and trade.

"At every post there was an intangible feeling of impending upheaval, something that would call for careful and fearless handling, a cry, as it were, from a people so distressed that conciliation by constitutional means, administrative tolerance, unfailing foresight and charity would be the only means of adjustment," John Peter Turner, the official N.W.M.P. historian, recorded of this period. Steele caught this same feeling in Calgary in the spring of 1884.

Though the Blackfeet were probably the best off of all the Indian tribes, their formerly amicable attitude towards white men had turned sour. Chief Crowfoot had grown especially sullen; and unlike most of his colleagues in the force, Steele did not trust the Blackfoot leader one bit. He also held the theory that Louis Riel had not, as he had announced, settled down to a quiet family life while teaching school in Montana. It was by accident that his worst suspicions were confirmed.

His orderly-room sergeant returned from a weekend leave on the Blackfoot reserve (presumably he had a girl friend there) and told him that he had seen a French-Cree métis going around and talking to the Indians. It happened that the sergeant spoke both Blackfoot and Cree and so was able to understand what was being said. He told Steele that he had overheard the man say that he had crossed the border from Montana with Louis Riel. The métis had gone on to declare that the land belonged to the Indians and that they had the right to kill the ranchers' cattle. He said that the whites should be driven from the land.

This report gave Steele reason to swear out a warrant for the arrest of the métis on a charge of vagrancy. The man went by the Indian name of Bear's Head, and he was picked up on a Blackfoot reserve. He admitted at his trial that he was one of Riel's agents. He was sentenced to a short jail term with a strong caution to desist in his agitation. (Steele says in his memoirs that the sentence was a month, but the records indicate it was fourteen days.)

It was April, time for the C.P.R. construction to resume. At the personal request of Sir John A. Macdonald, Steele was ordered to take charge of policing the line of construction through the Rocky and Selkirk mountains to the point where it would join the line being built from the West. Most of the work would be within British Columbia, and because that province was outside the N.W.M.P.'s jurisdiction, Steele was appointed a federal commissioner of police to equip him with the requisite authority. This represented another step towards making the North-West Mounted into a national police force, the forerunner of today's Royal Canadian Mounted Police.

Without waiting for his replacement in Calgary to arrive, he took a party to the end-of-track at Laggan, near Lake Louise. As he posted men at strategic points along the line, he could see that they were in for a hard year's work. He wrote: "Large numbers of gamblers, whiskey men, in fact almost every description of criminal, who had been plying their trade on the Northern Pacific Railroad, were wending their way from Sand Point and establishing their dens on every little creek along the line." Mindful of the rash of armed robberies on the Northern Pacific, he organized a system to guard against holdups of the payroll based on regular inspections of every possible ambush site. He then returned to Calgary, leaving Sergeant Fury in charge.

He was met in the town by the Indian agent for the Blackfoot reserve, who was anxious about recent developments. The Indians had grown even more sulky and hostile since a stout métis about thirty years old had come to stay at Chief Crowfoot's camp a few days before. The description fit that of Bear's Head, the agitator Steele had jailed earlier. He immediately sent Sergeant Fred Dann and a constable out to arrest the man. The two policemen went to the railway station at Gleichen, near the Blackfoot Crossing, and waited while a friendly Indian brought the métis to them on a pretext. He was indeed the man who called himself Bear's Head. They arrested him and caught the morning train back to Calgary.

They boarded the mail car with their prisoner. The train had gone only a few miles when Bear's Head slipped off the oversized handcuffs that held him while Sergeant Dann was preoccupied brushing his kit. He seized the sergeant's rifle and jumped from the train, which was moving at about thirty miles an hour. The sergeant jumped after him, but his knee went out of joint as he hit the ground. The constable landed safely, but he could not keep up with the escaper, who was wearing moccasins, while the policeman had on high leather riding boots. They last saw Bear's Head running in the general direction of Crowfoot's camp.

The sergeant and constable came to report this embarrassing occurrence to Steele just as his replacement, Superintendent William Herchmer, arrived at the Calgary barracks. Herchmer had come from the eastern part of the territories, where native unrest was noticeable everywhere. The presence of an emissary from Riel among the Blackfeet alarmed him; the Mounted Police dreaded the thought of this powerful and warlike nation joining in the métis-Indian revolt that seemed to be developing. The superintendent asked Steele to personally find the agitator and bring him in.

Steele did not want to excite the Indians further. Instead of taking a squad of policemen with him, he went in a buckboard with only two constables to the Blackfoot reserve. When they reached the main camp at the Blackfoot Crossing, they found that the Indians were elsewhere, holding a sun dance at a temporary camp built especially for that purpose. Sun dances always put the Indians in a bellicose mood, with their grisly initiation rites and their boasting sessions about the prowess of the tribe's warriors. The regular camp was practically deserted but for Chief Crowfoot's métis interpreter and confidant, Jean L'Hereux.

L'Hereux showed signs of trepidation when Steele told him he wanted to speak to Crowfoot. Steele was convinced that L'Hereux had some reason to fear a visit from the police. He assured the interpreter that there was no cause for alarm; he was a friend of

Crowfoot's and was there in the ordinary course of duty. L'Hereux reluctantly accompanied him to the sun dance camp several miles away.

He found Crowfoot's lodge at the camp and entered with L'Hereux. In it the headmen of the tribe were seated in a circle. Crowfoot was at the back, facing the entrance. On his right side, in the traditional place of honour, sat the escaped man.

Crowfoot glowered at Steele, who instructed L'Hereux to tell the chief that he had come to take Bear's Head to face trial in Calgary. Knowing that the fugitive spoke English, he then addressed him directly, ordering him to come along at once. Bear's Head would not move. Crowfoot then spoke in his own language with unmistakable hostility. The other Indians noisily expressed their approval of his words.

Glancing at the interpreter, Steele noticed that he was pale and trembling. He accused him of temporizing in his interpretation, and L'Hereux braced himself and rendered Steele's words in their original form. At this Crowfoot sprang up and charged at Steele. Steele warned him off by telling him sharply not to make another offensive move.

He then stepped up to the chief, at the same time telling L'Hereux to open the flap that served as a door to the lodge. When he was close enough to reach Bear's Head, he put his right hand on the butt of his revolver; with his left he seized the man by the collar, whirling him around and dragging him headfirst through the door. The two constables were outside waiting to grab the prisoner. As they bound him to the buckboard, a crowd of hundreds of belligerent Indians formed around them, screaming threats.

Speaking through the interpreter, Steele told this menacing throng that when the Mounted Police came for anyone, Indian or white, anyone who interfered with them would be in trouble. He shouted to Crowfoot that he wanted to talk to him outside. Crowfoot came, and Steele proceeded to berate him for breaking his treaty promise that he would help to uphold the law. Anything the métis had said was false, Steele declared. If Crowfoot did not believe this, he could attend the man's trial himself; he scribbled a note to the C.P.R. agent in Gleichen to give the chief a return ticket to Calgary for that purpose. He said that Crowfoot would find at the trial that he had been harbouring a disturber of the peace.

Steele and his constables drove off with their man. His high-handed manner in this affair may be open to criticism, but it had been a great show of firmness in the Mounted Police tradition. Crowfoot did attend the trial, but much to Steele's disgust the case was dismissed for lack of evidence. The incident served a purpose, however; it put the police on guard against agitation among the Indians inspired by Louis Riel. The fact that Bear's Head was half Cree and as such a hereditary enemy of the Blackfeet also demonstrated that the Blackfeet were capable of regarding the white men as their primary enemies. They would not be impervious to the appeal of the war drums of revolt.

16: THE CHALLENGE OF THE MOUNTAINS

By the spring of 1884 the Canadian Pacific Railway Company had blundered into deep financial trouble. It needed $22.5 million more than it could possibly earn or raise by selling stocks or bonds in order to finish building its line. It was rescued by a government loan of that amount after a bitter political debate that opened up perilous divisions within the ruling Conservative Party. Prime Minister Sir John A. Macdonald let it be known afterwards that it would be politically impossible for the government to lend the company one dollar more.

From then on the going got rougher both for the railway and for its chief guardian in the West, Inspector Sam Steele. After a comparatively easy drive over the prairies, the brunt of the construction effort had run up against Canada's great mountain barrier, with its sheer rock walls to be pierced, its roaring gorges to be bridged, its fantastic heights to be surmounted. The work proceeded in the shadow of death and destruction by avalanche—and in the shadow of financial disaster as the arduous mountain work swallowed up more and more money.

Steele's job was to keep the track moving forward against a powerful tide of disorder and criminality. And he was expected to do this virtually with one hand tied behind his back. Under the Act for the Preservation of Peace on Public Works, which defined the duties of Steele's special force, its jurisdiction extended over a strip only twenty miles wide (ten miles on either side of the C.P.R. right-of-way). The construction work was being impeded by the navvies' habit of walking to the fleshpots artfully positioned just outside of this strip and going on prolonged sprees that stripped them of their pay. It was an easy enough matter for bootleggers and the like to cross into the zone, do their business, then scurry back to their refuges beyond the limit. In any case the penalty for bootlegging prescribed by the act was a mere forty-dollar fine for the first and second offences. An offender might be jailed on a third conviction, but this could be avoided by simply transferring the ownership of a bootlegging outlet to another name.

Even within the zone, liquor could be possessed and consumed quite legally unless it was in a dive (an illicit temporary bar usually set up in a tent or shanty). The provincial government of British Columbia freely issued licences to sell liquor on the grounds that the province should not be deprived of tax revenue from liquor sales by a federal law.

For Steele and his twenty-five men it was a dangerous as well as a difficult situation. Far removed from the rest of the N.W.M.P., they could not hope to be reinforced if violence broke out. The danger lay in the kind of people they had to deal with. Gold-hunting prospectors, never the most law-abiding of citizens, prowled the mountains; many of the navvies were fresh from the Northern Pacific job in the western states, where rioting, robbery, and gunslinging were rampant. A ragtag retinue of camp followers came with them: bootleggers, cardsharps, confidence men, prostitutes, and what-have-you. Surveying the surroundings when he arrived at the end-of-track in the Rocky Mountains late in the spring, Steele resolved to enforce such laws as he was able to enforce to the limit. With the arrest of five prostitutes and five found-ins at a bawdy house in Laggan on July 1, he launched one of the most drastic cleanup campaigns in the history of the Canadian West.

Drunk and disorderly. Drunk. Assault. Drunk and using abusive language. Steele drew a fine legal line in the mountain camps, and anyone who stepped over it stood a good chance of finding himself in front of his makeshift magistrate's desk. In spite of the sparsity of his force it seemed as if the red-clothed arm of the law could reach out at any time from anywhere. No dive was safe, and it was futile to try to intimidate, bribe, or otherwise distract a member of the Mounted Police.

A pair of these imperturbable young men would stand up to a score of hostile drunks and drag anyone who got too obstreperous off to jail with the serenity of workmen shifting sacks of potatoes. It is recorded that a local tough once imported a whole railway carload full of whiskey into the camp at Golden, British Columbia, and invited a small crowd to sample the blend. They had barely started when Sergeant Fury and two constables appeared with written instructions from Steele to destroy it. The irate drinkers drew revolvers and shouted threats, but Fury and his men ignored them while they tapped keg after keg and spilled the contents onto the ground. The threats eventually subsided in the face of this characteristic display of determination by the men of the N.W.M.P.

As a judge Steele was a positive menace. He prosecuted sixty-seven cases within twenty-nine days in October 1884. In imposing this draconian regime, he was more concerned with deterrence than with punishment. Conscious of the national importance of the C.P.R. project, he was determined that nothing should delay it. To strengthen his hand, he telegraphed a strong appeal to the government to expand the dry zone bordering the tracks to forty miles. For once Ottawa acted positively and promptly, and Steele, with no little satisfaction, personally saw to it that dives on the outer fringes of the former twenty-mile belt moved outside of the new limit. From then on, navvies contemplating a spree also had to contemplate a twenty-mile hike in each direction. This was too much for even the most inveterate drunkards, so they stayed in camp under the eyes of Steele and his men.

He also applied the principle of deterrence to the task of guarding the C.P.R. payroll. The pack ponies carrying the sacks full of cash along the lonely mountain trails were escorted by patrols organized along the lines of operational cavalry. Scouts rode ahead to check out every possible ambush point. Two men rode directly in front of the ponies, two rode with them, and two brought up the rear. They were deployed in such a way that they could never all come under fire at the same time; the experienced Sergeant Fury commanded them. Professional holdup men from the States were known to be in the district, but they never dared to strike.

With the human element under control, the railway work ploughed ahead doggedly. Blasting tunnels and rock cuts, throw-

ing up huge bridges with timber cut on the spot, threading track along narrow ridges, the railway builders moved through the Kicking Horse Pass and across the Rockies to the forbidding Selkirk range. Steele kept his headquarters close behind the vanguard of the construction force, moving from Laggan to the first crossing of the Columbia River (this zigzagging river had to be crossed twice) at a place named Donald, British Columbia, after Donald Smith, one of the chief backers of the C.P.R. and the future Lord Strathcona. While at Donald, Steele was constantly backtracking to hear cases and visit detachments in the more easterly camps. He travelled on horseback over the tote road, a treacherous mountain track blasted out of solid rock, built to supply the construction crews.

One of his frequent brushes with death came one day on the tote road between Donald and Laggan. He was mounted on a fresh, high-spirited horse recently sent up from Calgary. He kept to the middle of the road in the knowledge that horses are usually less afraid of a precipice than of the wall of rock on the other side. At a point hundreds of feet above the Kicking Horse Pass, he recounted in his memoirs, "I met an Italian navvy with his bundle of blankets, and he, as was then the custom, instead of going to the right, planted himself against the wall of rock furthest from the precipice. At the sight of this extraordinary object, my horse, crazed with fright, whirled about, and I just saved myself and the horse by hurling myself on the road. I kept a strong hold of the reins and head collar and hung on to the animal, whose hind quarters were over the brink, with its body resting on the rocky edge. My companion, who rode a steady horse, ran to my assistance, and with our united efforts we dragged the brute on to the road."

In October Steele got a taste of law enforcement problems American Wild West-style. A group of the Americans on the job made a habit of gathering in a barber's tent in the camp on the Kicking Horse Flats. The barber and a railway conductor got into an argument over the U.S. presidential campaign then in progress. The discussion grew increasingly heated until the barber, in a rage, flew at his adversary with his razor; he had cut through the conductor's waistcoat and was about to make another pass to disembowel him when the conductor's friend, a brakeman, inter-

vened by shooting the barber dead. The brakeman fled east to the prairies before the police arrived, but was later apprehended. Steele decided that it was a case of self-defence because the brakeman presumably would have been next if the barber had disposed of the conductor. He was freed.

Another murder followed in December, this time outside of the Mounted Police's zone of jurisdiction. A respectable American businessman named Baird was shot and killed from ambush and robbed of four thousand dollars in cash collected from customers of his firm. The murder occurred near a roadhouse called the Hog Ranche (after the owner's collective pejorative for his customers), about twenty-two miles from Steele's post.

On hearing of it, Steele alerted all points from Victoria to Winnipeg and sent two constables to the Ranche to question Baird's companion, a blacksmith named Manuel Dainard, who had seen the murderer. After interviewing Dainard, the constables began to follow a trail of physical clues: some ejected rifle shells, an abandoned packsack that had contained the money, a spent campfire, and finally the murder weapon, a new Winchester rifle that had been dropped in a river ford. On the trail they camped overnight near the present site of Revelstoke, British Columbia, with a fellow traveller named Bulldog Kelly. Kelly in no way fitted the description of the murderer given by Dainard. When the trail ran cold, they returned to report to Steele, mentioning Kelly's name in passing. For some time afterward Steele maintained an alert for the murder suspect as he had been described, but no further clues turned up, and he admitted to being baffled by the case.

Broader problems were in the air. With another construction season past, the C.P.R. again had run out of money. The railway had long since been mortgaged to the last tie. In their frantic efforts to conserve every available dollar, the company's management evaded paying its suppliers, contractors, and employees. Contractors who were not paid did not pay their own employees. Going without pay understandably put the construction workers on the mountain line in a sore mood.

Sergeant Fury had already intervened in a disturbance in one of the camps when angry workers struck against a contractor who had failed to pay them. From time to time men would come to Steele to complain that they had not received their pay. He would

intercede with the company to meet their claims, counselling patience in the meantime. But the protests grew more frequent and serious as time went by.

He had no idea of just how desperate the C.P.R.'s financial plight had become. When he settled into a snug new log headquarters at a camp called Beaver, within a mile of the end-of-track, after Christmas, the company had scraped the bottom of the barrel. With nowhere else to turn, the president of the C.P.R., George Stephen, was again clamouring for money from the government. Early in January 1885, he telegraphed to the prime minister: "Imminent danger of sudden crisis unless we can find means to meet pressing demands. Smaller class creditors getting alarmed about their money. . . ." In fact the C.P.R. then owed its contractors more than four million dollars. Macdonald could do no more than speed up the subsidy payments already earmarked for the company. He knew that it would be political suicide to approach Parliament for yet another loan.

Steele was better informed about another crisis gathering to the east. Through regular contact with other Mounted Police officers he knew that Louis Riel had returned to Canada in July 1884 at the request of the métis people of the northern Saskatchewan region to lead a political struggle for their rights. The Mounted Police kept tabs on Riel throughout the remainder of the year. He held a series of meetings in métis communities, all of which seemed to be aimed at strictly legal agitation for the redress of the métis' legitimate grievances. Riel was the chief author of a petition to Ottawa calling in a reasonable tone for a set of overdue reforms in government policy towards the métis and the Indians. At the same time, however, he was known to have sent emissaries to agitate in much stronger terms among all the important Indian chiefs.

At secret meetings infiltrated by the Mounted Police, Riel's agents advocated taking up arms against the white men if the demands of the petition were not met. In fact these demands were scarcely even considered. Sir John A. Macdonald earned his nickname of Old Tomorrow anew as he shrugged off repeated attempts to move him to remedial action. Mounted Policemen, missionaries, and prominent white settlers who appealed for prompt recognition of the métis' just claims watched the danger grow

while Macdonald and his ministers sat. Riel personally offered the
government a chance to avert trouble by telling intermediaries
that he was willing to remove his disturbing presence from the
Northwest in return for a few thousand dollars he claimed the
government owed him. He was reliably reported to be positively
anxious to return to Montana provided the government made it
worth his while.

But the great procrastinator in Ottawa ignored this offer as the
menace of revolt festered. In the meantime Riel, who had
previously been in and out of mental institutions, apparently was
driven over the line of insanity by the adulation accorded him on
his return. He began claiming to have a personal communion with
God and telling his audiences of seeing divine visions. His super-
stitious followers were fascinated by his mystical claims. Although
the clergy and some of the cooler heads among the métis turned
against him, there could be no doubt that most of his people considered him their chosen leader. They presented him with a house
and a purse of sixty dollars as a token of their goodwill.

Although Steele was conscious of the mounting rumbling in the
Northwest Territories early in 1885, he had little time to brood
over it. His force was frequently shorthanded as men on detachment duty came down with mountain fever, which had always
been a problem on the construction line. And his new post at
Beaver, amid the towering Selkirks at the mouth of the Beaver
River, had turned out to be the wildest railway camp town he had
yet encountered. Keeping the peace in Beaver was a round-the-
clock task.

This settlement of more than seven hundred people had been
established for the express purpose of getting one jump ahead of
the railway's raffish camp followers. So many fleshpots had grown
up in Donald, the next major camp to the east, that C.P.R. construction chief James Ross had made an extraordinary effort to
push the track across the Beaver River in hopes of putting the
workmen beyond their range. But the rough element followed
with alacrity. A British Columbia provincial official indiscriminately peddled licences to operate saloons, and dance halls,
saloons, and brothels constructed of cedar logs were raised directly
across the bridge from Steele's police post.

A doughty Scot who would go on to become a millionaire in-

dustrialist, James Ross did all he could to get rid of these trouble-
some parasites. He would not allow food and other supplies for
them to be carried by C.P.R. trains. This only added to Steele's
problems, as they resorted to rampant thievery. Sleighs of supplies
left unguarded anywhere along the line were robbed. Steele's
policemen were kept on the run tracing stolen goods and arresting
the thieves. The campaign of deprivation was also thwarted by
subcontractors who black-marketed goods to the riffraff, knowing
that they could always go to the C.P.R. stores to replenish their
own supplies. The tenderloin district across the river flourished
more or less unaffected by Ross's move.

Every evening the mountains echoed with the sounds of carous-
ing as the dance halls and saloons filled up with navvies. The
revelry continued far into the night, punctuated by fisticuffs and
outright brawls. The denizens of the east bank managed to extract
most of the navvies' pay through crooked gambling games, prostitution, and "coffin varnish" whiskey at fifty cents a glass. Helplessly inebriated men often found that their pockets had
been rifled and any leftover money taken. Because of this Steele
ordered that men who were very drunk were to be locked up for
their own protection. They would be released with an admonish-
ment the next day.

On the morning after a donnybrook there might be as many as
thirty prisoners in the cells. Steele dispatched most of them, tried
the more serious cases in the afternoon, then spent the night in
readiness for sudden calls to step into the fray across the bridge.
He was obliged to stay on call until two or three in the morning
and to rise between six and seven, having breakfast at eight. He
liked to pass the time between bouts of action sharing a few quiet
whiskeys in his quarters with his friend George Hope Johnston,
the local civilian justice of the peace. Many years later Johnston
recalled: "I never met anyone with such a wealth of stories, especially about the characters whom he remembered from his boyhood days in the County of Simcoe, and his sketches of many of
the men who accompanied him on the Red River expedition were
so lifelike and telling that he held one spellbound."

It was hectic duty, but Steele's party of Mounted Police was
able to keep the whole line of construction in the mountains
under the sway of law and order. By the end of February the

C.P.R. stretched unbroken from the head of the Great Lakes to a point some two hundred miles west of Calgary. The line being built from the West Coast over the Gold Range Mountains was fast approaching a linkup with the end-of-track in the Selkirks. In central Canada a few stubborn gaps in the track north of Lake Superior remained to be filled before the line could be connected all the way from the mountains to its terminus in Montreal.

But high in the mountains glaciers shuddered and creaked, weakened by the incessant blasting on the railway. Fields of ice up to half a mile wide and fifty feet thick tore away from their foundations in the rock and came sliding down thousands of feet with an earsplitting roar. They devastated all before them, ripping stretches of forest asunder and demolishing whole sections of the newly built railroad. Thousands of tons of snow also came sweeping down from the mountain peaks, uprooting great pine trees, knocking loaded boxcars off the tracks, burying men alive. There were blizzards lasting for days on end, and these terrifying slides kept coming. To the men in the Selkirks that winter it must have seemed that the world was crashing down around them. The avalanches shattered men's nerves as they shattered forests and buildings and stretches of railroad. An ominous mood of disquiet filled the mountain camps.

The Canadian Pacific had run out of money, the long-dreaded rebellion had erupted in the Northwest, and according to the gossip
in the local saloons, Sam Steele lay on his deathbed. It was April
1, 1885.

For several weeks past Steele had been receiving increasingly
frequent and bitter complaints from the construction workers on
the mountain section of the C.P.R. about not being paid by the
company and its contractors. The quieter men among them
stressed that their lack of funds was causing hardship to their
families at their distant homes. The frequenters of the rowdy
shantytown across the bridge from Steele's headquarters beside
the Beaver River wanted cash to spend on gambling, whiskey, and
women. Steele could tell them no more than to wait for their
wages until the C.P.R. was in a position to pay up.

But the fact was that the company did not have enough funds
to meet its payroll or to recompense its contractors. The funds advanced to it by the government on an emergency basis the year
before had been consumed by the incredibly expensive construction work in the mountains and amid the rock and muskeg
of Lake Superior's forbidding north shore. The government had
supplied fifty-five million of the ninety-nine million dollars needed
to build the line up to that stage. This was thirty million dollars
more than Sir John A. Macdonald had originally bargained for.
With his own party split on the issue and the parliamentary opposition in hot pursuit, his government could not possibly advance
the company any more.

By March of 1885 only pledges of all the personal assets of the
C.P.R.'s two principal backers, George Stephen and Donald
Smith, stood between the company and bankruptcy. Rich as these
men were, however, the million-odd dollars they were able to raise
by mortgaging their fortunes was only sufficient to stave off a
financial collapse for a few weeks.

Then, on the clear, cold morning of March 26 about two hundred métis plainsmen and Indians under Louis Riel and Gabriel
Dumont met and defeated a mixed force of Mounted Policemen
and local volunteers at Duck Lake in the Saskatchewan Territory.
The government forces, led by Superintendent Lief Crozier, suffered twelve killed and twelve wounded, compared with five fatal
casualties among the rebels. The price of years of neglect and
procrastination was being paid in blood in the snow.

From there on the revolt spread rapidly to the Cree and Assiniboine Indians in the northeastern part of what is now Saskatchewan. They looted and burned Hudson's Bay Company
posts and murdered several white men before the majority of the
white settlers were able to gain the comparative safety of Mounted
Police forts. There was a real threat that the Blackfoot nation,
with all its formidable power to make war, would join the rebels
and extend the conflict throughout the Northwest Territories. As
Steele had suspected, Chief Crowfoot's loyalty to the Crown was
shaky. At the outbreak of the rebellion, he proposed to Chief Red
Crow of the Bloods that they jointly lead their people on the war-
path against the whites, a proposal which Red Crow rejected out
of hand.

The hostilities threw Steele and his tiny Beaver River force of
eight Mounted Policemen into an exceedingly precarious position.
The long-unpaid, disgruntled workers on the line were nearing the
end of their patience; there were rumblings of a general strike.
The trouble in the Northwest precluded all hope of help from
outside should the strike bring the expected rioting, sabotage, and
looting. Steele was less concerned with the danger from the workmen themselves than from the violently inclined people around
them. He was well aware that the small city of saloons, dance
halls, and brothels across the river held more than its share of potential killers. He had just been informed, in fact, that one man

in Beaver was the prime suspect in a triple murder case in Arkansas.

On the last day in March he learned from sympathetic contacts that a strike was being organized. He warned James Ross to be prepared for imminent trouble, but the construction chief was not impressed. Steele remained so concerned with the threat of an outbreak of rioting and looting that he sent a telegram directly to Sir John A. Macdonald. In it he stated bluntly that if the men were not paid immediately, violence could break out at any time.

He then summoned the federal civilian magistrate, George Johnston, to come to his post and arranged for Johnston to visit the camps along the route in an attempt to help the policemen stationed there to maintain order. He had a pressing reason to call for his friend's aid. He was feeling distinctly ill, and he knew why: It was his old nemesis, mountain fever. The disease had taken the lives of several men in the construction camps over the past few months.

It hit him the next morning so hard that he could not move out of bed. As he was limply sweating out the fever, workmen walked off their jobs all along the line.

Magistrate Johnston and the chaplain, Father Fay, made a tour of the work sites, urging the strikers to refrain from violence. While they were away, Steele received a telegram from Lieutenant Governor Dewdney of the Northwest Territories ordering him to withdraw all his men from the mountains and proceed east immediately to help suppress the revolt.

Steele was in no condition to go anywhere, but apparently he considered this fact irrelevant. He wired the governor to the effect that with a volatile strike in progress, it would be madness to leave. More than 1,200 C.P.R. and construction company employees had halted work and were holding rowdy meetings at which their hotheaded leaders talked about beating up officials, tearing up the track, and generally destroying company property. The strikers were highly excited, and many among them were armed.

A deputation marched on the Beaver police post and demanded to see Steele. He had a constable help him from his bed into a chair to receive them. In the official report of the incident to the commissioner, he recounted that he "assured them that if they committed any act of violence, and were not orderly, in the strictest sense of the word, I would inflict upon them the severest punishment the law would allow me."

He advised them to discuss their grievances once again with James Ross. The construction boss promised to do all in his power to see that they were paid in full promptly. He asked them to return to their jobs in the meantime, promising not to charge them for their board while they were waiting for their wages. Satisfied with this, several hundred agreed to return to work.

However, most of those who chose to remain on strike gathered in the shantytown on the Beaver River, with its large population of "loose characters ready to urge them to any mischief," as Steele put it. After a brief spell of ominous quiet he learned that about three hundred of the strikers, most of them armed with revolvers, had set out along the tracks to prevent the men who had accepted Ross's terms from proceeding with their work. They ordered parties of teamsters and tracklayers off the job at gunpoint. When a party of bridge builders defied them, the strikers slashed through a rope holding a block and tackle used to hoist materials, rendering further work impossible. They bullied construction foremen into ordering their men to abandon whatever they were doing. When a trainload of tracklayers set out for the head of steel, they forced the train to back up into the yards.

At this James Ross mounted the engine and ordered the engineer to drive forward. As it approached the spot where the strikers were massed on the track, Ross called for full steam. The train hurtled towards the strikers, who cleared off the track and started shooting. With bullets zipping around it, the train plunged through a narrow rock cut to the head of the line just beyond.

Sergeant Fury had stationed himself at the mouth of the cutting. With drawn revolver he stood straddling the track as the mob approached, chasing the train and firing their guns. Fury had positioned three constables up on the rocks with their revolvers pointing down on the strikers from good cover. As the mob drew abreast of him, Fury coolly announced that he would shoot anyone who attempted to pass. After some angry shouting but no further forward movement, the crowd turned back to the Beaver, leaving the tracklayers on the other side of the cutting to get on with their work.

While Fury was facing down the strikers, Steele, back in his sickbed, had received another telegram. It was from Mayor George Murdoch of Calgary: "For God's sake, come; there is a danger of attack from the Blackfeet." Steele dictated a reply: "Cannot leave. Telegraph the Lieutenant Governor." It was against his instincts, but it was all he could do.

When Sergeant Fury and his party returned from their stand at the rock cut, he rose unsteadily and sat up in a camp chair. He had sent Constable Kerr for a bottle of medicine from the dispensary at the main C.P.R. camp. Fury gave his report, then left the room while Steele consulted with George Johnston. Within minutes Fury was back.

The sergeant brought news of a fresh outbreak of violence. On his return from the dispensary with the medicine for Steele, Constable Kerr had come across a mob in the middle of the town. A so-called contractor name Behan, who was actually a suspected outlaw from the United States, was urging the strikers to attack the police post. Observing that the man was drunk and certainly disorderly, Kerr marched up to place him under arrest.

As he tried to haul Behan off to the police post, Kerr was assailed by a gang of toughs and strikers. They knocked him down and forced him to retreat while Behan resumed his position as the centre of the mob's attention.

Steele heard the sergeant out and said: "It is a pity that he attempted the arrest without sufficient assistance, but as he has done so we must take the man at any cost. It will never do to let him or the remainder of the gang think they can play with us. Take what men you require and arrest him."

Fury rounded up three constables, and they strode across the bridge. They found Behan in a saloon, surrounded by drunken admirers. The constables grabbed him and began to drag him bodily out of the building. But a howling crowd overwhelmed the Mounties and tore Behan from their grasp. Fury joined his colleagues in their attempts to recover the prisoner. They took a bad beating, but they persisted until members of the mob threatened to shoot.

"They took our prisoner from us, sir," Fury reported. He stood in front of the camp chair, bruised and bleeding, his tunic in shreds.

"That is too bad," Steele said. "Take your revolvers and shoot anyone who interferes with the arrest."

George Johnston went over to a window and watched as Sergeant Fury and Constables Fane, Craig, and Walters crossed the bridge again. Within a few minutes a shot rang out. "There is one gone to hell, Steele," Johnston intoned.

Despite his weakness Steele could stay in the camp chair no longer. He hobbled to the window beside Johnston in time to see Constables Craig and Walters dragging Behan across the bridge. Behan was struggling savagely to escape, but the two big Mounties held him firmly. Cursing and shrieking, a woman in a scarlet dress followed on their heels.

Sergeant Fury and Constable Fane brought up the rear, fending off a furious mob wielding firearms, clubs, and bottles. They had just reached the far end of the small wooden bridge.

His ailment forgotten, Steele exploded into action. He threw on his tunic, clapped his officer's wedge cap on his head, and strode to the door, calling back to Johnston to get a copy of the Riot Act and follow him. Snatching a Winchester rifle from the guard at the door, he ran down the hill, arriving at the bridge just as the crowd on the other side was about to make a rush for it. He levelled the rifle at them and warned them to halt or he would fire.

"Look at the bastard," someone exclaimed. "His own death bed makes no difference to him!" They hung back while the policemen hauled their prisoner the rest of the way across the bridge. Behan was still resisting wildly. Constable Walters raised a huge fist and knocked him out.

"You red-coated son of a bitch!" screamed the woman.

Steele snapped: "Take her in too!"

As the constables dragged their charges up the hill, Johnston passed them running down it. He had had to kick in the door of the orderly room to get the book containing the Riot Act because Constable Fane had the key. As Johnston drew up at his side, Steele stepped out onto the bridge. "Listen to this," he commanded, "and keep your hands off your guns or I will shoot the first man of you who makes a hostile movement." In a rich Scottish burr Johnston explained and read the act, which forbids participants in a riot from forming groups of more than twelve persons. When he had finished, Steele raised his voice again.

"You have taken advantage of the fact that a rebellion has broken out in the North-West and that I have only a handful of men," he said, "but as desperate diseases require desperate remedies, and as both the remedy and the disease are here, I warn you that if I find more than twelve of you standing together or any large crowd assembled I will open fire and mow you down! Now disperse at once and behave yourselves."

By this time a number of respectable civilians from the camp on his side of the river had lined up with firearms to support him. All eight Mounted Policemen, Fury in front, stood at the head of the bridge with revolvers cocked. Steele and Johnston waited a few tense minutes while the crowd broke up.

Pressing his advantage, Steele promptly sent a lone constable across the bridge to pick up the victim of the shot they had heard; Fury had put a bullet through his shoulder when he had tried to stop the police from taking Behan. The constable brought the man back without interference. He was sent to the C.P.R. infirmary to be patched up.

Night fell, but it brought no rest for the man who had been so weakened by illness a few hours earlier. Fearing an attack on the jail as long as Behan was in the cells, he borrowed a locomotive from Ross and sent the prisoner on it to the next detachment down the line. The next morning the Mounted Police were back in business rounding up the leaders in the attempt to obstruct Behan's arrest. Steele quickly fined them each a hundred dollars, then took a locomotive to the next detachment to mete out the same treatment to Behan. They got off lightly because, with rebellion raging in the Northwest Territories, he could not spare the men to escort them to the nearest prison several hundred miles away.

On that same day, the Holy Thursday of April 2, 1885, the rebellion took on a terrible new dimension. A band of Big Bear's Cree warriors, with Steele's old adversary Wandering Spirit in the lead, had invaded the tiny village of Frog Lake in the wilderness northeast of Edmonton and cold-bloodedly massacred nine men, including two mission priests. Taking two widows of the murdered men as hostages, they moved to besiege the small Mounted

Police post at Fort Pitt. To the east Fort Carlton had been evacuated, and a large body of Mounted Policemen had retreated to Prince Albert to protect the civilians who had taken refuge there. Rebellious métis and Indians were virtually in command of the whole eastern half of the Northwest Territories. To the west it was touch and go whether the big and restless tribes of the Blackfoot nation would also take up arms against the whites.

At the same time, however, the fortunes of the C.P.R. had taken a stunning turn for the better. The company had contracted to move more than three thousand troops from the East to quell the rebellion, despite the fact that they would have to march over the unfinished gaps in the line on Lake Superior's north shore. The revenue thus obtained, plus the public recognition of the railway's crucial importance to the nation brought about by the movement of troops, helped to revitalize its financial situation. Within six days of the Beaver River incident a pay car arrived with all the wages owed to the navvies. By then Steele had shaken off the mountain fever. Leaving Sergeant Fury with orders to follow him with the rest of his mountain police force as soon as possible, he headed east towards the sound of the guns.

18: ON THE WARPATH

Steele arrived in Calgary early in the morning on April 11 to find the railway station crammed with frightened women and children fleeing to refuge in Winnipeg. The local Mounted Police contingent had been reduced to a handful of men in order to reinforce posts in the heart of the rebel zone. Left to their own devices, agitated civilians, many of them the worse for drink, were milling about in abject confusion. The state of near panic was aggravated by rumours that the Blackfeet were massing for an imminent attack on the town.

Ironically, the effectiveness of the Mounted Police in preventing bloodshed in the past had rendered the white inhabitants of the western end of the Northwest Territories practically defenceless. Although surrounded by gun-toting Indians, the settlers and cowboys of southern Alberta had come to rely so much on the Mounties' protection that they were mostly unarmed. Previously, the police had been more than satisfied with this situation; they had always discouraged the possession of arms—and confiscated them at every opportunity—to avert the growth of a gunslinging society like the one across the border. But now that they were needed, weapons and ammunition were desperately scarce.

The most the government had been able to provide was a shipment of fifty old single-shot Snider rifles, which were too long to be used by men fighting on horseback. There was scant solace in the fact that 325 militiamen were on their way by rail; they were untrained city boys from Montreal, of dubious reliability in an Indian war. Surrounded by prophets of doom, Steele made his way to his friend General Strange, who had been appointed only the day before to command the Alberta District. The crusty old veteran of the Indian mutiny and many other campaigns was striving to bring order to the chaos that reigned.

Strange had already requested that Steele be released from his police duties to assist in forming a brigade to be called the Alberta Field Force. Strange wanted him to command his cavalry scouts. The general briskly put Steele in the picture. Although it was not quite so grim as the impression abroad on the streets of Calgary, the situation was serious. Thanks largely to the efforts of the Mounted Police in Fort Macleod and two former officers, ex-Inspector Denny and ex-Commissioner Macleod, the tribes of the Blackfoot nation seemed to have lost their inclination to join the revolt. But Big Bear's band, about six hundred strong, was still at large in the north and was even then moving against Fort Pitt, where twenty-two Mounted Policemen under Inspector Francis Dickens, son of novelist Charles Dickens, were preparing to make a desperate stand in defence of a handful of white traders and their families. Other Indians had plundered farms, missions, and stores in the vicinity of Red Deer, Beaver Lake, Saddle Lake, and Victoria. Ermine Skin's and Bobtail's bands of Crees, a notoriously bad lot, had allied themselves with Riel. Urgent pleas for protection were pouring in from the white settlements north of Calgary. It was feared that isolated settlers who had not made it to the doubtful safety of the villages would starve while hiding out in the woods—if the Indians did not kill them first.

Steele stayed with Strange while awaiting instructions. The next day the general received a telegram from the minister of militia: "You can take Steele with you." Appointed to the rank of major in the militia, Steele immediately went to work raising a corps of Mounted Policemen and experienced cowhands. The general named the unit Steele's Scouts.

In the meantime Steele arranged with magistrate George Hope Johnston to swear in a force of special civilian constables to police the C.P.R. construction line in the mountains. This would free his twenty-five-man detail there to form the nucleus of his scouts. Much red tape had to be cut before the policemen were released, and Bill Fury brought the men down to join him. Steele appointed Fury his squadron sergeant major forthwith.

The first militia unit, the 65th Voltigeurs of Montreal, had by then arrived, with about three hundred more hastily raised volunteers from Winnipeg to follow. Reassured that the Calgary area could be adequately garrisoned, General Strange planned to march as soon as possible against the Crees and other rebellious Indians in the north, relieving the imperilled town of Edmonton on the way.

Steele and Fury spent the next few days inducting recruits and employing their old soldiers' skills to the task of scrounging horses, saddlery, food, and ammunition. Scores of petty administrative details had to be attended to. At one point General Strange came and said, "Steele, the [red] jackets of your fellows are lined inside with brown cloth. Can't you have them wear the brown outside and thus be less inviting targets for the enemy?"

"My men are not turncoats," Steele smilingly replied to this impractical suggestion. On Strange's insistence he procured a supply of brown canvas working outfits to clothe his mounted policemen and had them issued broad-rimmed soft felt hats looped up at the side in the British colonial fashion that later became associated with the Australian Army. "He himself, a splendid-looking fellow and a good soldier, could not give up the swagger of his scarlet tunic, and I did not ask him to make the sacrifice, though it would have cost him his life in his first skirmish at close quarters had he not been so handy with a six-shooter," Strange later recalled.

The rapidly growing field force had to wait for more than a week before the general, making the telegraph wires burn with his indignant demands for more supplies, finally rounded up enough saddles, wagons, rations, arms, and ammunition for his expedition. Steele made use of this interval to drill the buckskin-clad cowboys under his command in the simple mounted infantry tactics of the Mounted Police. He improvised methods to train the men to fire a rifle from horseback, which was made the more difficult by the fact that most of the horses he had obtained were unbroken broncos. The animals were fitted with severe Mexican bits that would wrench their mouths if they attempted to move forward once a man had thrown down his reins in order to fire.

While Strange recruited some eighty local men to form the Alberta Mounted Rifles, twenty more Mounted Policemen arrived from Fort Macleod with the force's nine-pounder field gun. Three hundred and twenty-six militiamen of the Winnipeg Light Infantry reached the Calgary area, but they were unable to move north for the time being for want of transport and supplies.

On April 15 a detail of fifteen Steele's Scouts under a subaltern made a preliminary foray north to Red Deer, where they found the countryside free of marauding Indians and starving white refugees. On April 20 Strange was at last ready to march with the main body of his troops. Steele's Scouts, already dubbed the "Buckskin Cavalry," were to lead the column and guard the flanks. The 65th Voltigeurs and the Mounted Police artillery detachment with its field gun were to follow. The Alberta Mounted Rifles were to remain in Calgary with the Winnipeg troops until they could be fitted out with serviceable saddles and other supplies.

"The start in the morning was like a circus," Steele wrote. "The horses, with few exceptions, had never been ridden, and bucked whenever mounted, until two or three days had gentled them. This little performance interested the men from Montreal as they gazed at the gyrations of the cow-puncher soldiers and the Mounted Police." To add to the comic appearance of General Strange's motley miniature army, the nearest thing to a battle flag that could be found was a sixpenny cotton handkerchief printed with a Union Jack, which was attached to a buggy whip.

There was a further brief delay early on in the march because of the drunken incapacitation of the transport officer, who was left to sleep it off on the bank of the Bow River. Soon, however, the column pulled out onto the bald, burnt-over prairie, its 175 supply wagons stretching back for nearly a mile. Before long, a chinook wind melted the snow and flooded the streams and coulees. At every dip in the land horses sunk to their bellies and wagons to their axletrees. Guiding and shepherding this cumbersome convoy, Steele was acutely conscious that he had too few men for the tasks allotted to them. Yet he was highly pleased with his men, especially the cowboys, who abandoned their independent ways and took to military discipline as if they had been soldiers all their lives.

Despite the arduous labour of crossing swollen rivers and swamps, the column moved fairly swiftly. A new urgency had been lent to their mission by the news that the civilians at Fort Pitt, led by chief Hudson's Bay Company trader W. J. McLean, had left the fort to surrender to Big Bear's band. Relieved of their responsibility to protect the civilians, Inspector Dickens and his men had evacuated the post, escaping in a leaky scow down the North Saskatchewan River to the strongly fortified garrison at Battleford. There had been no news yet of the anticipated defeat of Louis Riel and his 200-odd métis and Indian guerrilla fighters at the hands of some 1,300 eastern militamen under General Officer Commanding the Canadian Forces Frederick Dobson Middleton. A British Army colonel who held the local rank of major general, Middleton had been in the West for nearly a month while the strength of his army steadily mounted. He was confidently expected to destroy Riel's ragged little legion with one mighty blow.

In fact, though, Middleton had suffered a stunning reverse at Fish Creek on the very day Strange's column set out. The militia forces suffered six killed and forty-nine wounded, four mortally, in a fight against a raiding party led by the great plainsman Gabriel Dumont. The rebel casualties were only four men killed and thirteen wounded. Out of communication with Middleton's headquarters, the men of the Alberta force were not to know about this for some time, which was probably just as well for their morale.

Theirs was an exceedingly hard and dreary march, first over many miles of fire-ravaged prairie offering no feed for the horses, then through a thick forest of poplars and alders strewn with swamps, creeks, and muskegs. Wagons often had to be manhandled across watercourses, and the men had to build their own roads and bridges with axes and spades. They worked on a skimpy and monotonous diet of canned corned beef and hardtack. Heavy snowstorms blew up to add to the hardships of the trail.

Steele knew from spotting signal fires and mirror flashes that unfriendly Indians were following their movements closely. He was in personal charge of selecting campsites that would be secure in the event of an attack. He deployed night patrols to keep a constant eye on the horses; creating stampedes was a standard feature of Indian warfare. Reveille was at 4:30 A.M., and they camped at about 5:00 P.M.; but Steele stayed in the saddle, scouting, long after dark.

When they reached the Battle River on April 29, they found welcome evidence that Indian enthusiasm for the rebellion, faint as it had always been in the broad scheme of things, was waning. Chiefs Ermine Skin and Bobtail, accompanied by Fathers Lacombe and Scollen, appeared at the camp to make the peace and apologize to General Strange for having temporarily given in to the temptation to encourage their bands to loot farms and Hudson's Bay Company stores. Gunner Jingo Strange, as the troops called him, refused to shake hands with the miscreants, saying he would do so only after he had dealt with Big Bear, and only if they behaved themselves in the meantime. What impressed Steele was that he knew these chiefs for a pair of thoroughgoing rogues who had obviously thought matters out and opted for the winning side.

On May 1 Steele led the way into Edmonton amid cheering settlers and refugees from the outlying area. "That the Force reached its destination, safely," recorded Strange, "was, I believe, due to the precautions taken, but especially to the careful scouting of Major Steele's Force, as a handful of Indians could have easily stampeded horses not carefully guarded. The horses were not picketed, but allowed to graze all night, being herded by mounted patrols, otherwise they would not have stood the work. . . . The Indians could also have inflicted a heavy loss on a Force of 160 Infantry, who were trying to guard a convoy of 175 waggons and carts, which often stuck in the black mud or broke down, and at times extended a distance of one or two miles."

At Edmonton Steele was reunited with his three brothers, Dick, Godfrey and Jim, who had been ranching in the vicinity. They all joined his scouts, as did a number of men relieved of duty in the Edmonton Home Guard. General Strange chose to stay in Edmonton to await the arrival of reinforcements from the Alberta Mounted Rifles and the Winnipeg Light Infantry. Steele used the four-day delay to give his men target practice and train his half-wild horses. He had his troopers gradually ease their mounts close to the lines of infantry taking target practice, and hit upon the idea of firing a pistol as a signal for feeding to accustom the animals to the sound of gunfire so that the men could shoot from their backs.

The general, true to his unconventional spirit, put plans into effect to move his troops and supplies downriver by barges "armoured" with a lining of stacks of pork and flour barrels. When the colonel of the newly arrived Winnipeg militiamen expressed doubt about the scheme, saying that the effectiveness of the protection should be tested, Strange replied in a formal order that the experiments on the penetration of flour sacks were to be left to enemy fire. Steele was to command a land column composed of his scouts and two companies of the 65th and move northeast to the trading center of Victoria, where there were reports of Indian trouble. They embarked on the morning of the sixth after a minor squabble with the civilian teamsters, who demanded to be armed. The reports of an Indian attack on Victoria, like the earlier reports of settlers starving while hiding in the bush, proved to be groundless.

Steele's task was to pick up Big Bear's trail and at the same time try to protect Strange's flotilla from attack along the banks on the North Saskatchewan River. Only one attack, a harmless and none too determined one, was made. But the soldiers were on edge now that they were on Big Bear's home ground. One night the Voltigeurs' sentry sounded the alarm for attacking Indians. The men seized their rifles and charged up a hill with a cheer, spraying the prairie with hot lead. Five of Steele's scouts were forced to take cover in a hollow until it was realized that the "Indians" were actually poplar saplings waving in the wind.

For Steele it was a return to the familiar hard trail he had followed to Edmonton when the police first brought the law to the West eleven years earlier. He approached it cautiously, aware that, from then on, hostile Indians would be watching his every move. To fight fire with fire he enlisted friendly Indians and métis to help in the scouting. This was doubly necessary because his cowboys were now in bush country greatly different from their usual surroundings.

On the night of May 24 they arrived at Frog Lake, where Wandering Spirit and his gang had murdered the nine white men. All the buildings in the deserted village had been burned. One of the men present, a cowboy scout named Joseph Hicks, recounted,

"The troops went to work looking for the dead and found them all. Some in shallow graves and some lying just where they fell. All mutilated with all kinds of indignities and the two Roman Catholic priests all dismembered and thrown into a deep well or cellar. Two men went down and handed up the parts to those above who then buried them. The men who went down to get the bodies wore gas masks consisting of a sponge saturated with army rum. They had the freedom of the camp that night."

On the morning of the twenty-sixth they came to Fort Pitt, which had been looted and burned to the ground after Dickens' Mounted Police unit departed. Outside the gates they found the body of Constable Cowan, a police scout killed in a skirmish with Big Bear's Indians while the fort was under siege. The corpse had muskrat spears sticking into it and had been scalped; the heart had been cut out and impaled on a stick driven into the ground. From the evidence gathered at Frog Lake and Fort Pitt, the officers calculated that the Crees must have taken about twenty-five white prisoners, including a number of women and children. Some métis were also presumed to have gone with them, but whether as prisoners or allies was not known.

Steele personally scouted the area surrounding the fort for the trail the Indians had taken. On the south side of the river there was a heavy cart track and the prints of a white woman's shoe. He concluded from the pigeon-toed tracks that the shoe had been worn by an Indian woman who had taken it from the fort, which had been thoroughly looted. To the north of the river he found a letter written to Mrs. McLean, the chief trader's wife and a prisoner of the Crees, by her daughter in 1880. Coincidentally, Mrs. McLean had shown the letter to Steele when she first received it. The McLeans were then his neighbours at Fort Qu'Appelle.

The prevailing theory was that Big Bear would move south to join forces with Poundmaker, the other Cree chief whose band had joined in the rising. Steele disputed this on the strength of having found Mrs. McLean's letter on a trail leading north and other clues. So confident was General Strange in his chief scout's ability that he overrode the other officers and ordered Steele to move northward. The next day Steele found a clear trail made by hundreds of ponies exactly where he suspected it would be.

Strange ordered him to travel fast to gain contact with the enemy. Taking ninety mounted men and two other officers, Steele pushed quickly north. They rode through the silent woods until close to midnight, when a Chippewa scout with them said that he "smelled" Indians. Having no wish to bump into the mass of Big Bear's warriors, Steele decided to camp. He halted the troops and took a small party of officers and NCOs with him to look for a bivouac where the horses could not be stampeded. They rode down a hill into a little valley. Steele reined up and said, "This is just the thing!"

Suddenly an Indian sprang up from the grass and snapped off two shots that whisked past his nose. He drew his revolver and was about to fire when Corporal McLelland moved between him and the Indian. The corporal shot the man dead at eighty yards.

Out of the corner of his eye Steele saw another Indian on a horse. The man fired at him. Then the woods came alive with Indians loosing off with their rifles in the dark.

Their war whoops mingled with the shouted curses of the NCOs as Steele and the others returned their fire. He was afraid of hitting his own men in the melee. In a minute or two the Indians galloped off.

The Indian who had been killed turned out to be Meeminook, a brave hunter and a gentle soul who had helped and protected the Crees' white captives when Wandering Spirit wanted to kill them. His party had gone out to stampede the horses from the main army camp. He died with a Queen's medal for Indian headmen on his chest, clad only in a breechcloth, his face smeared with vermillion and yellow war paint. He measured 6 feet, 4½ inches minus his scalp, which was taken by one of the scouts.

Steele sent back word of the encounter to General Strange and camped until dawn. The scouts then picked their way slowly along the Indian trail. They found an abandoned campsite where Steele counted the remains of 187 recent campfires, indicating that there were six to seven hundred people in Big Bear's group.

He was examining the site when he heard war whoops and looked up to see his advance scouting party, under a métis named John Whitford, galloping towards him with a pack of howling Indians chasing them. He ordered Fury to ride forward with a squad to cover the retreat and formed his dismounted men into an extended firing line. The Indians pulled up at a respectful distance and wheeled away.

Steele was amused by Whitford's breathless report. He had gone ahead of the party into some dense woods when he heard a horse stamp as if bothered by mosquitos. Then he heard an Indian say, "Wait, wait, let them come a little further."

"Shall we fight or fall back?" whispered Whitford in Cree.

"Let us draw them; to fight is no good. We were not sent for that," said the unseen Indian in the woods beside him. Whitford then took off with the rest of his party as fast as their horses could carry them, the Indians only yards behind them. As General Strange put it, Whitford lost his hat and barely saved his scalp.

Steele sent back word that they were coming very close to the Indians and waited until Strange brought the infantry and the field gun forward. The force advanced about two miles in the late afternoon, with Steele's men probing ahead. They came to him with a report that the Indians had established a fortified position on a promontory named Frenchman's Butte. Steele rode up to take a look. "A fine-looking band of Indians appeared on the summit of a large round butte about 1,500 yards distant," he recorded. "They were galloping in a circle to warn their camp, their excellent horsemanship and wild appearance making a remarkable picture as they were silouetted against the blue sky."

The main body of troops arrived, the gun was instantly unlimbered, and Strange called for a bombardment. Shrapnel ripped up the earth of the butte a split second after the Indian horsemen had disappeared over the top. Steele led a mixed party of Mounted Policemen, scouts, and Winnipeg Light Infantry to clear the wood bordering the open field at the foot of the hill. They drove the Indians away without casualties. Author R. G. MacBeth, who was a lieutenant with the Winnipegs, recalled of this engagement: "I have a vivid recollection of being advised by Steele to take cover when in an exposed position, while at the same time he was beside me, seated on his great bay horse seventeen hands high, with his colossal figure, red-coated, clearly outlined against the sky-line."

Steele pushed his men forward under the cover of the woods to a point where he could see a large Indian encampment. Darkness

The main street of Winnipeg in the 1880s. (*Glenbow-Alberta Institute*)

Calgary's main street, circa 1886. (*National Photography Collection, Public Archives, Canada, PA-66540*)

A camp of Plains Crees (Assiniboines) during the 1880s. (*Glenbow-Alberta Institute*)

C.P.R. construction camp and North-West Mounted Policemen at Moose Jaw, winter, 1882–83. (*Manitoba Archives*)

Two views of the Beaver (Beavermouth). *Above:* Winter scene, 1884–85, showing Queen of the West Hotel at left. *Below:* Sam Steele and detachment of N.W.M.P. in summer, 1885. (*Glenbow-Alberta Institute*)

C.P.R. right-of-way construction on the Columbia River, 1884.
(*Glenbow-Alberta Institute*)

Railway construction crew in the Rockies. (*Glenbow-Alberta Institute*)

Completion of C.P.R. through the Rockies. (*Glenbow-Alberta Institute*)

The last spike, November 7, 1885. (*Glenbow-Alberta Institute*)

Big Bear. (*National Photography Collection, Public Archives, Canada, C-17430*)

Steele's Scouts, 1885. (*R.C.M.P. Museum, Regina*)

Major General F. D. Middleton. (*Glenbow-Alberta Institute*)

Polo team at Fort Macleod in 1892. (*Glenbow-Alberta Institute*)

Officers of the force, around 1890: (*left to right*) Inspectors Baker, McDonell, Begin, Steele, Starnes, Wood. (*Glenbow-Alberta Institute*)

fell. Throwing a strong ring of piquets and patrolling scouts around the wagons and horses, the force bivouacked for the night. The troops were short of food, the more so because a large number of Voltigeurs had rushed to the scene from their barges on the riverbank, leaving behind their dinners. The cowboys, Mounted Policemen, and Winnipeg men cheerfully split their rations with the French-speaking troops from Montreal.

At daybreak on the morning of May 28 Strange ordered an advance with Steele and his men in the lead on foot. Nearing the butte, Steele realized that they were up against a very strong defensive position indeed. A creek bounded by thick bush and muskeg ran in front and on both sides of the butte, with a swampy field at the foot of it. The slopes were bare, providing a clear field of fire from its crest. The crest itself was coated with brush, affording good cover. The Indians had improved on it by digging deep, concealed rifle pits fronted by logs.

From observations made of the camp the night before, Steele estimated their fighting strength at almost six hundred. They now opened fire on a squad he had sent ahead to reconnoitre the creek. His men sunk to their waists in the mud on its banks. An Indian bullet hit Constable McRae in the leg while he was attempting to cross this obstacle. It was a bad wound, but the policeman insisted on firing all his cartridges at the enemy before he would allow himself to be moved.

The infantry opened out in skirmishing order at the edge of the woods and moved forward towards the foot of the hill. The Indians poured a withering fire on them. Luckily many of the Indians were armed with shotguns and obsolete muskets that were ineffective at this range. The soldiers reached the scanty cover of the willows along the creek and steadily returned the fire.

Strange started to bombard the summit of the butte with the N.W.M.P.'s nine-pounder. This made the Indians keep their heads down, but not enough to prevent them from maintaining a daunting rate of fire down the slope. They got the range of the gun with powerful Sharps rifles, pinging bullets off the barrel while the gunners loaded and aimed kneeling or lying down.

At one point an Indian appeared on the crest of the butte with a blanket on a pole. The soldiers ceased fire, but the Indian fusillade got all the hotter. Lieutenant Strange, the general's son, who was in charge of the artillery, asked his Irish gunner, "Can you hit that man?"

The gunner replied, "Be japers I'll ate what's left of him." He literally blew the Indian to pieces with a shell.

The general rode over to Steele and told him to take his men back to their horses on the ridge behind them, mount, and make a detour under the cover of the bush on the left to see if they could find a place where they could cross in behind the enemy. They rode under heavy but ill-aimed fire for a mile and a half without discovering an opening. The Indians had well-concealed riflemen posted all along the way.

Meanwhile another party of scouts reported that an Indian raiding party was working its way around to the rear of the militia position, where fire could be brought to bear on the wagons. Steele came back to Strange to report that there was no chance of turning the enemy's left flank. Strange told him about the threat to the rear, but Steele was doubtful that the Indians could have moved that far. He urged the general to ignore the report and put in an attack from the right side of the Indian position. He was convinced that this would have a good chance of succeeding, albeit with casualties.

Earlier in the day one of his scouts, a Mounted Police sergeant named William Parker, had climbed a tall pine tree overlooking the Indian camp. Parker now reported that the Indians were leaving their firing line and fleeing north in twos and threes. But Strange, swayed by the cautious advice of his two infantry colonels, had already made up his mind on a withdrawal to Fort Pitt, about five miles away. From his point of view there were good reasons for breaking off the action: Ammunition was scarce, it would have been dangerous to camp overnight in full view of the enemy, the men had not eaten since daybreak, and the horses had not been out of their harnesses for eight hours.

It had been a remarkably bloodless affair, with only three wounded among the whites and (as far as could be ascertained) two killed and three wounded among the Indians. As one observer tartly remarked, the engagement "was noted for loss of good ammunition rather than the destruction of the enemy." There had been almost as much shouting back and forth as shooting, with each side calling rudely on the other to come out and fight like men. Wandering Spirit played a prominent part in the verbal hostilities. Every time a shell dropped near his rifle pit, he would bob up and shout, "Tan at ee!" The Cree war chief had witnessed troops drilling on both sides of the border, and he knew that the words "stand at ease" had the effect of putting soldiers in an inoffensive position. Evidently he thought it was worth trying this war whoop-in-reverse.

19: HUNTING THE BEAR

The back of the Northwest rebellion was broken on May 12, 1885, with the fall of Batoche, the tiny métis capital. Louis Riel was subsequently captured, and Gabriel Dumont fled to the United States. The battle of Batoche was won in spite of General Middleton's dithering. After three days of inconclusive skirmishing, a sudden bayonet charge planned by his subordinates without his knowledge carried the day.

The general officer commanding—an imperious, walrus-moustached man of sixty—now turned his lugubrious attention to Big Bear. He moved leisurely northward by steamboat with some four hundred militamen to link up with General Strange's force at Fort Pitt. By then the maverick Cree chief had become public enemy number one. The Fort Macleod *Gazette* expressed the feelings of western whites towards him and his people. "Big Bear is reported to be at Sounding Lake, with four white women, who have been terribly outraged," the *Gazette* recorded. "General Strange has gone after him with blood in his eye, and it is believed and hoped will not give any quarter to these Indians, but clear them off the face of the earth."

Strange expected Middleton to arrive the day after the engagement at Frenchman's Butte, when he planned to make a fresh move against the Indians. He waited in vain for the steamboats for two days before sending Steele and his scouts back to the butte on a reconnoitring patrol. They found the place deserted. The camp, protected by no fewer than three hundred two- and three-man rifle pits, obviously had been hastily evacuated. It was full of loot from Frog Lake and Fort Pitt which the Indians would not have left behind if they had not pulled out in some panic: wagons, barrels of flour and bacon, tools, furniture, silverware, and a fortune in furs plundered from the Hudson's Bay Company stores.

It was later learned that the seemingly ineffectual artillery bombardment had done its work after all. Running low on ammunition and terrorized by "the gun that speaks twice" (once when it fires and once when the shell explodes), the Indians had begun retreating in large numbers before Strange had called his withdrawal. A strong rush on the right flank, as Steele had suggested, would have won a decisive victory.

He had little time to ponder this, however. Having dispatched a report to Strange, he rode on to direct the scouts following the trails leading out of the camp. There were seven in all, deliberately devised to confuse pursuers, describing circles and crisscrossing one another. Through diligent tracking the scouts eventually were able to find a spot where the seven trails converged into two.

That night, the night of June 1, some of Steele's scouts recovered five white prisoners. They had been set free by a party of Wood Crees who had taken one of the two remaining trails. The Wood Crees had been reluctant partners of Big Bear's kindred Plains Crees since the Frog Lake massacre, and this particular group had decided to break away from them. The freed prisoners reported that Big Bear's band, still with some Wood Crees and most of the white prisoners in tow, had headed northeast.

So Steele now definitely knew the right trail. He sent back word of this to Strange and awaited instructions. In time orders arrived from the general to ride after Big Bear and attempt to make contact. The message implied that though Middleton's force had not yet landed, it would march immediately to come to Steele's support. Strange himself could do nothing; his force's ammunition stocks were too low to mount another offensive, and even if he could, he was under orders from Middleton not to move.

Steele was short of ammunition himself, and he had only sixty-two men with him. On the other hand, he now knew that Big Bear's fighting strength had been depleted by the desertion of a considerable number of the Wood Crees who had been at Frenchman's Butte.

"It was about two o'clock in the morning when the major came around to our tents simply roaring," wrote Joseph Hicks, the cowboy-scout who had been at Frog Lake when the bodies were discovered. "GET UP MEN. GET UP. TAKE EIGHT DAYS HALF RATIONS AND FOLLOW ME. And up the trail Steele went as hard as his horse could lope. Accordingly every man in the camp got up, got whatever rations he could handle and filled everything with ammunition and up the trail after Steele."

He led them in the dark through rugged bush country choked with small trees and intersected by creeks, swamps, and muskegs. The Indians had set brush fires on the trail and dug hazardous traps. Large trees had been felled across it and had to be manhandled out of the way. Horses had to be pulled and pushed across the swamps and muskegs. The animals suffered terribly, covered with mosquitos and deerflies, with no feed but slough grass, which the men pulled up by the handful. From constantly moving through swamps and bogs, many had developed a disease of the hooves that in some cases caused them to drop off. Of the seventy-five horses that started this trek, only forty-seven survived.

While Steele pushed through the wilderness, General Middleton at last arrived at Fort Pitt on the morning of June 2. Besides his infantry and artillery (consisting of two Gatling guns, primitive machine guns mounted on wagon wheels) his force included two hundred mounted men. Strange's independent field command had been abolished, so he had to request that Middleton send mounted troops to support Steele's scout detachment. Sergeant William Parker had escorted Middleton to Strange's camp at Frenchman's Butte and was present at the meeting of the generals. According to Parker, Middleton exploded on hearing Strange's request: "Not a man! Not a man! Who is this Major Steele? It should not have been done."

An officer who went strictly by the book and never advanced unless he had his enemy grossly outnumbered, Middleton was annoyed that Steele would risk a battle with Big Bear with so few soldiers. But after storming on for a few minutes, he finally agreed to follow Steele—with his slow-moving infantry, his unwieldy Gatling guns, and in his own good time.

Back in the forest Steele had been finding notes from chief trader McLean saying that all was well and that the Indian band was moving in a northwesterly direction. These were useful because the Indians had laid a number of false trails to throw the scouts off the scent.

On its second day out Steele's party was preparing to move out of a clearing where they had stopped for lunch when a couple of shots sounded in the woods ahead. Steele leapt on his horse and charged across the meadow into the bush. He heard a bloodthirsty war cry and looked around, fully expecting to meet a Cree warrior. But it was only Canon George Mackay, the frontier minister who had joined the scouts as a chaplain, leading a chase after a couple of Indians with rifle in hand.

A scout named Fisk passed Steele going in the other direction, his arm smashed by an Indian bullet. Steele wheeled and ordered the men behind him to scour the woods, then galloped on to catch up with the men ahead. The two Indians fled over a rise; there was no hope of catching them. The men in the woods found no others. As it happened, Canon Mackay had ridden ahead of the advanced guard and surprised the two Indian scouts in the thickets. He took two wide shots at them, and scout Fisk, who had ridden to his aid, was shot by the Indians in turn.

Steele pressed forward immediately to cut down on the time the main body of the Crees would have to react to their rear guard's warning. He kept his men on the march from noon until just before dawn on June 3, when they stopped to eat their half rations of biscuits and take a short rest. Sergeant Butlin, a Mounted Policeman, had gone on ahead with an advance patrol. It was still dark when he came to a ridge and sighted the Indians' camp.

The sergeant sent for Steele, who led the rest of the men forward. He reached the ridge and looked down on a beautiful big body of water known as Loon Lake. The Indians had pitched their teepees on the near shore. A narrow and shallow stretch of water separated the camp from a heavily wooded peninsula. To one side of the camp was a dry swamp dotted with spruce and tamarack trees; directly in front was a small prairie. Dense bush stood between the ridge on which Steele lay and the open approach to the camp.

In the dim light he saw some Indians crossing the ford between the camp and the peninsula beyond, as if abandoning the campsite. This seemed to make sense, as only three teepees were left. But Steele suspected that the movement was a ruse to draw his men into an ambush in the woods on the hillside below them. He knew that they were heavily outnumbered. At the Indians' last campsite he had counted fifty-three extinguished campfires, indicating about two hundred people. The situation called for a calculated bluff.

He summoned Canon Mackay and asked him to tell the Indians in Cree to surrender. He was instructing the gunslinging preacher on what to say—that all the other rebels had been defeated and that only the ringleaders and murderers among them would face trial—when an Indian outpost in the bush below them opened fire. Steele jumped up with a revolver in his hand and called on his men to follow him. They surged down the hillside with war whoops, putting to flight the Indians who had laid an ambuscade on the trail.

The Indians formed a firing line at the foot of the hill. Steele heard a chief urging his warriors to advance upwards again, telling them that they faced only six soldiers. They started crawling up under the cover of the brush. The leader got within ten feet of a teamster in Steele's party, who shot him dead. Two more Indians were killed in their rush up the hill, and one was dropped by bullets as he emerged from a teepee.

As they hit the bottom of the hill and started to climb a slight rise to where the camp stood, Steele's men divided, by prearrangement, into two wings of thirty men each. The left was to charge the camp and the right to clear the swamp. The Indians ran for cover in the bush behind the camp and resumed shooting. Luckily, the shotguns that some of them carried were so weak that although several of Steele's men were hit, the buckshot bounced harmlessly off their clothing.

Nevertheless, enough Indians were bearing Winchesters and long-range Sharps to keep up a dangerous volley. Bullets were ripping the bark off the trees around Steele and his trumpeter, a carefree young man named Chabot. Chabot offered his rifle to his commander to take a shot or two at the redskins, but Steele thanked him and said he had other things to attend to. He had heard an Indian chief leading his men with shouts as they worked their way around a crescent of hills to the left of his position. To meet this threat Steele sent a squad up a hill after them. At the head of the charge was Sergeant Major Fury, who was hit in the chest by a bullet from a Sharps rifle just as he reached the crest of the hill.

The others in the squad surged over the top and flung themselves to the ground, opening rapid rifle fire on the Indians. Seven Indians were killed and one wounded before the rest fled over the ford to the peninsula. The squad on the right attacked the swamp, killing five Indians. The survivors scampered across the ford.

The Indians launched a heavy fire from the thick bush of the peninsula, forcing the white men to stay under cover. Concerned about the lack of ammunition, Steele ordered the trumpeter to sound the cease fire. He took Canon Mackay—who, he said, "had been very forward in using his rifle"—to the highest hill above the camp. There they hoisted a white flag. All the Indians ceased firing except for one man, armed with a good long-range rifle, who continued to snipe at them methodically. Every time this excellent marksman found his range, Steel and the canon had to scramble for new cover. In between these undignified excursions, however, Mackay delivered Steele's call for surrender in a ringing ecclesiastical voice.

The Indians made no reply—they seemed to be uncertain about what to do—until a few scattered voices shouted defiance, and they all resumed firing. Steele issued orders to fire at anyone moving in the vicinity of the ford and had Mackay shout across his message again. One Indian appeared near the ford, and a scout shot him in the elbow; he hastily withdrew into the bushes. The Indians shot sporadically at any of the white men who moved.

Steele's plan was to wait there for Middleton's force to catch up with him; he had been led to expect that they would arrive that morning. Without reinforcements his party could not possibly attack the strong Indian position across the ford. He had sent Sergeant Butlin and a couple of other scouts back on the trail to meet the general's column. After almost four hours, Butlin returned to report that there was no sign of anyone. Steele knew then that he had no choice but to withdraw. His troops were down to fifteen rounds of ammunition and one day's rations each;

they were eighty miles over a difficult trail from their base. Only three men had been wounded in the attack. Although he was bearing up just as courageously as Steele would have expected, Fury was in critical condition and great pain. Ordering a buckboard to be fitted out as an ambulance for the wounded, Steele prepared to pull out.

He ordered the teepees, which contained ammunition, to be set on fire, and posted a small party on the ridge to prevent the Indians from returning. Then the main body moved down the trail for some twelve miles. They did not camp until close to midnight. By then their horses were almost too played out to move.

The rear guard on the ridge opened fire on men moving on the other side of the ford on several occasions. Had they only known it, they might have rescued the white captives there and then. The Indian who had been shot in the elbow during the stalemate was, in fact, carrying a letter from Mr. McLean to Steele saying that the Wood Crees among the Indians were prepared to surrender and that Big Bear's Plains Crees were pulling out for the south in an attempt to reach the American border. The men the rear guard shot at were Mr. McLean himself and another prisoner, named Simpson; they had been attempting to raise a flag of truce on behalf of the Wood Crees after Big Bear had gone.

Thwarted in their attempt to surrender, the Wood Crees struck out for the north, taking the prisoners with them. Wandering Spirit went along with this group, presumably because he thought it was safer than going south with his own band of Plains Crees. According to one account Wandering Spirit feared that his kinsmen would turn on him and kill him for leading them into trouble. Big Bear personally had good reason to hate his war chief. Pathetically enough the old Cree leader had been swept unwillingly along by the bloodthirsty impetus of Wandering Spirit and the other young warriors in his band. He had joined the exodus partly to use his authority to prevent them from killing or molesting the captive whites.

From Loon Lake on, Big Bear knew that the game was over. He encouraged his followers to split up and slip away in small groups. He must have realized that, with the whites back in control of the country, he had little chance of reaching the border undetected. Half starving, he wandered around the Battleford area, eventually accompanied only by his young son and a loyal tribal councillor with the perplexing name of All and a Half.

In a single thrust, Steele had smashed to pieces the savage band that had terrorized Alberta. He had also sprung loose the white prisoners, who were later released by the demoralized Wood Crees on their trek north (the women, incidentally, had not been raped). But Steele had no way of knowing this at the time, and his impatience grew as he waited at his camp on the Loon Lake trail for the dilatory General Middleton. The general finally appeared on the morning of the fifth at the head of two hundred men and an artillery detachment manning the Gatling guns. He might have been even later if he had not jettisoned his infantry on the way.

The GOC had no cause to be pleased with Steele. First of all he had a petulant contempt for Mounted Policemen. He also knew that among his disgruntled troops, his elephantine methods were being compared unfavourably with those of the hard-riding Major Steele. The two men had a cool interview at which Steele crisply but politely gave his report of the Loon Lake engagement. Middleton then ordered him to take his scouts and report to Strange's force.

Steele gave the general full particulars of how to proceed on the trail, although he must have been inwardly seething. The order meant the withdrawal of the only men who knew the country and the only men there with battle experience against the Crees. But Steele dutifully made his preparations to return to Fort Pitt, only to have the General change his mind and order the scouts to go with him. The whole ponderous column then retraced the steps of the scouts to Loon Lake, arriving at the bluff overlooking it on June 6.

Any Indians there were dead. Across the ford—now called Steele's Narrows and the site of a Province of Saskatchewan historical park—were the freshly dug graves of the men who had fallen in the June 3 battle. Middleton ordered the graves to be opened in case they contained the bodies of the captive whites. They did not, of course, but by digging them up, it was discovered that Cut Arm, a prominent Wood Cree chief, was among the casualties.

The advance scouts came across another body, that of an eld-

erly Indian woman who evidently had hanged herself because she
had been wounded and could not keep up with her people. They
called for Steele to examine a muskeg across from where her body
was found. Cutting through the muskeg was a clear trail where
Big Bear's band had crossed. Yet Middleton's own chief scout, a
former British Army officer and gentleman farmer named Boulton, declared the bog impassable. When the general rode up for a
personal reconnaissance, his horse stepped on a particularly soft
spot and sunk up to its saddle girth.

Steele made a careful examination and found a place where
there was a solid bottom two feet below the surface. He sent two
men ahead from this point, and they picked their way across without difficulty. Still, Middleton and his staff officers stuck to the
theory that it was impassable. Steele pointed out that it had not
proved a barrier to the delicate women and children in Big Bear's
band, who had crossed it only a few days before.

Apparently convinced by this argument, Middleton decided to
go ahead. He ordered Boulton and Steele to lead the way across
the muskeg the next morning. They were about to do so when
word reached them that the general had changed his mind again.
He did not want to put such an obstacle between his troops and
his base.

Wearily and bitterly, Steele's party rode with Middleton's army
all the way back to Fort Pitt, which was about as far away as anyone in that part of the West could get from Big Bear. Their appearance doubtless drew disapproving glances from the pukka general. Weeks of scouting in bush country had worn and torn their
clothing to tatters. Some of the men had made shirts out of abandoned flour sacks by cutting holes for the neck and arms. Their
horses—those that survived—had been reduced to skin and bones.

They led a life of boring inactivity in the tent camp at Fort Pitt
for almost another month before Middleton ordered them to return to Calgary to be disbanded. By this time Big Bear, Wandering Spirit, and other Indian murderers had been arrested without
further strife. The Northwest rebellion was over once and for all,
thanks in no small part to Steele's steadfast pursuit of Big Bear's
band and the stunning effect of the action at Loon Lake.

But there were no rewards for him and his men as they
awaited the end of their service. Supplies at the fort ran out, and

they might have starved if they had not killed Indian cattle to eat. According to Joseph Hicks (who tended to exaggerate, but whose memoir nonetheless left a good private soldier's view of the campaign) Middleton threatened heavy punishment for any eastern Canadian soldiers caught sharing food parcels sent by eastern organizations with their western counterparts. "This cost the General his wagon load of private food supplies and every man in our troop was a party to the theft," Hicks wrote. "Steele committed every kind of offence trying to get his men better treatment but every request was preempterly [sic] refused by Middleton; it was then that our officers shut their eyes [to] everything we did and enjoyed their meals all the better for the loot. The General's ham tasted all the better because he knew we took it and he knew that the men were supported by their officers even up to General Strange."

Steele himself was distinctly bitter. On the way back to Edmonton he was informed that some of the civilian teamsters on the trail ahead were planning to loot the Saddle Lake Indian Reserve. He dispatched Sergeant Parker with a party to prevent it. "He was in the nick of time," Steele recorded. "Many of them had their teams loaded up with [farm] machinery and other articles, which Parker compelled them to restore before they left. This action saved the government the loss of several thousand dollars' worth of property. One of my men, however, on the march to Pitt, had accidentally damaged a set of weighing scales. Of that the Indian department took due notice, but not of the action to save their property. Such is life!"

Despite such irritations, however, Steele's Scouts were in high good humour as they marched victoriously back to Calgary.* An anecdote related by Sergeant William Parker in his memoirs catches the mood: "On going into camp one evening between Edmonton and Calgary, a prairie chicken lit in some long grass about seventy yards from me. There was an order against shooting in camp so I went to Major Steele and asked permission to shoot it with my revolver, as I wanted it for supper.

"He laughed and said, 'I'll tell you what I will do, Parker. If

* The memory of this unusual unit is commemorated today by a private organization of the same name in Calgary whose members annually take to horseback to duplicate its trek north.

you shoot it the first shot, I will give you a gallon of whiskey on arrival in Calgary.' I said it was difficult to shoot a chicken with one shot with a revolver, and to allow me two shots, to which he agreed. A large number of scouts were watching me as I threw myself down on the grass and started to crawl towards the chicken; just its head was showing above the grass. When within about thirty-five yards, I took careful aim and fired. It was a lucky shot, as the head of the chicken flew in the air and all the boys cheered. The major came out of his tent to find out what the cheering was about and was told that Parker was going to have chicken for supper!" Parker did not record whether Steele ever gave him the whiskey.

For his part, Steele officially reported that his scouts were "the best body of men I have ever had anything to do with." They were greeted like heroes in Calgary, where the grateful citizens held a banquet for the officers and presented Steele with an expensive diamond ring. Strange praised him highly in his final report on the Alberta campaign and recommended him for a companionship in the Order of St. Michael and St. George (C.M.G.). But as Steele noted, there would be no official glory for anyone who served in the rebellion except General Middleton himself. The GOC's own report on the campaign belittled the importance of such engagements as Loon Lake and conveniently neglected to include Strange's more relevant dispatches. When he was not downright condemnatory of the performance of N.W.M.P. officers during the rebellion, he damned them with faint praise.

And Middleton was the man of the hour in Ottawa. Parliament voted him a $20,000 reward, and on the say-so of the Canadian authorities he was knighted and promoted to the rank of major general in the British Army. In his enmity towards the Mounted Police, he lobbied to have the force disbanded and replaced by a military corps of mounted infantry under his own ultimate command. He publicly excoriated Commissioner Irvine for choosing to concentrate on protecting white settlers rather than risking disaster by attempting an offensive with the inadequate forces at his disposal.

Nothing came of the general's effort to get rid of the Mounted Police, but that seems to be primarily because a parsimonious government dreaded the expense of replacing it. Although Steele emerged from the rebellion with his personal reputation enhanced, he was hurt and angered by this assault on the reputation of his beloved force.

In a rare instance of real-life poetic justice, General Middleton was soon to come under a cloud himself, though too late to save the careers of several senior Mounted Policemen. The general was accused of looting a large quantity of furs belonging to a métis prisoner. The weight of the evidence was such that the Canadian Government quietly let him know that he ought to return to Great Britain. There Queen Victoria, who could not believe that a British officer could do such a thing, gathered him to her metaphorical bosom and appointed him to the sinecure of keeper of the crown jewels.

20: THE LAST SPIKE

On the day after Steele paid off his scouts, he received a telegram from Controller Fred White in Ottawa informing him of his promotion to the rank of superintendent. It was long overdue. Promotion in the Mounted Police in those days was a plain matter of political patronage; although he was a declared Conservative Party supporter, Steele had been passed over several times in favour of officers with more influence in Ottawa. He had not been backward in pointing out his loyalty to the party and political connections, but he seemed to lack the political pull necessary for advancement. Now, after his well-publicized performance in the rebellion campaign, his qualifications for a higher rank apparently could no longer be ignored.

He was under orders to return to his command in the mountains, but he had a long spell of accumulated leave coming, which he chose to spend among friends in Winnipeg. The burgeoning metropolis of western Canada held a special attraction to him as a keen judge of horseflesh and a man who liked to make the occasional, strictly legal bet. The first racecourse in the West had just opened outside of town, and Steele was an avid spectator. He travelled back and forth between his hotel and the track by train.

He had just returned from the races one day when his orderly knocked on the door. The young man asked excitedly if Steele had any reason to have a warrant for the arrest of the man known in the mountains as Bulldog Kelly. Steele said no.

The constable explained that he, too, had caught the train back from the racecourse that day and had taken a seat in the same car as Bulldog Kelly. The two recognized each other from the mountains and had a talk. The constable mentioned that he was in Winnipeg accompanying Steele. Kelly asked why Steele was there. Had he come to arrest him? The young man said he thought not, and Kelly abruptly left him. Later he spotted Kelly jumping from the train as it slowed down to enter the station.

Steele mentally ran over the details of the case of Mr. Baird, the American businessman who had been murdered the year before at the Hog Ranche near Golden. It had seemed to him at the time that the evidence given by Baird's packer and companion, Manuel Dainard, was uncommonly vague. He had entertained suspicions of Kelly when the constables investigating the case told of camping with him. It struck Steele now that the most likely reason why Kelly should fear that he had come to arrest him was that Kelly had killed Baird.

He hurried to the Winnipeg city police station, where he talked to Chief Murray, an old acquaintance. They jointly decided that Kelly should be detained. The chief sent men out to look for the suspect, but they reported back that he was nowhere to be found in Winnipeg. Murray resolved to track Kelly down, and Steele took the first train back to the mountains to work up a case.

On his arrival he again questioned Baird's companion, Dainard, who—much to Steele's disgust—admitted to having given the police false information. At the time of the murder Dainard had been afraid that Kelly would kill him if he told all he knew. He was now willing to swear that Kelly was the murderer. Steele wired Chief Murray to that effect.

Murray had not been idle. By then Kelly was behind bars in a small town in the Dakota Territory, the Winnipeg chief having traced him there and captured him by bursting into his hotel room in the middle of the night. The evidence gathered by Steele was brought before an extradition hearing at which the investigating commissioner ruled that Kelly should be returned to British Columbia to face trial.

But the Canadian policemen had hooked a bigger fish than they imagined. Kelly (an alias for his real name of McNaughton) had connections with a powerful gang of criminals in Chicago and with the anti-Canadian Fenian movement. The Fenian lobby in Washington saw to it that his extradition papers were not signed.

The British Columbia attorney general's department later made another attempt to extradite McNaughton after having him arrested in Minneapolis. The Chicago gang and the Fenians spent a large amount of money on his defence. Again the investigating commissioner ruled in favour of extradition, and again Washington declined to ratify his extradition papers. Because both the killer and his victim were American citizens, British Columbia authorities saw no point in pursuing the matter. Steele drew some consolation from the thought that the Canadian police had done their duty according to their own traditions of justice. The following year he heard that McNaughton had died a violent death in the United States.

On his return to the mountains Steele found that the construction camps had grown wilder than ever. The vacuum in law enforcement left by the absence of the Mounted Police during the rebellion had attracted an even larger criminal element than before. Heading a hastily raised force of untrained special constables, magistrate George Hope Johnston had done a remarkable job of maintaining order. Steele was amazed that there had been no killings or holdups, considering the bad characters who inhabited the camps.

It was all the more amazing in the light of a farcical squabble being waged by the resident representatives of the federal and provincial governments. The British Columbia Government continued to defy Ottawa and to undermine federal efforts to maintain the peace by granting licences to all comers to sell liquor in saloons and gambling dens in the camp towns along the line. The provincial government had appointed its own magistrate in the region, and he had raised his own private police force of special provincial constables. Moreover, the British Columbia magistrate considered it his personal duty to promote provincial rights.

While Steele was away, one of the federal "specials" arrested a smuggler bringing a consignment of liquor over a mountain trail by packtrain. Alertly taking advantage of the competition between the two levels of government, the man went to the British Columbia magistrate and persuaded him to issue a warrant for the arrest of the federal constable on a charge of highway robbery for having confiscated the booze. When a provincial constable set out to arrest his federal counterpart, the two got into a fistfight. As a result the federal constable had the federal magistrate, Johnston, charge the provincial constable with assaulting an officer of the law. Johnston sentenced the provincial man to seven days in jail.

At this the provincial magistrate charged Johnston with obstructing the course of justice. A posse of provincial specials, sworn in especially for the occasion, grabbed him on the street in Beaver and hauled him into the provincial court. The ensuing trial must have been very funny indeed. Both magistrates were hot-tempered, stubborn Lowland Scots, and Johnston was furiously angry at his countryman. He was allowed to go free only after depositing a heavy bail.

This was the situation that awaited Steele when he arrived back at Beaver. He was accosted in turn by the two fuming Scots, each blaming the other for having started the feud. He could think of nothing better than to suggest that the case be referred to an impartial third party. The magistrates agreed, and Steele telegraphed an urgent call for his old commander and magistrate in the Northwest Territories, Colonel Macleod.

Although doubtless bemused by Steele's plea for help, the former Mounted Police commissioner came promptly. Steele introduced him to the warring parties. "He sized them up in no time," Steele recorded. "The accused [Johnston] appeared in court, and eloquent and feeling addresses caused the disputants to shed tears over the fact that 'twa chiels frae the borders' should have such a 'fa' oot.' They were soon reconciled over a glass of hot Scotch and a pipe, and the gallant and tactful Colonel Macleod departed, well-pleased with the success of his mission."

With federal-provincial peace thus restored, Steele moved his headquarters to the new end-of-track at Farwell (later Revelstoke) and resumed his duties. His men had all returned, with the exception of Sergeant Fury, who was in hospital in Regina making a successful recovery from his wound. A whole new batch of confidence men, petty thieves, and the like had congregated in the mountains to extract what they might from the augmented work force employed on the last big push in the construction of the Canadian Pacific. It was time for another sweeping cleanup in the mountains. The procession of wrongdoers through Steele's courtroom started at nine in the morning and ended when he had supper well after dark.

The long, hectic job of policing the construction of the C.P.R. was coming to an end. On the misty morning of November 7, 1885, Steele boarded a westbound train at Farwell. It had come all the way from Montreal entirely on Canadian territory, carrying a large party of C.P.R. and government officials. They were on their way to a spot in the Eagle Pass called Craigellachie to witness the ceremonial driving of the spike that would connect the two sections of track laid from the West and the East across the mountains, the last spike on the railway that would finally link Canada together from coast to coast.

Steele had been chosen to attend the historic event both in recognition of his own contribution to the achievement and as the representative of the North-West Mounted Police. There could have been no better choice, for no man so personified the superb police force that had done so much to bring about this triumphant day. He was greeted warmly on the train by some of the leading figures in the building of the railway: Donald Smith, the pioneer financier who had held the company together when it seemed as if nothing could save it; Sandford Fleming, the magnificent engineer and surveyor who gave the world the first practical system of standard time; and W. C. Van Horne, the master railway builder. They were at Craigellachie within an hour.

There Steele watched from the fringes of the crowd of dignitaries as Donald Smith hammered home the last spike with blows that echoed through the mountains. The burly man in the red coat does not appear in the famous photograph taken on this occasion, but he was there, just as he had been there for many months past enforcing the peaceful conditions that enabled the track to reach that point at that time.

When the spike was firmly lodged, a cheer went up. Someone called for a speech by Van Horne. "All I can say is that the work has been well done in every way," said the great railroader. If he did not include the work of the Mounted Police in this statement, he should have, for it was as valuable as any work done in building the line.

"All aboard for the Pacific!" the conductor called. With the rest of the party Steele climbed aboard the first transcontinental train ever to run in Canada. It passed slowly over the join between the last track from the East and the first from the West and picked up speed as it steamed through the Eagle Pass.

From there on it was a ride that Steele would never forget. Making fifty-seven miles an hour, the train roared up and down hills and plunged through tunnels. Steele was on the last car, which whipped around the sharp curves like the tail of a kite. He was one of only three passengers on the car who were not trainsick.

Steele enjoyed this hair-raising jaunt immensely, and he was delighted by the rest of the tour laid on for the guests of the railway. At Burrard Inlet on the Pacific they boarded the steamship *Olympia* and explored Cold Harbour and English Bay, stopping to take soundings along the lonely shore where the future city of Vancouver would soon rise. The ship then headed for Vancouver Island, where crowds greeted the railway builders enthusiastically. They stayed in the pretty city of Victoria for several days, taking short boat trips, visiting the Chinese quarter, and going to the theatre, at which, to Steele's amusement, "about one thousand Chinese expressed their satisfaction with the play and music by maintaining solemn silence throughout."

As is natural on such excursions, the members of the party came to know each other well. Steele struck up a friendship with Donald Smith, the future Lord Strathcona, telling him of how he was present at a meeting between Smith and Lord Wolseley at Fort Garry in 1870 as a private soldier standing sentry at the gate. They returned by steamboat up the Fraser River to Yale, British Columbia, where Steele took the train back to his mountain post.

His duties as dominion commissioner of police had expired with the driving of the last spike, and his contingent was due to leave. After spending a few days putting his affairs in order, Steele and his men joined a group of engineers and contractors on an oversized train headed east. As the train emerged from the Bow River Pass, with the prairies stretched out below, one of the engineers exclaimed, "Hurrah! Civilization at last!" This may have been a little premature, but civilization was now well on its way to the Canadian plains.

The railway may have been complete, but it was still no more than a thread of modern transportation amid the vastness of the Northwest Territories. Ordered to move to Battleford after they had come down from the mountains, Steele and his men had to leave the rail line at Swift Current and form a mounted column with horse-drawn wagons to haul their supplies. The weather was cold and snowy, but when they came to cross the South Saskatchewan River, the ice had not grown thick enough to support the horses and wagons. Steele improvised a kind of a bridge by spreading hay on the ice and pouring water on it to freeze, repeating the process until the surface was strong enough to carry them across.

On the trail they camped in a wooded grove where they met three men travelling in the opposite direction. One of these was the hangman who had been to Battleford to execute Wandering Spirit and seven other Indians convicted of having committed murder during the rebellion. Louis Riel had already been hanged for high treason in Regina, despite his evident insanity. Big Bear and the other rebellious Cree chief, Poundmaker, had each been sentenced to prison for three years.

The tension left over from the rebellion had still not died in Battleford when Steele arrived. The fort was in the heart of the former rebel territory, and the white settlers thereabouts were afraid that the Indians and métis might yet go on a fresh rampage. The Indians had been relieved of their firearms, but they were still capable of mounting a massacre with their traditional weapons. To guard against renewed hostilities, two Mounted

Police divisions totalling about 225 men had been stationed at the fort.

In the official vernacular of the day, the natives were in an "unsettled state." Steele observed that they regarded the Mounted Police with terror. They also showed a contempt for the police which unfortunately was well earned. The Battleford post was a shambles. It contained a high proportion of the five hundred recruits enlisted in a crash program to build up the force's strength during the rebellion. This hastily raised mob had more than its share of drunkards, misfits, malingerers, and troublemakers.

They were crowded together chaotically in wretchedly inadequate huts. The officers on the scene seemed to be incapable of exerting control. Men were openly insubordinate, and some were engaged in bootlegging and black-marketing. Superintendent Lief Crozier was in overall command of the two divisions of the Battleford District, as well as being assistant commissioner of the force. But that outstanding officer appeared to have lost his grip. Crozier had never recovered from the public humiliation of the defeat he had suffered at the outset of the rebellion. He had let the Battleford command go to pot.

Steele was placed in charge of D Division, which incorporated most of the recruits. This was a job that called for all his leadership qualities. He first did some quick weeding out of drunkards and physically unfit men who should never have been allowed to enlist, shipping twenty of them back to Winnipeg. Then he went to work on the insubordinate ones, letting offenders have a long look at the inside of the guardroom. Four men deserted during this period, and two of them were subsequently captured and faced punishment. It became clear to those who remained that they would have no choice but to knuckle under to Steele's rigid rule.

He set about the trying task of training a division of men which included many who in normal times would never have measured up to his standards. He reverted to his old role of the merciless sergeant major, drilling them constantly and swooping down on the slightest fault. Much to Steele's relief, Crozier moved to the Regina headquarters at the end of the year, leaving Steele in command of the Battleford District as well as D Division. Now he had a free hand to deal with the serious problems of the police in the area. Things began to look up.

A round of transfers brought him two first-class officers to help him clean up the mess he had inherited. These were Superintendent Alex Macdonell (the tough Glengarry Scot who told Sitting Bull he would ration him with bullets) and Inspector Zachary Taylor Wood. A tall, elegant graduate of the Canadian Royal Military College, Zack Wood was the grandson of Zachary Taylor, the twelfth President of the United States, and son of John Taylor Wood, commander of the famous Confederate blockade-runner in the American Civil War, the *Tallahassee*. He would one day go on to become assistant commissioner of the force and the father of another distinguished Mounted Policeman, Stuart Taylor Wood, commissioner of the R.C.M.P. from 1938 to 1951.

Steele did his best to maintain a strong police presence in the district, but he realized that the inferior forces at his disposal were unprepared to meet real trouble. And the threat of trouble would persist as long as the Indians and métis were in a state of unrest. So he turned his attention to the reconciliation of the natives. This began with a personal tour of the nearby Cree reserves to talk to the Indians and listen to their complaints.

The Crees were without an agent (the representative of the Crown who could play such a crucial part, for good or ill, in the Indians' welfare). Steele's plan to fill this vacancy was positively inspired. He approached the resident Anglican archdeacon, John MacKay, one of the many prairie-born, Cree-speaking MacKays whose names crop up so often in western Canadian history. Steele had difficulty in talking the popular clergyman into accepting the Indian agent's post. Finally, though, MacKay agreed, and the Mounted Police commandant then diplomatically secured the consent of the clergy of other denominations. The appointment worked wonders. The Indians felt that at last they had an agent who really knew them and had their best interests at heart.

Steele took a further step to show the Indians that the government was serious about improving their conditions. At his insistence, two unsympathetic and possibly corrupt government farm instructors were summarily fired. He handpicked their successors: two former Mounted Police NCOs of broad experience in dealing with Indians. The Indians were also mollified by the news that Chief Poundmaker was to be reprieved after serving a few months of his prison sentence. Poundmaker had been something of a victim of circumstances in the rebellion, and everyone knew that the stiff sentence originally meted out to him was unfair.

Over the winter Steele gently put an end to the practice of Indian women coming into the Battleford settlement to prostitute themselves. He assigned a métis interpreter to do the rounds of the town daily, advising any woman found there without a legitimate reason to return to her reserve before she was charged. Steele discovered that a local white man was keeping a brothel of Indian women. He had the man arrested and hit him with a sixty-dollar fine.

The métis population constituted a separate problem. Although their land claims were now being settled, as they should have been years before, many had had their homes destroyed during the rebellion, and some were destitute. Steele instituted a policy of hiring distressed métis to work on a major expansion and rebuilding of the fort, including new barracks, officers' quarters, and stables. The first task to be undertaken in this project was to haul lumber to the treeless site from Prince Albert over a trail of 150 miles. "People who had lost property during the late rebellion were employed irrespective of the part taken, those who were in the most need getting the first chance," he reported. The freighting contracts provided enough cash to keep these people going over the winter, with a comfortable surplus to buy food and seed grain for the summer ahead.

The winter was exceedingly cold, so cold that much of the drill and instruction of the raw troops had to be conducted inside the barracks. Nevertheless Steele was able to raise the efficiency of his force to the point where he could launch a system of widespread horse patrols to keep in touch with the reserves and regularly check on every homestead within hundreds of miles.

Late in March the officers at Battleford and at every other post were stunned to hear that Commissioner Irvine was resigning. In reality this able officer had been given a political push by General Middleton (still the toast of Ottawa) and Lieutenant Governor Dewdney, with whom Irvine had never seen eye to eye. Steele himself was among the candidates for the commissioner's job, his

cause being championed by such notables as Father Lacombe and
W. C. Van Horne. There could be little doubt that he was the
best man available. But neither he nor any other experienced
officer was to become commissioner. To their surprise the government reached outside to make the appointment. Their new chief
was a civilian civil servant with a total of four years' military experience named Lawrence Herchmer. All that was known about
him within the force was that his brother was one of its officers,
the same Superintendent William Herchmer who had taken over
command from Steele at Calgary in 1884.

Steele was upset by this turn of events not only on his own account but on Irvine's. He was not without his criticisms of the
former commissioner—he considered him too lax and too susceptible to the wiles of sycophants—but on the whole Irvine had
done a difficult job well. There was no apparent reason for his removal except that Middleton had picked him as a scapegoat for
his own professional shortcomings during the rebellion. In his enduring concern for the Indians, Irvine successfully appealed to be
appointed Indian agent on the Blood reserve.

If Irvine was a victim of politics, Lawrence Herchmer was a
beneficiary. After the American Revolution his United Empire
Loyalist family had settled on a farm near Kingston, Ontario,
where his father was a boyhood friend of the neighbour's son.
This was none other than John A. Macdonald. As Prime Minister,
Macdonald later saw to it personally that his old friend's children
did not suffer. Having evidently failed in trying to run a brewery
in Winnipeg, Herchmer had been appointed to well-paying positions with the government Boundary Commission and then
with Sir John's own personal ministry, the Department of Indian
Affairs.

At first Steele put aside his resentment of this remarkable appointment and went about his duties with the resignation of a
professional. But the new commissioner, who quickly gained a
reputation as the worst kind of martinet, would not leave him
alone. Perhaps Herchmer saw Steele as a potential rival. In any
case he seems to have set out to drive the Battleford commandant
into resigning. He began to harass Steele on matters that normally
would have been left up to a post commander. He upbraided
Steele for keeping liquor in the post dispensary. He charged that

Steele was wilfully overlooking malingering among his men. He complained that Steele had overstepped his authority by buying too many potatoes from a civilian supplier, an accusation that made Steele furious. His men were entitled to so many potatoes in their rations, he retorted, and if they did not get them, it might damage their health.

Herchmer learned to his dismay that he had picked the wrong man; Steele was not the type to be nudged out or intimidated. He lashed back at the commissioner in his correspondence: "Your language has continued to be such as neither I nor any other officer in the force had been in the habit of receiving from anyone. . . . If any officer not recently appointed had treated me as you are doing, I would have complained and remonstrated at once."

It rankled Steele that this amateur soldier should introduce a British mounted infantry drill routine to replace the American-style single-rank drill that he, Steele, had devised for the force ten years earlier. The new drill was unsuited to the work of the Mounted Police and the high standard of horsemanship he wanted to instil. In the manner of disgruntled soldiers he took his orders and bent them. "When we had adapted it to suit our purposes," he wrote of the new drill, "the father of the work would not have recognised his child."

Things came to a head when Herchmer heatedly charged him with misconduct and threatened to have him transferred. Steele would have none of this; if anyone was guilty of misconduct, it was the commissioner himself. He demanded his right to have his case brought into the open through an inquiry and hearing under the Police Act. Herchmer backed down; he must have realized that he could only lose an open battle with Steele and that the loss might well result in his own dismissal. He ceased his harassment, and in return Steele did not press his case.

But the fight with Herchmer cost Steele his chance of promotion. It was still raging at the end of June, when the hapless Crozier resigned from the assistant commissionership. Steele was clearly in line to fill the vacancy, but Herchmer would not even consider it. Instead he used his political pull to have his own brother appointed to the number-two post.

This manoeuvre entailed abolishing the title of assistant commissioner and giving the younger Herchmer the title of inspecting superintendent. William Herchmer was also promoted to the military rank of lieutenant colonel, ever after to be known as Colonel Billy within the force. Having secured his flank, Lawrence Herchmer prepared to launch an attack on his intramural enemies. Heading the list of these, even higher up than Steele, were the members of the tradition-minded "Macleod clique," which bucked the new regime at every turn and ran the Macleod District as a separate fief.

Meanwhile Steele got on with his work at Battleford. He supervised the construction project at the fort. He introduced a system of detailed reports for an ever increasing number of wide-ranging patrols, an innovation for which Lawrence Herchmer later took credit. And he strove to bring the inexperienced and undisciplined mob that had been wished on him up to the highest standards of the Mounted Police.

He set them a grinding schedule and kept them at it. Within weeks the recruits could jump their horses over hurdles in column like a crack cavalry troop. They learned to swim their horses across rivers and perform dozens of other routines necessary to the hard-riding life of a Mounted Policeman. Before Steele was finished with them, they could find their way without a guide or compass across the empty prairies for hundreds of miles around.

The training was hampered by an intensely hot summer, with temperatures exceeding 100° F. Outdoor drills had to be discontinued because men were collapsing from the heat. The scorching weather brought with it an outbreak of typhomalarial fever; Steele himself was mildly stricken. Two men died from it, and several others, including the post doctor, fell desperately ill.

The commissioner took the offensive against his opponents in the force in September. His chief target was Superintendent John Cotton, commandant of the Fort Macleod District and leader of the Macleod clique. Steele disapproved of Cotton because the latter had won promotion by currying favour with ex-commissioner Irvine and had feathered his nest by acting as collector of customs in Fort Macleod, adding the commissions from the duties collected to his Mounted Police salary. Steele and Cotton were very different types of men, but they were bunched together in Herchmer's scheme to kill two birds with one stone.

The commissioner wanted to get Cotton as far away as possible from his confederates at Fort Macleod. At the same time he wanted to humble Sam Steele and diminish his influence. So he ordered the divisions commanded by Cotton and Steele to change places. This meant that both officers would go from commanding districts of two divisions to commanding one division under other district commandants appointed over their heads.

Steele could not have been happy as he rode off early in September from Battleford with his hundred men, heading for Fort Macleod. They faced a terribly difficult march of thirteen days across the desiccated prairies. The heat was all but unbearable. Lakes and creeks that had always contained water were found to be bone dry. Two of the men fell gravely ill with typhomalarial fever. They died shortly after reaching Fort Macleod.

If there was any consolation for Steele in this move, it was that Herchmer had not succeeded in forcing his resignation. He was determined to stay in the force, even though friends had offered to set him up in a civilian business career. He had become too much a part of the N.W.M.P., and it of him, to let a man like Herchmer make him leave it. His threat of bringing his mistreatment at Herchmer's hands out into the open caused the commissioner to treat him with some circumspection from then on.

It also helped to ease his distress that the commandant of the Fort Macleod District under whom he had to serve was Percy Neale, a friend since they had served together in the artillery in Kingston. The two had been together for some time at Fort Walsh, where their names had been linked in an out-of-the-way bit of Canadian history. In 1878, on behalf of the Mounted Police, they had jointly registered the first cattle brand in Canada: NWMP.

Neale sympathized with Steele's dilemma. Before long he arranged to have Steele restored to a semi-independent command, moving his headquarters and part of his division to Lethbridge, which then had a population of two thousand as the centre of a land and coal-mining boom.

Steele moved into brand-new quarters there in January 1887 and set up a system of far-ranging patrols on the outlying prairies. His duties in Lethbridge were light compared with his previous experience; his biggest problem was enforcing the "detestable" liq-

uor laws. For the first time he began to take an active part in social activities. He had always liked square dancing and playing
bridge and whist, and Lethbridge offered both the spare time and
the opportunity for these diversions. In this quiet outpost, where
he occupied his most comfortable quarters in years, he more or
less settled down to enjoy the easy pace.

It was not to last. An ugly and dangerous situation, chillingly
reminiscent of the prelude to the rebellion in Saskatchewan, had
reared up beyond the Rocky Mountains in the Kootenay District
of British Columbia. Small numbers of white settlers engaged in
placer gold mining and ranching had begun filtering into the district several years before. The local Indians were at first highly
hospitable, but then they bridled at the application of the white
man's law.

In 1884 two white placer miners had been robbed and murdered. In March 1887 the lone British Columbia provincial constable in the territory arrested a Kootenay Indian named Kapla
for the crime. Kapla was locked up in the jail at Wild Horse
Creek to await trial. When word of his arrest reached the Kootenay Indian reserve, the tribal chief, Isadore, led twenty young
braves to the jail. There the chief confronted the constable and
the local justice of the peace, claiming that Kapla had been
wrongfully arrested. Isadore pointed out that when two Indians
had been killed by white men a few years earlier, no one had been
charged.

When the white officials insisted that Kapla must stand trial,
the Indians forcibly relieved them of the keys to the jail and
released the prisoner. Isadore then ordered the constable and the
JP to leave the district if they valued their scalps. They left—and
left behind a thoroughly frightened white population. The settlers
barricaded their homesteads and called for government help.

The Kapla incident served as an outlet for the feelings of bitterness that had been seething among the Indians. They had accepted a reserve from the government on which to graze their cattle and horses but then had realized that it was too small. For
some years this had not been an issue because the white owner of
a large tract of land called Joseph's Prairie (on the site of the present city of Cranbrook) had allowed them to graze their livestock

there as they had for generations. But the land had lately been sold, and the new owner wanted it for himself.

The man who had bought the land was a retired British Army officer named Colonel James Baker. The colonel was a typical imperialist, a brother of the famed African explorer Sir Samuel Baker and of Baker Pasha, who had recently become a general in the Turkish Army after many years of fighting Queen Victoria's colonial wars. With all the high-handedness of his kind, Baker ordered Chief Isadore to get his stock off Joseph's Prairie. Isadore flatly refused, and the animals stayed where they were.

Encouraged by this defiance, the young men of the band had grown belligerent towards the settlers. The Indians were being liberally supplied with liquor by white and Chinese traders just across the border in Washington State. The Kootenays could be enthusiastic warriors, having won many battles in the past against the Blackfeet. Sent to investigate the situation, Inspecting Superintendent Herchmer estimated they could field 350 well-armed fighting braves.

The government decided to send a troubleshooting force of Mounted Police into the district, and Steele's division was chosen. Late in May 1887 he received orders in Lethbridge to hold himself in readiness to move. After several false starts he was finally told definitely to leave for the mountains late in June. On his departure he was presented with an address of appreciation from the citizens of Lethbridge to the officers and men of D Division. It read in part: "Much as we regret your departure, we assuredly know that in the discharge of your duties which entail hardship, danger or diplomatic skill, the Department could not have chosen, from the entire force, men who would more faithfully carry out their commands." Steele could only hope that the men he had so recently forged into Mounted Policemen would live up to the Lethbridge citizenry's high opinion of them in the unpredictable mission ahead.

22: A NAME ON THE MAP

Horses and all, D Division crossed the Rocky Mountains on a special train, arriving at Golden, British Columbia, on the morning of June 28 and making camp on the left bank of the Kicking Horse River. Inspector Zack Wood and Sergeant Major Tom Lake joined them the next day, having attended to the last-minute details of handing over the Lethbridge post to another unit. So did Commissioner Herchmer, full of unnecessary orders and advice for Steele, who, after all, had more experience in this kind of assignment than any other Mounted Police officer. The commissioner inspected the men and left, instructing Steele to stand by for orders from Inspecting Superintendent Herchmer. The commissioner's brother was then in the Kootenay District as a member of a commission sent to negotiate with Chief Isadore.

Colonel Billy arrived on the steamboat *Duchess* on the morning of July 5 with the other members of the commission. They told Steele that in return for a promise to enlarge his reserve, Isadore had agreed to hand over the suspected murderer, Kapla, and another Indian suspected of being an accomplice named Little Isadore (not related to the chief). But the situation was still very tense, Herchmer reported. He ordered Steele to prepare to ride south to the Kootenay District as soon as possible, transporting his supplies on the *Duchess* on its return trip.

The expedition got off to a bad start. A man charged with being drunk and disorderly deserted. No sooner had the supplies been loaded on the *Duchess* than Colonel Herchmer issued a counterorder to remain in Golden until further notice. Steele patiently

had the ammunition unloaded, leaving most of the other supplies
on board to be picked up at the landing at the head of the Columbia Lakes, about one hundred miles to the south.

Early in the morning of July 7 the camp was aroused by the
sound of a shot. Alone in his tent, Sergeant Major Tom Lake had
committed suicide. Lake had been a companion of Steele's on and
off since the N.W.M.P. was formed. They had lived and worked
together at Swan River in 1876 when Lake had been sergeant
major of a troop and Steele RSM of the force. Lake had served as
Steele's senior NCO in Calgary, Battleford, and Lethbridge. An
unassuming man, he had organized the first voluntary Mounted
Police band in Swan River and had acted as bandmaster in several
other posts. He had been suffering lately from acute neuralgia,
and nothing the medical officer could do had any effect on his
painful condition. Like many the soldier and policemen before
and since, he sought final relief in his gun.

The shock of his old comrade's death had not worn off when
Steele was faced with new trouble. The *Duchess* had started up
the river (the Columbia flows north at this point) with the police
supplies. One of the men had remarked to Steele when the boat
embarked that she was carrying too much bilge water. Now the
overloaded vessel had capsized a few miles from Golden, and the
supplies were floating away.

Steele dispatched a party of men to save what they could. But
their hard work in the water was mostly fruitless. Almost everything they recovered was ruined, including a much-needed carload
of oats for the horses and the officers' uniforms and personal
effects.

Steele sent out volunteers to help raise the boat, but its owner
seemed in no hurry. It was still sitting askew on the bottom when
he finally received orders to march on the night of the seventeenth. The division rode off at 5:30 the next morning, each man
carrying his lunch ration and a feed of oats for his horse; the food
for their evening meal was on a small steamboat that Steele had
hired at an exorbitant price from a merchant in Golden named
Hayes. At 5:00 P.M. they reached the Hog Ranche, twenty-five
miles south of Golden, but there was no sign of the steamboat,
which should have arrived several hours earlier. It did not appear
with its supply of food until ten o'clock that evening. The men

and horses had not eaten since before noon. "It appears that Hayes' cupidity was too much for him, as he had waited for some passengers," Steele wrote scathingly in his report.

For the rest of the trip to the head of the Columbia Lakes the steamboat trailed irritatingly behind the land-borne column. It was not needed on the next stage of the journey, and Steele viewed its departure with relief. He sent Wood back to Golden to supervise a second voyage with more supplies, exhorting the inspector not to be gentle in his dealings with the greedy Mr. Hayes. From there on the supplies were carried by an efficient packtrain of mules and horses. The division reached its destination near the Lower Kootenay Indian Reserve on July 30, making camp in a ghost town left over from the Kootenay gold rush of 1864.

Steele's orders were to build a post "selected with a view to defence, and if possible in the proximity of hay, wood and good pasturage." After viewing two unsuitable sites, he selected a ten-acre field on high ground overlooking the confluence of the Kootenay River and Wild Horse Creek. "From a military point of view it is perfect," he reported. It was "the most central point from which to communicate with the Indians and protect the settlers in the event of an uprising." The owner relieved him of one dollar for an indefinite lease on the land.

He moved his troops to the ferry across from the site the next morning. As they were about to dismount at the riverbank, he called them to parade. The men smartly formed ranks with their horses, and Steele rode out in front and addressed them. He emphasized the delicate nature of their duty and the need for unexceptionable conduct in their relations with both the Indians and the whites.

Before nightfall he had organized a courier service to Golden and purchased a fully equipped packtrain of twenty-seven fine native ponies. A Mounted Police work party had already started sawing and hauling timber to build the post. Over the next few days hundreds of long pine logs were piled on the site, although they were extremely heavy and had to be hauled from several miles away. Groups of not unfriendly Indians looked on as the policemen started constructing the buildings. Fifteen cents a day was added to the pay of the Mounties engaged in this work.

As soon as the camp was running smoothly, Steele sent a message asking Chief Isadore to come and see him, but the chief put off his visit until the twentieth of August. Isadore was a stately old man who enjoyed a great reputation as a military leader in his tribe's wars against the Blackfeet in the recent past. He was rumoured personally to own more than thirty thousand dollars worth of livestock. His industrious band combined hunting for food and furs in the mountains with large-scale farming and ranching. The senior members of the tribal hierarchy were very prosperous, but the younger braves had little property, which meant that they had little to lose by going to war against the whites.

The chief and the big redcoat parleyed warily. Isadore expressed a belief that Kapla had been arrested without proper authority, on the whim of the white constable; this, he said, was why he had forced Kapla's release. In his briefing by the government commissioners in Golden, Steele had been told that the humiliation of having to hand over Kapla and the other suspects to the law would be punishment enough for the proud Isadore and a vindication of white justice in the eyes of the Indians. That statement was hypocritical. The commissioners knew perfectly well that the arrest of the chief might touch off the revolt they feared. In talking to Isadore, however, Steele used it as a bargaining counter, saying that he would not proceed against the chief if he delivered the fugitives. The old man agreed to do so. To add to Isadore's loss of face, Steele sent the same provincial constable the Indians had earlier ousted to collect the prisoners and put them back in the same jail.

On August 25 Steele, in his capacity as magistrate, went to Wild Horse Creek to read the charges against the two Indians and hold a preliminary hearing. He remanded them for eight days while the provincial constable gathered further evidence for the prosecution. It had not taken Steele long to observe that this man was an incompetent, disrespected by the Indians and white settlers alike. Rumours of plans for a fresh assault on the jail caused him to have the prisoners moved to the Mounted Police camp. On September 2 he again had them brought before him, and again the constable asked for a remand to enable him to detain two Indian boys as witnesses. Three days later the hearing was finally held.

"There was no evidence of consequence," Steele reported, "the only evidence showing that they had passed along the trail some days after the white men." He dismissed the case there and then and provided parcels of food for the former prisoners and witnesses on their trip back to the reserve. Isadore had been a keenly interested observer at the hearing. Steele's prompt dismissal seemed to have the effect of showing the chief that there was such a thing as white man's justice after all.

Steele's personal opinion was that the murder probably was committed by a white man to whom the miners had bragged about how much money they were carrying. It had occurred during the construction of the C.P.R., a time when the Golden area teemed with criminal types. His report was bitingly critical of the provincial constable and justices of the peace for not investigating the crime when it occurred and for then charging two innocent Indians three years later. After the hearing he conducted an exhaustive reinvestigation of the case, with no results.

A few days after the hearing Isadore came to see him at the camp and bluntly asked him about his intentions. Several white men and Chinese, presumably whiskey traders, had told the chief that the Mounted Police had come to make war on the Indians and were preparing for an attack. Given the record of the U. S. Army just across the border, it is not surprising that Isadore should give credence to this story. In this isolated valley, Steele's red coat did not symbolize the tradition of evenhanded dealing with the races that it did in the Northwest Territories. The Kootenays were unfamiliar with the Mounted Police; Steele and his men would have to prove themselves all over again.

Of this interview he reported: "I informed him that such was not the case, I came here to maintain law and order, both whites and Indians were all the same to us, and would be fairly treated, but that any breach of the law would be severely dealt with, no matter who the offender might be. I told the chief to pay no attention to any statements made to him by anyone, if they were to the effect that hostility towards the Indians was the feeling of the

Police. Before going he promised to inform me if anyone attempted to stir up trouble between the whites and Indians."

By this time Fort Steele, as the settlers named it, was growing into the best constructed of all Mounted Police posts. It included a barracks, officers' and NCOs' quarters, a hospital, a guardhouse with cells, stables, and blacksmith and carpentry shops. It was all built with more than 1,400 stout yellow pine logs of up to thirty feet in length.*

Although Steele had paid great attention to the water supply and other health considerations in choosing the site, he could not evade that scourge of the West, mountain fever. As the summer went on, three men died from it, and a number of others became seriously ill; another died near the end of the year. As so often happened, the medical officer contracted the disease. His name was Powell, and he was the son of another physician, who was the Indian commissioner of British Columbia. The senior Dr. Powell was visiting the district at the time. When his son was stricken in September, he stayed on to fight the epidemic for almost a month until another police surgeon could be brought in from Calgary. But for his fortuitous presence, many more lives would have been lost.

Dr. Powell had come to the district as a member of a three-man British Columbia government commission sent to deal with Chief Isadore's complaint that the reserve allotted to his people was inadequate. This remained a volatile issue among the Indians, one that could still bring them out in arms. With a sharp eye on his future negotiating stance, the wily Isadore made a point of being absent with all his councillors on a trading trip across the U.S. border when the commissioners conducted their study. They waited for the Indian leaders for some time but finally decided that it was futile and went back to Victoria to write their report.

It fell to Steele to deliver their decision to Isadore. He met with the chief and the band councillors early in November, reading them a long letter from the commissioners that started out with a reprimand to Isadore for having broken into the jail. The letter

* Fort Steele was to become a thriving civilian community in the 1890s. The village and police post have now been authentically reconstructed on the thirty-seven-acre Fort Steele Historical Park, one of the most popular tourist attractions in British Columbia.

said that Isadore would no longer be recognized as chief by the
government if he gave any more trouble. Such a loss of prestige
would be a serious blow to any Indian chief. After rebuking the
Indians for not making good use of the land already reserved for
them (they let hundreds of horses run wild on it), the commissioners offered them extensive new parcels of land with better pasturage than they had before.

The award did not, however, include Joseph's Prairie, the field on
Colonel Baker's ranch which Isadore claimed for his people. The
most the commissioners offered in connection with this land was
to pay for the fences and other improvements that the Indians
had made. When Steele had finished reading their decree—"We
wish to see you improve your reserves, and your breed of horses,
raise more cattle and crops, become wealthy and prosperous, and
do your duty to the Queen"—Isadore objected to giving up the
prairie. He said the Indians had occupied it long before the white
men ever came to the country. Steele told him that the decision
was irrevocable and that the land must be vacated right away.

After a pause Isadore agreed that he must accept the decision,
provided the government agreed to meet his claim for the improvements before the stock was moved off the property. In parting he asked Steele to have an irrigation ditch dug at government
expense on his personal land. Surprised that the encounter had
gone so smoothly, Steele said he would recommend that this be
done.

But Isadore could be an exasperating man. When they next
met early in December, a full three weeks after Steele had
requested to see him, the chief reversed himself by saying that the
new lands allotted by the commissioners were too small. He complained that the commissioners should have met with the Indian
leaders in person. Knowing that Isadore had deliberately absented
himself while the commissioners were doing their work, Steele
was astonished by the temerity of this last claim. Isadore then said
he had changed his mind about the land on the Baker ranch. He
did not wish to give it up after all.

Smoothbore Steele was noted for his control of his temper, but
he must have come close to losing it then: "I told him he had
acted in a shameful manner, that his action was foolish, and that
he could not now expect much consideration," Steele wrote to the

Indian commissioner. "I also asked him to say if he meant that he would not give up the prairie or simply that he did not like to do so. He simply spoke of the smallness of the reserve, and said he did not wish to give up the prairie. I permitted the chief to leave then as I did not deem it advisable to say any more on the subject."

It was time for a little forceful diplomacy. The next day Steele sent an interpreter to the chief with a note saying that the government had agreed to pay for the irrigation ditch he wanted for his land. He took this opportunity to press Isadore on the question of Joseph's Prairie by requesting him to name an arbitrator to agree on the value of the improvements with an arbitrator appointed by Colonel Baker. Knowing his man by now, Steele went on to say that if Isadore did not appoint an arbitrator, he would take it upon himself to appoint one on the chief's behalf. Whether Isadore named his own representative or not, he said, the decision of the two arbitrators would be binding. He concluded by threatening to withdraw his recommendation to dig the irrigation ditch if the chief persisted in refusing to give up the disputed land.

Isadore duly appointed an arbitrator, but he was by no means beaten yet. Within a few day he arrived in Steele's office, accompanied by all his tribal councillors. Steele began the interview by saying that he was pleased that Isadore had at last seen sense and that he would pay him the amount of the award for the improvements the minute the arbitrators came to an agreement. The chief heard him out, then said flatly that the improvements were worth a thousand dollars and that he would not take less. Steele retorted that the whole prairie was not worth half the money. Again his temper was tried.

"I told him . . . that in consequence of his obstruction there was an absolute certainty of his being deposed and another chief appointed in his stead," he reported. "I found it necessary to speak thus plainly to him, as I am positive that if I had not dealt firmly with him he would have kept the matter in suspense until the spring, and then would give more trouble."

The chief backed down. The arbitrators awarded him $490 for the improvements. Steele paid him at 10:30 on the night of their decision, having him sign an elaborate receipt that legally bound him to vacate the land. Steele recorded: "I am of the opinion that the settlement of the dispute between Colonel Baker and Chief Isadore disposes of what might, if not settled amicably, have caused serious trouble in Kootenay, if not an Indian revolt, the consequence of which would be lamentable should no military force be there at the commencement." He began to make plans to vacate Fort Steele in the spring.

He could afford to relax now, attending the week-long Christmas celebrations at the Roman Catholic mission church that had become a tribal tradition. Among the customs was the practice of soundly flogging anyone in the tribe found guilty of any offence such as gambling, theft, or drunkenness over the year. Regardless of age or sex, the guilty parties were tied face downwards on the ground, and the councillors gave them forty or fifty lashes with a rawhide whip. Such was Isadore's moral authority that the offenders never failed to appear at the church to take their punishment. Steele noted with satisfaction that one of those flogged was a band councillor who had failed to report some cases of gambling to the Mounted Police.

Aided by the strictness of the tribal law, the police had very little trouble with the Indians. Crime was rare among them, and they avoided heavy drinking, even though they were often employed to pack liquor to the white merchants' stores. Steele fielded regular patrols to all the principal points in the area to create a psychological climate of law and order. Although some of his men might raise hell among themselves, they "strictly attended to the line of conduct laid down by me with regard to their intercourse with both the white and Indian population." The Indians became distinctly friendly towards the cheerful men in the red coats.

A form of safety valve existed in the proximity of the United States; the most undisciplined men deserted across the border. In September three of them had made a spectacular departure by taking off with two boats belonging to some English tourists. Another three skipped out in October, and four more deserted in the early months of 1888.

All seemed to be going smoothly when, in the spring, Isadore again began to grumble. He still wanted more land. Late in May Colonel Baker returned to his ranch from Victoria, where he

served as a member of the provincial Parliament, to find that the
Indians were not only grazing stock on a corner of his property
but had erected corrals and milk sheds. He huffily called on Steele
to evict them. Steele sent Zack Wood to investigate, and the inspector ascertained that the Indians had been given permission to
use the land over the summer by the colonel's son.

To avoid a recurrence of disputes over the land, Colonel Baker
offered to show Isadore its exact boundaries. The two took a ride
around the property, in the course of which Isadore accused the
colonel of trying to steal the whole countryside. A raging argument followed. Baker stormed off to complain to Steele about the
"insolent" behaviour of the chief.

Although the incident must have had its comic aspects, Steele
felt that it might bring on another crisis. He brought Isadore and
Baker together the next day. Isadore admitted that he had indeed
insulted the colonel, but only after the colonel had ordered him
to get his stock off the land in two days. Baker claimed that the
chief had reversed the sequence of the offensive remarks.

Steele sided with his fellow imperialist, believing that Isadore
had provoked the dispute; he had a weakness for British gentlemen, and it was quite in character that he would automatically
take the word of one over that of a native. Perhaps the colonel
reminded him of his father—an ex-officer and MPP, a transplanted
squire trying to live in Canada in the old English manner. Elmes
Steele had called his place Purbrook; Colonel Baker called his
Cranbrook.

In the presence of his natural ally Steele reproved the old Indian in a patronizing, imperialistic tone: "I warned the chief that
his conduct would lead him and his tribe into trouble if persisted
in," he wrote. "Colonel Baker, I said, was one of their best
friends, and by acting as he did the chief was going contrary to
the wishes of the Great Mother, whose desire was that her children of all colours should live together in peace. When I had
finished speaking Isadore arose and shook hands with Colonel
Baker, saying that he would never again trespass on his land, a
promise he faithfully kept."

Steele was able to report that the Kootenay affair was over. He
recommended that the Mounted Police be replaced in the district
by a provincial force of five men. At his suggestion feed grain and

farm implements were being supplied to Isadore's band, and the government was paying for more irrigation ditches. An industrial school was about to be constructed. The Indians were content, and the white people were no longer afraid. It was time to go.

He organized a sports day at the fort in July as a farewell gesture. He pointedly had Colonel Baker take the salute in the opening parade. Most of the Lower Kootenay band turned up to enjoy a hearty lunch. Steele acted as starter for the races; the Mounted Policemen beat the Indians at the sprints, and the Indians ran away from them in the long-distance events. There was wrestling on horseback, at which the Indians were matchless. The one-mile horse race was won by an Indian on a buckskin pony in the remarkable time of one minute and fifty seconds. Steele asked the rider to get on the scales. He weighed 190 pounds.

At the end of that pleasant day Isadore gathered his band around him and called for silence. He approached Steele, who later wrote: "The Chief, in a speech on behalf of his people, praised the division generally for the moral and manly behaviour of its members, and stated that when we came into the district the Indians regarded us with suspicion; but now all that was changed. He hoped that when we returned to the North-West we should look back with pleasure to our stay among them, as the Indians themselves would do, and that they would never forget us as long as they lived; that when the division came in, and for years before, there had been a mutual distrust between the white and red men, but now all that had gone, chiefly owing to the good advice received from the officers of the Police force and the excellent demeanor of the men toward the Indians."

The division marched out of Fort Steele at 5:30 A.M. on the ninth of August. Instead of riding north to Golden, Steele led it east on an old Indian trail through the Crowsnest Pass. He wanted to test the feasibility of this route over the Great Divide, and he kept careful notes on the journey. His diary entries stressed the coal-mining potential of the region; he also observed that "the Pass appears to be a first-class one for railway purposes, grades being very light and there being very little rock work."

Some of the horses got sick from eating a poisonous weed on the trail; others stampeded. Nevertheless the division covered the 195 miles to Fort Macleod in nine days. Steele's exploration of the pass led to regular police patrols to keep the trail open, and it soon became the preferred route for civilian travellers into British Columbia. The coal deposits were later developed, and Canadian Pacific later built a line through the pass.

In 1889 Marie Elizabeth Harwood came to Fort Macleod to
spend the summer as the guest of her aunt, the wife of Superintendent A. R. Macdonell. A tall, slender woman of twenty-nine
with a pleasant if not pretty face, Miss Harwood hitherto had led
a rather sheltered life. She was the eldest daughter of an active
country gentleman and man of affairs, Robert William Harwood.
Her father was the Member of Parliament and seigneur of the
county of Vaudreuil, Quebec. Her mother's family, the Lotbini-
ères, had been in Canada from the time of her great-grandfather,
a French marquis who, as General Montcalm's chief engineer, supervised the construction of such historic fortifications as Fort
Ticonderoga. The Lotbinière-Harwoods were among the last of
the noble seigneurial landowning families in Quebec, and they
lived the part.

To Marie the rough Mounted Police post in the foothills of the
Rockies was a bright new world; she was delighted by all about
her. When the high winds blew off the mountains, she would
watch with amusement as chickens caught out on the barracks
square frantically dug themselves into the ground to prevent
being blown away. It was a refreshing diversion to help her Aunt
Min serve the steady procession of colourfully dressed Indians
who dropped in for tea in the kitchen. One regular visitor was the
Blood war chief Calf Shirt, who was on familiar terms with the
police by dint of having served a jail term at the fort for horse
stealing. This sociable brave habitually kept a nest of pet rattle-
snakes next to his chest. "Calf Shirt, you've got to put your nasty

snakes away or you'll get no tea," Aunt Min would admonish. It was a long way from the formality of the Harwood seigneury at Vaudreuil.

Alex Macdonell was in command of H Division at the fort, and Zack Wood commanded the other resident unit, D Division. Sam Steele was in general command of the Macleod District, which took in both. Steele was a long-standing friend of the Macdonells, having been Alex's superior officer in Battleford. He was very fond of this rambunctious Glengarry Scot, and he called Mrs. Macdonell Aunt Min just as Marie did. As a lonely bachelor he spent much of his leisure time in the Macdonell's home.

If he had time on his hands now, it was because the West was steadily growing tamer. The last wild buffalo had met its doom the year before. White settlers were filtering into the region, notably Mormons from Utah and other peaceable immigrants arriving in covered wagons from the United States.

The Macleod District was, to be sure, still wilder than most of western Canada. It remained distant from the main railway line, and the Indians on the two vast reserves in the vicinity, the Bloods and Piegans, had yet to be weaned of their habit of stealing horses and cattle—often, it seemed, just for fun. The village of Fort Macleod, dominated by Kamoose ("Squaw Thief") Taylor's Macleod Hotel, retained its frontier atmosphere, with cowboys and Indians strolling the rutted main street and stagecoaches and mule trains coming and going. But civilization was inexorably advancing, much to the dismay of old-timers like Steele's friend chief scout Jerry Potts who had been heard to grumble, "this country's getting too damn soft for me."*

A relaxed atmosphere prevailed around the fort, and Steele took advantage of it to court Miss Harwood. He escorted her to the dances held by the officers and their civilian friends. She liked dancing as much as he did; they were always the first couple on

---

* Among the Macleod Hotel's rules and regulations, posted in the lobby, were: "Quarrelsome and boisterous persons, also those who shoot off without provocation, guns and other explosive weapons on the premises, and all boarders who get killed not to be allowed to remain in the House. . . . When guests find themselves or their luggage thrown over the fence, they may consider that they have received notice to quit." More than a century after its founding, the hotel is still there, and cowboys and Indians still whoop it up in the bar.

the floor. On quiet evenings at the Macdonell's home, they would sing together at the parlour piano. He took her to rodeos, to cricket and polo matches, and to the parties held afterwards. In the manner of her class she was a capable horsewoman. On the long summer evenings they would go riding in the hills.

They were a well-suited pair. Marie had a robust sense of humour and liked a good anecdote, and one of the great pleasures of Sam Steele's life was to delve into the treasury of amusing stories he had collected in his years of pioneering. His rugged service had done nothing to rub the polish off his manners; they had the affinity of gentlefolk. Her father was, like him, a good Conservative Party supporter. They shared a love of the outdoors and of reading. One may speculate that Aunt Min was not unconscious of the possibilities of bringing together the thirty-eight-year-old bachelor officer and her spinster niece.

There seemed no reason why they should not be married except the prevailing prejudices of the day. She was a French-speaking Roman Catholic whose family was prominent in church affairs in Quebec; he was an Anglican and a Mason. When some of his associates warned him against getting involved with a Catholic, he brushed them off lightly; he had no use for the taboos of religious discrimination. He proposed to her, and she accepted. They agreed that their offspring would be raised as Roman Catholics.

She returned to the East after they had set a tentative date for the wedding and had arranged for him to take the long leave that was due to him to spend on their honeymoon. It must have crossed his mind at that time that he should seriously consider leaving the Mounted Police. He had received several offers of jobs in civilian life from such friends as Jim Mitchell, his companion in the artillery and later in the Mounties, who had done well in business in Winnipeg. In any case a man of his notability would have no difficulty finding well-paying work outside of the force. Despite his heavy responsibilities his annual salary of $1,400 was the same as any other superintendent's, and it was very low by civilian standards for a comparable position. There was little prospect of any significant increase in his income unless he was appointed commissioner or inspecting superintendent, the only two posts in the N.W.M.P. higher than his own.

Besides, he was in a degree of hot water. He had become the subject of controversy merely for acting as he always had—striking swiftly in the face of impending trouble. But this time, instead of winning praise for his dynamic action, he had come under criticism for going beyond the law.

It all began in April 1889, when a party of Indians from the Blood reserve crossed the border on a horse-stealing foray. They drove off about a hundred horses from a reservation in Montana and killed and scalped an American Indian on the way. When, in June, a Mounted Police constable attempted to arrest one of the raiders, the Indian held him off with a rifle. The horse thief fled and could not be found until a report came in that he had appeared at a sun dance festival on the Blood reserve.

Indian outlaws had often sought sanctuary in the camps erected for sun dances in the belief that the rituals, which could last for several days, constituted religious ceremonies at which they could not be arrested. Because fugitives from justice could sow disrespect towards the law at these bellicose affairs, Steele decided to take advantage of the occasion to show that this was not the case. He dispatched three men to pick up the horse thief. In traditional Mounted Police fashion they burst into the sun dance lodge and seized the fugitive while the rituals were in progress. Their intrusion enraged the other Indians. They were overpowered in a fierce struggle with some two hundred tribesmen, who tore their prisoner from them. Only through amazing coolheadedness did they escape with their lives.

Steele's reaction to the news of this debacle was quite in character. He sent Inspector Wood to the camp with a small party of policemen, in the meantime putting his whole force of about one hundred men at Fort Macleod on the the alert to ride out against the Bloods at the sound of a bugle call. Wood arrived outside of the sun dance camp and sent a message to the Blood chief, Red Crow, informing him that Steele was prepared to use force to take both the horse thief and those who had been the leaders in resisting the policemen. After a tense spell of waiting Red Crow appeared with five deliquent tribesmen, including the wanted man.

The chief accompanied them to Fort Macleod, where Steele stood waiting. He took Red Crow into his office and gave him a severe telling off for harbouring a criminal and obstructing the police. Red Crow departed, apparently chastened. Steele presumed that the old redcoat magic had worked again.

It was not that simple. Red Crow was a farsighted man whom Steele rated as the greatest of all Canadian Indian leaders. On this occasion the Mounted Police commander might have wished that the chief was not so progressive. For Red Crow chose to fight the case the white man's way.

The chief and the Indian agent on the reserve demanded and put up bail for the accused tribesmen. The agent defended them when the case came to trial. He maintained that the police had not only violated a religious ceremony against legal usage but had also attempted to make an arrest without a warrant. Steele argued that such action was necessary among the Indians, "there being so many bad Indians wanted at times that unless a man takes every chance offered he will likely lose his man altogether."

The press caught on to the case, and it ballooned into a cause célèbre. Letters and telegrams coursed between Fort Macleod and Ottawa. Eventually the officiating judge declared the arrests illegal. Steele's position was subsequently vindicated in a ruling by the minister of justice that, as legal wards of the government, Indians could be arrested at any time.

Judging from the tone of his official reports on the affair, Steele had found the experience upsetting. To add to his uneasiness, things were going badly within the force. Lawrence Herchmer's approach to Steele personally had been wary ever since Steele had threatened to resort to the Police Act, but the commissioner was making life hell for the other officers. He was overbearing, unreasonable, foul-tempered, partisan, and given to such absurd vanities as having the flag at the Regina headquarters lowered when he was not in residence. Steele had few serious complaints about Herchmer directly, but he could not avoid being the subject of pressure from other officers to join in a campaign to depose the commissioner. Thus he was caught in the middle of a battle of nerves between his brother officers and the head of the force.

The thought of toppling Herchmer from his perch—and perhaps assuming that perch himself—must have been tempting. Although the commissioner was making obvious efforts to maintain good relations between them, he could still not restrain himself from occasionally saying things that got Steele's goat. A fanatic on the subject of drinking in the force (although he was no teetotaller himself), Herchmer had nagged Steele about the large proportion of "drunkards" in the Macleod command when Steele was doing all he could to stamp out heavy drinking. Herchmer had taken it upon himself to investigate a report that Steele and an old friend from Fort Steele days, Inspector Huot, had been drinking and making noise in a hotel in Fort Macleod village. After assuring the Fort Macleod commandant that he had found this rumour to be groundless, Herchmer could not resist adding a gratuitous admonition: "I think it would be advisable to meet your friends in a private house where practicable when you propose to spend a social evening. Certain parties in this country are only too happy when they can get the slightest chance of vilifying the police, and it behoves us to be circumspect."

Steele must have mulled over these vexations on his long train journey east to be married in January 1890. The wedding was held on the fifteenth of that month at Marie's family seat of Vaudreuil, outside of Montreal. The newlyweds began their wedding trip among the bright lights of New York City. Steele had arranged in advance to visit the New York Police Department. To his surprise he and his bride were treated as visiting dignitaries. The fire department turned out sixty engines in their honour.

They spent an enjoyable winter touring the eastern United States and Canada, during which time Steele had a cordial meeting with Sir John A. Macdonald in Ottawa. They returned to a warm welcome at Fort Macleod in mid-May.

He soon found that with two excellent divisions under his command, everything at the fort functioned "with almost monotonous regularity." The crime rate had dropped as a result of a well-organized system of intensive patrolling. As a married man with a more or less routine job, Steele joined in the active social life of the post and civilian community, although he gave up drinking in order to keep fit. He played host at musical soirées at which Marie, with her good voice, would lead the singing; they attended every dance and party. He spent an increasing amount of time bird shooting and trout fishing. But he seems to have been a bit restless, looking forward to getting out on the trail again while doing the rounds of his detachments by horse-drawn wagon, often with Marie at his side.

He stayed overnight regularly at the Mormon settlement of Cardston, where his hosts would make a point of having their extra wives stay elsewhere for the duration of his visits. He had abandoned his initial prejudice against the Mormons and had come to hold them in high regard as hardworking folk. His attitude towards polygamy had gradually softened. Although it was illegal, he saw no reason to press cases against the Mormons as long as they were circumspect about it and otherwise obeyed the law.

The highest excitement for the Mounted Police over the next few months had nothing to do with crime. It came when the disaffection within the force finally burst into public view. Ever since Lawrence Herchmer had taken over as commissioner, members of Parliament had received an outpouring of complaints from officers and men over his officiousness, political partisanship, and unfairness. In time the commissioner's behaviour and the poor morale it engendered became an open scandal that even Old Tomorrow Macdonald could no longer ignore. One of the prime minister's last public acts was to commission an inquiry into the conduct of his family friends, the Herchmer brothers. It began belatedly in November 1891, several months after Macdonald's death.

The judge appointed as a one-man commission patently set out to whitewash the Herchmers' reputation, finding numerous legalistic excuses to throw out charges against them. Before the inquiry was fully under way, Inspecting Superintendent William Herchmer dropped dead, and complaints against him were suppressed by mutual consent. In the end the judge heard 137 charges against Commissioner Herchmer and with great reluctance found fourteen of them proved and twenty-three proved partially. These included illegally interfering with officers, improperly sentencing constables, and using threatening and abusive language. All these offences, however, could be traced to Herchmer's unstable personality rather than incompetence or dishonesty. The government had no real reason to remove him from his post.

Steele stayed out of the affair as far as he could, even though by joining the dissidents he might have tipped the balance in favour of having himself appointed commissioner. He had made it a rule not to take part in the internal politics of the force. His attitude was that hard to take as Herchmer's manner might be, he had brought to the force a much-needed new degree of efficiency. Steele agreed entirely with Herchmer's policy of tightening up drastically on discipline while at the same time making life in the ranks more tolerable by raising the pay, improving the food and accommodations, and introducing canteens and other amenities. He was all in favour of running a tight ship. Rankers grumbled about the "endless succession of drills, parades and guards" at the Fort Macleod garrison. Recalling how the commandant drilled his men "morning, noon and night," a Fort Macleod veteran later wrote: "Some men will stand almost anything, but there were twenty-four who couldn't or wouldn't stand old Sam and his methods—for that number deserted in one month."

He had reconciled himself to Herchmer's ways to the extent that he was willing to serve under him as assistant commissioner. When that position became open with the death of William Herchmer, he put in a written bid for it, stressing that the promotion should be his on the grounds of seniority alone. He enlisted the support of his Conservative MP father-in-law to press his case with the ministers in Ottawa. Harwood's efforts were unavailing. The new assistant commissioner (the title of inspecting superintendent had been dropped) was J. H. McIllree, who had once served as a sergeant under Steele. Steele had nothing against McIllree, whose nickname among the rankers, Easy-going Old John Henry, spoke for his personality. Still, it hurt to be passed over yet again for a promotion he obviously deserved.

Steele's curious lack of advancement in the force seems to have resulted directly from his reputation as a man of unbending integrity. The powers that be in Ottawa evidently presumed that he could never be sufficiently malleable in the political sense to make the kind of N.W.M.P. commissioner they would want. Steele could be highly undiplomatic when it came to points of principle. He once, for instance, forced the principal of a boarding school on the Blood reserve to stop locking the pupils in at night by telling him he would charge him with manslaughter if any of the children should be killed in a fire. The principal complained vehemently that Steele was interfering with the affairs of the Indian Department. It brought the displeasure of the government down on Steele's head, but that did not matter. He had done what was morally, though not politically, right.

In any case his career was now taking second place to more personal considerations. In his forties he was at last making up for the family life he had missed in his lonely years of duty on the far frontiers. Marie had adapted smoothly to life at the fort, enjoying the sociability of the western folk and making a gracious hostess for his roughhewn bachelor friends, who, in the manner of the West, would come to stay as houseguests for a month or more. She had given birth to a healthy baby girl, and another child was on the way. In these comfortable circumstances Steele seems to have grown resigned to spinning out his days as a Mounted Policeman in relative serenity. His only problem was financial. His enthusiasm for the development potential of the West had led him to invest heavily in some shaky gold-mining ventures in the Fort Steele area. He lost a good deal of money in these plunges. He had to borrow money from the bank to make up for the savings that had thus gone down the drain.

He was not, of course, inactive in his police work. He still had the thankless task of administering the despised and contradictory liquor laws. Each summer seemed to be taken up with a running battle between the Mounted Police and rampaging prairie fires. He made strenuous efforts to combat cattle rustling by so-called settlers who built up sizable herds by stealing their neighbours' stock. It was difficult to secure convictions because the stolen animals could seldom be identified conclusively enough to warrant laying charges. He came in for some criticism locally for his seeming helplessness in this matter, but by maintaining a constant watch on known offenders, his men managed to catch and convict many rustlers in the long run.

He took a growing interest in the equipment, dress, and ordinance of the force, and his prestige lent great weight to his opinions on these subjects. He brought about a number of changes in the system, among them the adoption of the Stetson hats that later became the trademark of the Mounted Police. He permitted the men in his command to purchase a standard pattern of Stetson out of their own pockets and to wear them in place of the unsuitable helmets and pillboxes. The rank and file had long since taken to wearing an assortment of cowboy hats in their day-to-day work, but this was the first time that the standard pattern, still worn today, was adopted and sanctioned in use.

He kept busy enough, but it was still a somewhat dull existence for a man so accustomed to action. So when a case came up that took him back to more rousing days, he tackled it with some zest.

The "hero" of the story, to use Steele's own descriptive noun, was a Blood Indian best known by his nickname of Charcoal. He made a fitting adversary for Sam Steele at his best.

Charcoal's "pluck and endurance were a wonderful example of what the greatest of natural soldiers is capable of, when put to the test," Steele wrote in his memoirs. "He was at least the equal if not the superior in character and prowess of the ideal Indian of Fenimore Cooper's novels, and for some years before we met the Bloods was spoken of by them as one of their most remarkable young warriors, a hero in their eyes from every point of view. In those days he rarely slept in his camp, was generally on the war-path or on horse-stealing expeditions against the hereditary ene-mies of his tribe, a restless brave who for a long time hated the whites. To many he seemed a myth, but when we came into the wilderness we found him only too much alive. He gave us much trouble, but as time went on our just treatment had the effect of making him friendly, and for some years he had been well-behaved."

In mid-October of 1896 Steele received a report that a Blood named Medicine Pipe Stem had been found shot dead in a cowshed. That same day the farm instructor on the Blood reserve was shot and wounded. A tribesman told the Indian agent that Charcoal had done the shooting in both cases. The late Medicine Pipe Stem had been the lover of one of Charcoal's four wives, a girl named Pretty Wolverine. The aggrieved husband had killed him after catching the pair making love.

By this time the Mounted Police had so cemented good rela-tions with the Bloods that the Indians frequently arrested law-breakers on the reserve of their own volition. The Bloods formed a posse to deliver Charcoal to the police. But before it got under way, he had vanished with all four wives and two of his children. When he left, he let it be known that he intended to kill Chief Red Crow and the Indian agent to pay off old grievances. That night the chief took to sleeping on the floor of his new house in case Charcoal tried to shoot him in his bed.

An inquest was held, and Steele issued a warrant for the fugi-tive's arrest on a charge of wilful murder. He sent out mixed par-ties of Indian scouts and Mounted Policemen in pursuit. He then rode to the detachment at Big Bend (near the present Waterton Lakes National Park) in the heart of the search area. There a settler told him that an Indian fitting Charcoal's description had stolen his overcoat while he was working in the woods a few miles away.

At dawn the next day Steele sent out a party to scour the woods where the theft had occurred. Removing their hats and boots, the men proceeded to search noiselessly. They found a tent Charcoal had pitched in a hollow choked with trees, but a twig cracked under someone's foot just as they were closing in on it. Charcoal emerged and fired at them without scoring a hit. The policemen and Indians returned the fire but had to stop for fear of hitting the women and children who had scampered into the open. Charcoal darted off into the dense forest, followed by two of the women and a boy, leaving behind the rest of his family, several horses, and a two-month stock of food.

They were in a pine forest five hundred acres square at the foot of the Rocky Mountains. Steele sent orders for a party to come in from the west to prevent Charcoal from penetrating into the mountains and posted a cordon of patrolling sentries around the woods. The day passed without further contact with Charcoal. Steele ordered another sweeping search to commence at dawn.

The inspector in charge of the party on the west side of the forest had sent his horses to a vacant ranch six miles away because the animals were encumbering the foot search. When a constable went to feed them at daybreak, they were gone.

The general opinion was that Charcoal had taken the horses back into the forest, but Steele thought otherwise. This was confirmed by a telegraph message later in the day saying that Charcoal had been spotted forty-five miles to the east. He had covered an incredible total of fifty-five miles, six of them on foot, since escaping from his tent.

Steele sent a message calling for thirty more Blood volunteers to act as scouts, along with an issue of ammunition, blankets, and woollen underwear. If Charcoal continued to move as fast as this, it was going to be a long hunt.

The next morning brought more news of Charcoal's movements. He had entered a ranch house and, in the presence of the rancher's wife, had wordlessly helped himself to some food and departed. The woman had hastily informed the police, who tracked him to a point where they found the horses he had purloined from the police. But from there on they could not trace the prints of his moccasins on the hard, dry ground.

Steele rode to the ranch house and bedded down there for the night. He was roused by word that a Piegan Indian who had tethered his horse near the house had been shot at, presumably by someone trying to steal the horse. This indicated that Charcoal was in the immediate vicinity. Steele sent out a patrol to search the woods thereabouts, but again the will-o'-the-wisp renegade eluded them without leaving a sign.

The days went by while reports poured in that Charcoal had been sighted here and there over half of southern Alberta. Steele kept up the pressure, employing about seventy-five Blood scouts and up to a hundred Mounted Policemen in a continual search. The eastern newspapers got word of the great manhunt. With little concrete news to go on, the newspapers manufactured reports that the settlers were alarmed because Steele had been arming the Indians. This, he retorted, was nonsense. Far from being uneasy, the settlers were pleased that the precedent of mobilizing the Indians on the side of the law had been set.

The first break in the case for some time came when Charcoal's young son was discovered hiding out on the Piegan reserve to the west of Fort Macleod. The boy said he had come there with his father to steal a horse. He was hiding in the woods when he heard a shot and assumed that his father had been killed. The boy was talked into leading a party of Indians to Charcoal's hiding place in an attempt to negotiate his surrender. But Charcoal saw them coming and again slipped off into the woods.

Steele then took drastic action. He knew that Charcoal's relatives had been supplying him and informing him of the movements of the search. He rounded up twenty-two of them, including two of Charcoal's brothers, Left Hand and Bear's Back Bone, and had them taken to the Fort Macleod guardroom. There Left Hand said that he could find his brother and perhaps induce him to give himself up. Steele had his doubts about this, but he released Charcoal's two brothers regardless. As they were leaving, he threatened to prosecute them and all their relatives for aiding and abetting a criminal unless they promised to try to disarm Charcoal and bring him in.

On November 2, three weeks after the manhunt was launched, Charcoal shot and slightly wounded the corporal in charge of the detachment at the Mormon settlement of Cardston. Later he was heard rummaging in the storeroom of a farmhouse, from which he took a large quantity of food. From that point an expert Indian tracker picked out his trail from among the hundreds of horse tracks on the high prairie. It led nearly fifty miles to the northeast.

On the way Charcoal had abandoned his played-out horse and lassooed another. Hot on the trail once more, Steele put a pack-train in the field to allow the hunt to be pressed day and night.

Charcoal was spotted within a few days in the Pincher Creek area and trailed by Sergeant William Brock Wilde and a party of Indians. This was the same Wilde who, as a young corporal, had coolly kicked down Chief Piapot's teepees on the railway line in 1883. Although he had a reputation for hard drinking, Wilde was cast in the old Mounted Police mould: trail-wise, dedicated, and courageous. On November 11, riding at the head of his party, he sighted Charcoal in the distance, riding a horse bareback and leading another loaded with supplies.

Churning through deep snow, Wilde galloped forward, followed at a considerable distance by the Indians. Within minutes his powerful horse carried him to Charcoal's side. As Wilde reached out to grab him, Charcoal pulled up sharply and wheeled about. In the same movement he shot Wilde off his horse.

A cowboy who had been rounding up cattle nearby saw Charcoal dismount and fire another bullet into Wilde's body. Then Charcoal waved his hat at his distant pursuers, shrilled a war whoop, and galloped off on the dead man's horse.

A Blood scout named Many Tail Feathers Around His Neck sped up on foot. The unarmed cowboy who had witnessed the killing offered the scout his horse. Precious moments were wasted when the horse, barely broken, balked as the scout tried to mount it. Finally Many Tail Feathers took Charcoal's abandoned horse and rode off on his trail.

The scout pursued him at a distance into the night, but Charcoal was too fast for him. A posse of cowboys from Pincher Creek eventually joined in the hunt. They tracked Charcoal into the mountains, where, in the nick of time, Many Tail Feathers spotted him standing behind Wilde's horse in a wooded bluff, aiming his carbine across the saddle to ambush his pursuers. The scout called for Charcoal's surrender and fired on him when he failed to answer. Charcoal then faded into the woods again, evading the posse and another search party not far away.

In the next couple of days he covered seventy miles of rugged country, heading back to the Blood reserve. There his brothers, Left Hand and Bear's Back Bone, heard a knock on their cabin door. They opened it to be confronted by Charcoal, who declared: "You have betrayed me." He glowered at them for a moment, then turned back to his waiting horse.

They pounced on him as he was about to mount and dragged him inside after a vicious struggle. They gave him a smoke to calm him, but he was able to stab himself with an awl that he had hidden in his clothes. He would have bled to death in silence if they had not noticed the blood in time to bandage him. They sent for the police, who took him to the guardroom at Fort Macleod as soon as he was well enough to be moved.

Steele noted that in all his month-long flight, Charcoal never left the Macleod District. He could have escaped to the United States at will. "He knew, no doubt, that he would eventually be captured, but he was determined to leave a name that would not be forgotten, and in this he certainly succeeded," Steele recorded. It was his opinion that Charcoal would never have faced the death penalty had he not killed the sergeant. There was ample evidence that Medicine Pipe Stem had provoked his own doom.

As it was, Charcoal went to the gallows like a true warrior, chanting his death song. Although he mourned Sergeant Wilde, Steele could not help feeling a curious sympathy for this intrepid brave who had outlived his time.

Part Three

CALLS OF DESTINY

24: THE TRAIL OF '98

As he celebrated the New Year of 1898 with his family and friends at Fort Macleod, Sam Steele looked forward to another year of more or less routine service. True, he was once more responsible for policing a frontier railway construction job, this time on the line the C.P.R. was building through the Crowsnest Pass and up the Columbia River valley over the route he had suggested ten years before. But to his relief, the pack of human scavengers that usually followed construction camps in the West had not materialized in any proportions. He surmised that most of the worst of that breed were off after richer pickings in the great Klondike gold rush then under way.

That was about as much thought as Steele gave to the frenzied stampede to the fabled river of gold in the Yukon; as far as he was concerned, it was a blessing. But on January 29, a cryptic telegram came from the commissioner posting him to duty in the Yukon forthwith. He was told to take the first train to Vancouver and there await detailed instructions which were being wired from Ottawa. He had no idea of how long he might be expected to stay in the distant gold country, so he arranged to leave his wife and family of two small girls and a boy at Fort Macleod until he could make further plans.

He moved so fast that his successor in the Macleod District command, Superintendent Burton Deane, was only able to nod to him as they passed each other in their buckboards on the road to the railway station. He took the train over the new line from Fort Macleod to Calgary, thence to Vancouver, arriving there at 1:00

P.M. on the thirty-first. Superintendent Bowen Perry was waiting on the station platform. Perry had come over from Victoria with sealed orders from Ottawa, which they opened there and then.

The orders came from Clifford Sifton, the dominion minister of the interior. The two officers were to supervise the immediate establishment of border posts manned by the Mounted Police at the heights of the White and Chilkoot Passes, the principal gateways to the Yukon through which the bulk of the gold rush would surge. Steele was to take command of these posts and of the police in the main staging area of the rush at the headwaters of the Yukon River. Perry was to ensure that the border posts were put into operation, then return to Vancouver to telegraph a report to Ottawa confirming that this had been done.

Sifton was to say later that this move saved the Canadian government twenty years of negotiations with the United States over the location of the boundary between the Yukon and the strip of U.S. territory that blocked it off from the Pacific Ocean. Canada claimed that the border cut across the tops of the passes; the United States claimed that its Alaskan Panhandle stretched some thirty miles beyond. It was vital to Canada's territorial integrity to secure control of the passes before the main body of the gold-rushers, most of them American citizens, arrived in the disputed territory. Sifton had decided to use the Mounted Police to enforce Canada's claim unilaterally on the premise that possession is nine points of the law.

Perry left for Skagway, Alaska, on the next boat out of Vancouver. Such was the crush of people clambering to get to the goldfields that Steele was not able to sail for another week; even then he had great difficulty booking a berth. He finally took passage on a small converted sealing vessel named the *Thistle*. The 120-foot craft was packed to the gunnels with more than two hundred gold-crazed stampeders, then popularly known as *Klondike argonauts*. A fellow passenger commented that the boat was well named because it offered no place to sit down.

Steele's bunk above the propeller was in a cramped cabin with "a strong odour of ancient cheese," but he counted himself lucky. The boat was seaworthy, the boiler was sound, and the captain and pilot were old salts from Newfoundland, skilled in sailing stormy northern seas strewn with ice and rock. This was more than could be said for many of the so-called ships pressed into service for the gold rush. As the *Thistle* moved up the coast, they passed the shattered remains of several vessels which had run aground on rock islands. Scores of lives were lost in the freezing waters off British Columbia and Alaska that year.

It may have been safe, but it was an exceedingly rough and uncomfortable voyage. Steele landed at Skagway on February 15 in −30° F. weather sharpened by a howling wind off the White Pass which seemed to cut to the bone. Skagway was a raw shacktown hunched beneath a towering wall of mountains with a floating population of about five thousand. Passing numerous saloons and gambling dens, Steele found his way to the shack which served as the Mounted Police office; it had been established there on U.S. soil to forward supplies to police posts in the Yukon interior and provide information and advice to the Klondike argonauts.

His friend Inspector Zack Wood was in charge of this setup, but at the time of Steele's arrival Wood was on the other side of the mountains conducting business with the newly appointed commissioner of the Yukon. The commissioner (in effect the governor of the territory) was weathered in for the winter at an outpost on the Yukon River called Big Salmon. He was none other than Steele's first troop commander in the N.W.M.P., James Morrow Walsh, who had been called out of retirement to rule the Yukon on behalf of the Canadian government during the Klondike rush.

The policeman minding the office informed Steele that Superintendent Perry had hurried through Skagway to organize the border posts on the summits of the passes. These would be manned by Mounties already in the Yukon. The force had been in the territory in a small way since 1894, and the Yukon contingent had recently been reinforced up to a strength of some 250 men.

Steele laid out his sleeping bag on the floor of the office cabin and settled down to wait for Perry. With time to kill, he had a look around Skagway, which in his expert opinion was "about the roughest place in the world." In the absence of any sort of law enforcement, the town was totally controlled by a smooth-talking gang boss named Jefferson Randolph Smith, known to all by his nickname of Soapy.

Smith's mob of about 150 hardened thugs preyed remorselessly on the gold stampeders passing through Skagway and the mountain passes. Steele later recalled: "Robbery and murder were daily occurrences; many people came here with money, and the next morning had not enough to get a meal, having been robbed or cheated out of their last cent. Shots were exchanged on the streets in broad daylight, and enraged Klondikers pursued the scoundrels of Soapy Smith's gang to get even with them. At night the crash of bands, shouts of 'Murder!' cries for help mingled with the cracked voices of the singers in the variety halls; and wily 'box rushers' (variety actresses) cheated the tenderfeet and unwary travellers, inducing them to stand treat, twenty-five per cent of the cost of which went into their own pockets. In the dance hall the girl with the straw-coloured hair tripped the light fantastic at a dollar a set, and in the White Pass above the town the shell game expert plied his trade, and occasionally some poor fellow was found lying lifeless on his sled where he had sat down to rest, the powder marks on his back and his pockets turned inside out."

In the midst of this wanton lawlessness Steele must have pondered the immensity of the task before him. For this was only part, albeit the largest part, of the huge army of gold seekers and their camp followers that would converge on the Yukon from all directions as soon as the ice broke on the lakes and rivers the following spring. It would be Steele's job to maintain order on the Canadian end of the "trail of '98" and in the vast camps beside the lakes at the headwaters of the Yukon bloated with people waiting to sail up the river to Dawson with the spring breakup. This greedy mass would surely incorporate the greatest concentration of lawbreakers ever to migrate to one place. The Americans among them—and they were in the vast majority—would have their own idea of enforcing the law with drumhead justice and lynchings. Steele's powers as a tamer of wild humanity would be tested as never before.

Superintendent Perry arrived back in Skagway on the morning of February 16. He had moved two strong parties of Mounted Policemen to the "true boundary" on the tops of the passes. He had been just in time. On the far side of the mountains there were organized groups of Americans who were convinced that the fact that the nearest Mounted Police post was sixty miles to the east constituted a recognition by the Canadian government that all the land in between belonged to the United States. They had elected their own mayors and justices of the peace in the staging camps on Lakes Bennett and Lindemann, and they planned to claim American sovereignty over the whole staging area. They were surprised and indignant when the Canadian police parties marched past them laden with lumber to build the border posts on the peaks to the west.

The party on the White Pass was under Inspector D'Arcy Strickland, a beefy veteran of Yukon service. The one on the Chilkoot was commanded by Inspector Bobby Belcher, a close friend of Steele's since he had served as the sergeant of Steele's troop at Fort Garry in 1873. They had moved tents up to the summit sites as well as a six-month stock of provisions. To show they meant business, they had set up Maxim machine guns at the border lines.

The Mounties had gone to work immediately in an appalling blizzard to build a cabin at each post to serve as a combination customs house and officer's quarters. As soon as these buildings were ready for occupation, they would raise the Union Jack on the peaks.

It was literally a case of showing the flag. Perry was under orders not to return south until he was able to report to Ottawa that the flags were flying. This would denote under international law that all the country to the east was under Canadian control.

It fell to Steele to make sure that the flag was flying on the Chilkoot. He set out on the famous trail of '98 only hours after Perry returned. He and his orderly, Constable George Skirving, crossed the bay from Skagway to Dyea, at the foot of the Chilkoot, in a small tugboat in violent sub-zero weather. The dock at Dyea was coated with glare ice. Several of their fellow passengers slipped and fell in the water as they were disembarking. Steele and Skirving helped to retrieve them and rush them to shelter before they froze to death.

Steele had dinner that evening at the local hotel with an American Army officer in charge of a relief expedition to Dawson, which included many tons of provisions, a herd of reindeer, and steam-driven snow locomotives. Rumours had spread of mass starvation among the people in the vanguard of the gold rush that had reached Dawson the autumn before. But neither the American relief expedition nor anyone else would reach the isolated gold rush capital that winter; extremely cold and stormy conditions put travel out of the question. Thanks largely to the efforts of the Dawson Mounted Police contingent, no one starved there, although the food supply was severely limited. As for the expedition, the reindeer starved, and the snow locomotives proved incapable of climbing the slightest grade.

At first light on the seventeenth Steele and Skirving began to walk up the Chilkoot Pass. The wind howling down the canyon was so cutting that at times they could make headway only by dashing from the shelter of one tree trunk to the next. They joined a convoy of sleighs from a cartage company engaged in hauling supplies for an aerial tramway then being constructed to carry goods to the summit. Every so often they had to crouch in the lee of the sleighs for a few moments' respite from the excruciating blizzard. The trail was lined with tents, but no one was moving. Even the horses were almost stopped in their tracks by the force of the frigid blast.

By noon they were only halfway up the thousand-yard track, which rose at a thirty-five-degree angle. The wind made it impossible to go on. Luckily they were near the cartage company's stables. The jolly old ex-prospector in charge gave them hot food and offered them shelter. They slept that night on beds of straw made up in vacant horse stalls which offered some protection from the deadly cold.

The storm raged on the next morning with only slightly diminished intensity. They heaved themselves into it, moving at a snail's pace up the trail. They soon reached Sheep Camp, where several thousand people had cached their supplies, which they carried in stages up the steep slope to the summit. Such was the power of gold fever that many had ventured out into the savage blizzard, bent double from the loads on their backs as they staggered along. Some had stumbled off the trail and were groping to find it. Steele and Skirving helped to set them back on the track; to drift too far off in such conditions would have meant certain death.

At the foot of the final ascent to the peak the storm was utterly blinding. Try as they might, they could not find the lifeline that had been rigged to guide people up the steps cut in the ice to the top. They had to turn back to the tramway construction camp, which they had passed coming up. That also nearly proved impossible to find. The threat of death by exposure was growing when Skirving called, "Here it is, sir!" and led Steele down a tunnel into a vast snowdrift which completely covered two large tents.

They spent the night in the cheerful company of the tramway construction engineers. The insulating effect of the blanket of snow on the tent made it quite cozy, but two men were constantly employed shovelling snow out of the tunnel lest the occupants suffocate.

The blizzard was still blowing fiercely the next morning. Just as it seemed that no living creature could survive in it, a constable from Belcher's camp on the summit appeared. The Chilkoot detachment was ready for duty, he reported. This was so even though the water on the frozen lake in a crater where they had been forced to pitch their tents had risen and soaked all their clothing and equipment. They were having to sleep on dogsleds inside the tents to keep dry. The wood for fuel had to be hauled seven miles up the mountainside from below the tree line.

After a brief rest the young man cheerfully set out for the summit with orders from Steele to Belcher to hoist the flag and commence collecting customs duties the next day, February 25. As soon as he heard the flag was flying, Steele retraced his steps down the pass to Dyea. It was bitterly cold, but the weather had cleared; thousands of argonauts were toiling up the slope of the Chilkoot. As many as forty round trips were required to pack all their supplies and equipment to the peak. Commissioner Walsh had ordered that no one would be allowed into the Yukon without sufficient provisions for a year; this meant that each had to pack over the passes at least 1,150 pounds of food, plus tents, cooking utensils, tools, and other equipment. If they did not bring their quota, the police turned them back to Alaska. Among people without the faintest notion of the hardships they would encounter, this regulation saved many lives.

Steele had sent a message over the tramway company's telegraph line asking Perry to meet him at Dyea. The two met and crossed the bay to Skagway in a small sailboat. On disembarking at low tide, they were forced to wade through pools of icy water up to their thighs; their clothing froze instantly. Perry had to catch his boat to Vancouver that afternoon, and Steele had to write some dispatches for him to take along. They did not have time to change into dry clothing when they returned to rush through the paper work at the office. As a result Steele contracted a severe case of bronchitis that lasted several weeks.

There was no chance of staying in bed to recover, even if a proper bed had been available. Steele was busy letting contracts for the transportation of supplies to the foot of Lake Lebarge, where the Mounted Police were building boats to transport them to Dawson in the spring. He was joined in Skagway by Inspector Wood, who returned from his meetings with Walsh at Big Salmon. Wood also had a pile of work to do. After putting in a long day dealing with administrative matters and talking to argonauts seeking information, they slept on the floor of the office shack.

As an example of just how wild a place Skagway was, Steele once told of how, early on a Sunday morning, he and Wood were roused from their sleep by the shouts and curses of a mob outside having a pistol fight. Bullets ripped through the thin walls of the shack, but it was such a common occurrence that they did not bother to get out of their sleeping bags. "Wood jocularly suggested that we should get up and take a hand in the scrap, but that was all," he wrote. "The pursued left for some other part of town, followed by the others, who were most likely men who had been robbed by Soapy Smith's gang and were trying to get even."

On another occasion a contractor Steele had engaged, "a soft young man," spent an evening in a dance hall where he was enticed by the girls and otherwise bilked into spending $3,000 for drinks and $750 for a single box of cigars. The proprietor had the effrontery to claim that the young man owed him yet another $1,000 and to come to the Mounted Police office to collect. Fuming, Steele told him he was lucky he was not in the Yukon. He invited him across the border sometime to find out why.

The Americans had not taken Canada's arbitrary occupation of the summits graciously. The U.S. commissioner in Skagway, a notoriously corrupt judge, was preparing to raise a company of volunteers to march over the passes and take Lake Bennett by force.

The commander of a contingent of black U.S. troops that had arrived in a futile attempt to establish order in the Skagway-Dyea area sent Steele a stiff note asking why the Canadian government "found it necessary to exercise civil and military authority over American territory." Steele forwarded this to Walsh, who replied just as stiffly that Canada had a legitimate claim to the territory all the way to Skagway but had refrained from asserting its full rights. The army commander persuaded the judge to call off his invasion and leave the matter to international arbitration. A year later the U.S. government quietly gave in and acknowledged that the true boundary was almost exactly where the police posts had been placed.

The weather was cold but clear through the last week of February. During this lull many thousands surged over the passes, all to be greeted at the spine of the divide by Mounted Policemen who briskly examined their kits and charged them duty on anything not purchased in Canada, down to and including their underwear. The mountains echoed with howls of complaint as the argonauts were obliged to hand over an average of 25 per cent of the cost of each dutiable article. The protests met with that implacable courtesy for which the Mounted Police were famous. For the most part the tirades had the virtue of brevity; the stampeders were anxious to push on before another storm hit.

Even in clear weather the living conditions the policemen endured in these mountain perches were just short of unbearable. On the Chilkoot, fine snow drifted constantly through the cracks between the warped green boards of Belcher's grandly named Customs House and Quarters for the Officer in Command. The roof was a canvas tarpaulin. A thick layer of frost would form on the inside surface at night and melt when the fire was lit in the morning, making Belcher's office "like a shower bath." Clothing, bedding, and official papers were sodden. The light canvas of the men's tents let in an unremitting cold, wet spray.

The temperature rarely climbed above −40° F. Yet they carried on—collecting duties, screening and turning back undesirables and people with insufficient supplies, prosecuting thieves and argonauts who mistreated their animals, rescuing people from exposure and aiding them in a variety of other ways. Soapy Smith's gang operated right up to their doorstep. On several occasions Smith's heavily armed desperadoes chased people all the way to the boundary. They would glare in anger at the coolheaded

Mounties standing by with Winchesters and Maxim machine guns as their quarries stumbled safely over the line.

Three days into March another howling blizzard descended. It was still blowing intermittently on the twenty-fifth when two doctors passing through Skagway reported to Steele that Inspector Strickland, in charge of the White Pass post, had an extremely serious case of bronchitis and should be relieved. Steele was still suffering from bronchitis himself and under doctor's orders not to leave the building. However, when he heard about Strickland, he felt compelled to go to his aid. He struck out for the summit, accompanied by the newly arrived Inspector F. L. Cartwright, whom he had chosen to replace Strickland. He had to go along to familiarize the new commander with his duties at the pass.

They rode uncomfortably up the White Pass trail on pack horses; no saddle horses were available. There they passed thousands of people hauling supplies. At every sheltered spot Soapy Smith's shell game operators and gamblers were busy bilking the tenderfeet. Steele half-expected gunfights to break out at any time. He knew that it was common for argonauts who had been cheated to "fire their ill-aimed revolvers at the expert, who occasionally got impatient at the fusillade and returned the fire with fatal effect."

He was appalled by the conditions at the White Pass post. Enormous quantities of supplies had piled up all around the encampment while their owners waited for the policemen to check them through in the flaying cold wind. Teams of constables took turns shovelling snow away from the entrances to the tents, which were submerged many feet below the level of the snowdrifts. Others were at work cutting and hauling wood from the nearest source, twelve miles away. Many of the men were on the brink of pneumonia. Strickland's condition was virtually critical. Steele immediately arranged to have him sent down to Tagish to recuperate in the clear, dry weather that prevailed in that sheltered post below the hills.

Steele remained on the summit for several days to acquaint Cartwright with the routine. "While there," he wrote, "I noticed the difference in the demeanour of the people of all nationalities when they arrived under the protection of our force. There was no danger of Soapy Smith or his gang; they dare not show their faces in the Yukon. The 'gun,' the slang word for a revolver or pistol of any description, was put in the sack or the valise, and everyone went about his business with as strong a sense of security as if he were in the most law-abiding part of the globe."

When Cartwright had settled into his work, Steele went down the Canadian side of the mountains to organize his district head-quarters at Lake Bennett. Now that the border posts were functioning satisfactorily, his main task would be to police the camps at the head of the Yukon River and to shepherd the rush downstream in the spring. Lake Bennett was well suited to his purposes because it was at the junction of the White and Chilkoot Pass trails and at the head of navigation. Before reaching the lake proper, he called on Yukon Commissioner Walsh.

Walsh was camped on a hill that afforded a panoramic prospect of the headwaters area. As Steele looked down on it, he thought, Here is a scene never likely to be repeated in history. As far as the eye could see, people were camped along the shores of the lakes and rivers with their tents, supplies, and prospecting gear. From the valley came the incessant noise of axes, hammers, and whip-saws at work. Klondike argonauts building boats by the thousand for their spring journey had turned the wilderness into a vast ship-yard. The rash of tents, supplies, sawn lumber, and partly built boats stretched like one long anthill for almost sixty miles.

Steele took up quarters in a log building on the shore of Lake Bennett that also served as his office. It was furnished with a wooden trestle bed, a rough board table that he used as a desk, another of the same type for his orderly-room clerk, a few homemade chairs for visitors, and a sheet iron stove. Bennett was perhaps the most remarkable outgrowth of the whole remarkable gold rush era: a tent city of more than 10,000 souls with hotels, cafes, saloons, barbershops, bakeries, gambling dens, churches, a hospital, and dozens of other urban amenities, all under canvas. Steele was to see little of it, however. He had to work so hard that he could scarcely move from his headquarters for the next two months.

He rose at 4:00 or 5:00 A.M. every day, did paper work until 9:00, and then had breakfast. For most of the rest of the day until midnight he was besieged by gold-rushers who came to consult him on a bewildering variety of questions, problems, and disputes. It was split-up time in the Yukon; the relationships among men who had formed partnerships to join in the gold rush had been strained to the breaking point. After agreeing to disagree, the erstwhile partners invariably quarrelled petulantly over how to divide up their joint belongings. They turned to Steele as an arbiter. He was proud of the fact that in most cases he succeeded in talking the disputants into reconciliation. If he could not restore reason, he left them go to it, tearing a tent down the middle, sawing a canoe in half, dissecting a frying pan with an axe.

Although fisticuffs were common, there was very little trouble in this strangest of all habitations, despite the presence of innumerable rough characters who had spent time behind bars elsewhere. Steele capitalized on the psychological ascendency of the redcoat tradition to keep the peace. His men, many of them young English gentlemen, rarely raised their voices. No matter how roughly they were accosted, they behaved fairly in setting matters right. They demonstrated that they had the best interests of the stampeders at heart by going around the improvised boatyards and advising the unskilled argonauts on how to build their boats safely. Their sincerity and good manners had a gentling effect on those around them. But anyone who knew of Steele knew what was inside his velvet glove.

One evening he was working in his headquarters when two shots sounded. He sent a sergeant out to investigate. The sergeant returned to report that the shots had come from a man who said he had been cleaning his gun. The sergeant added, though, that the man looked suspicious. He was possibly one of Soapy Smith's gang.

Steele ordered a search of the suspect's kit, which turned up a deck of marked cards and a rigged gambling outfit. In the meantime another policeman at the post positively identified the gambler as a henchman of Soapy Smith's. When he was brought before Steele, he adopted an air of indignation. "I'll have you know you can't lock up a United States citizen and get away with it," he roared. "My God, sir! The Secretary of State himself shall hear about it!"

"Well, seeing you're an American citizen, I'll be lenient," Steele said mildly. The man's face brightened. ". . . I'll confiscate everything you have and give you half an hour to leave town."

Before the crook could say anything more, he was hustled out

Commissioner Lawrence William Herchmer (1886–1900). (*Glenbow-Alberta Institute*)

Fort Steele, circa 1888. (*Glenbow-Alberta Institute*)

Sam Steele and bride, 1890. (*Glenbow-Alberta Institute*)

Digging out after a snowslide at the Chilkoot Pass, spring, 1898. (*National Photography Collection, Public Archives, Canada, C-26413*)

Sam Steele aboard the steamer *Willie Irving* as she runs the rapids of Miles Canyon on the Yukon River. 1898. (*Glenbow-Alberta Institute*)

First stores in Dawson, 1898. (*National Photography Collection, Public Archives, Canada, PA-13406*)

Front Street, Dawson, July 4, 1899. (*National Photography Collection, Public Archives, Canada, C-14258*)

Steamers arrive at Dawson, 1900. (*National Photography Collection, Public Archives, Canada, PA-16202*)

Sam Steele and daughter Flora, circa 1899. (*Glenbow-Alberta Institute*)

First mounted review, Strathcona's Horse, Ottawa, March 7, 1900. (*National Photography Collection, Public Archives, Canada, PA-28911*)

Lieutenant Colonel Samuel Steele, C.B., March 1900. (*National Photography Collection, Public Archives, Canada, PA-28146*)

The 2nd Canadian Division in Belgium, February 1919. (*National Photography Collection, Public Archives, Canada, PA-4129*)

Major General Samuel Benfield Steele, Folkestone, Kent, England, in 1915. (*Glenbow-Alberta Institute*)

of the door by the sergeant. Another Mountie marched him straight to the border, a hard uphill hike of twenty-two miles.

When real estate speculators claimed to have bought up the land around the lakes and tried to charge rent for it, Steele meted out similar treatment. But to people in real distress—and they were legion—the Mounties could be as gentle as they could be tough. They loaned or gave money, food, blankets, and even dog teams to those who were short of cash or had lost part of their kits in accidents. Their generosity extended down to their own clothing. Once a honeymooning couple crashed through the ice of a creek, soaking all their belongings. The bride later appeared before Steele clad in the scarlet jacket and yellow-striped riding breeches of the corporal in charge of the outpost near the creek.

They ministered to the dead along with the living, acting as the administrators of the estates of the many who never made it as far as the Klondike. They kept a careful count of the possessions of the deceased and wrote to the next of kin enclosing last messages and statements of what had occurred. They auctioned off their effects and sent the proceeds to the survivors, together with any small items they considered to be of real or sentimental value.

Their efforts all too often met with crass ingratitude, but they were sometimes rewarded indirectly. Steele would never forget a girl named "San Francisco Belle," a waitress in the log cafe. The terrible conditions at the mountain posts and Bennett had taken their toll in several cases of pneumonia, bronchitis, and pleurisy among the policemen. The invalids were placed in a makeshift hospital. Although she had plenty to do at the restaurant, Belle gave of her time to help the doctor, bring medicine and food, and generally cheer the patients up.

As the harsh winter progressed, the parade of people into Steele's office continued unabated. He remarked that no two were alike. They came from around the world and from every occupation. Among them was the future manager of the Bank of Commerce branch to be opened in Dawson, who had with him $2 million in bank notes. He asked Steele to put them in safe keeping. For lack of a better place Steele stuffed them under his bed.

It was a huge task simply to keep track of everyone in this chaotic community. One of Steele's first orders on his arrival was that every boat, scow, and canoe in the area must be registered, with its number painted plainly on it as soon as it was built. The names and home addresses of every man, woman, and child in each boat were taken down and entered in the registers. This was no easy undertaking, with people continuing to stream in, but Steele saw to it that no one could die or go missing on the Canadian side of the boundary without the police knowing who they were and whom to inform.

On April 27 disaster struck on the American side. A blizzard had been blowing for weeks on end, burying the customs house and supply caches on the summit of the Chilkoot under a huge hill of snow. At about seven o'clock that morning the wind died, and the stampeders on the trail below hastened to take advantage of the respite and move their burdens. But the storm soon hit the summit again with renewed ferocity, making it impossible for the trek to go on.

The stampeders were forced to turn back and descend the ice steps from the top. As they were doing so, a tremendous avalanche thundered down the mountainside. Sixty-three people were buried alive in it. Of these only ten survived.

As the commander of the only organized authority in the region, Steele responded quickly to word of the emergency. He ordered Belcher to send a party of his men to the scene despite the fact that it was in the United States. To prevent Soapy Smith's gang from looting, Steele instructed Belcher to organize a committee of trustworthy American citizens on the trail to look after the property of their dead countrymen. He permitted members of the committee to recover any of the victims' belongings cached on the Canadian side. The Mounted Police were to care for the property of any British subjects among the dead.

The grim operation went off smoothly. Steele obtained a list of all the victims and took the time to write personally to all the next of kin of the dead and injured, in whatever country they were. The tragedy touched him personally. Among the dead were several of the kindly young engineers who had taken him and Constable Skirving into their tent when they were stranded on the Chilkoot Pass.

Early in May the Mounted Police were called upon to deal with the first murder of the gold rush in the headwaters district when a prospector on an isolated trail was shot dead and his companion seriously wounded. The survivor said they had been ambushed by four Indians. Corporal Rudd led a party of eight to bring the murderers in. The Mounties trailed their men for two weeks through deep snow and rotting ice in unknown country. But they came back with the Indians, who had been found with the dead prospector's stolen effects. It was a salutary demonstration to all concerned of the rule of law on Canadian soil.

Spring came slowly. The ice was still rotting on Lake Bennett as a crowd gathered for a field day on May 24 to celebrate the Queen's birthday. Then, on the twenty-ninth, the ice cleared and, to quote Steele, "the wonderful exodus of boats began. I went up to the hill behind the office to see the start, and at one time counted 800 boats under sail in the 11½ miles of Lake Bennett." It was perhaps the most fantastic flotilla in history, including dugout canoes, Chinese junks, homemade paddle-wheelers, and huge scows packed with oxen, sled dogs, cows, and horses. The crazy craft bore such wistful names as *Lucky Star*, *Golden Horseshoe*, and *Seven-Come-Eleven*. Steele watched them sail off into the brilliant spring sunshine with a sense of foreboding, for he knew that the majority were pitifully unprepared for the hazards ahead.

Later that day he embarked on a little forty-foot iron steamer named the *Kilbourne*. The weather was fine, with a light breeze blowing off the snow-capped mountains above. As it steamed down the lake, the *Kilbourne* passed thousands of boats off on the four-hundred-mile voyage to the fabulous Klondike gold creeks near Dawson. After about fifty miles the engine broke down, and they were obliged to put ashore for repairs.

They were unable to move again until the next morning, when they reached the approaches of Miles Canyon. Here the Yukon River squeezed into the treacherous Whitehorse Rapids, five miles of tumultuously rushing water, whirlpools, rock reefs, and sandbars bound on either side by sheer black rock walls a hundred feet high. The year before nineteen large boats had capsized in these furious waters. No fewer than two hundred lives had been lost.

At the head of the gorge Steele found several thousand boats tied up, their occupants roaming the shores dazedly. He had earlier posted a detachment at this point headed by Corporal

T. A. Dickson, an experienced "white water" man. An entrepreneur had built a wooden tramway across the five-mile portage consisting of carriages run on wooden rails and drawn by horses. Half a dozen rivermen and sailors engaged in piloting boats through the rapids had pitched tents on the shore.

Steele cursed the breakdown of the steamer the day before when he was told that about 150 boats had already been smashed in attempting to run the rapids. Five people had been drowned, and there would have been more if members of the Mounted Police detachment had not waded in to save several women and children from death. If this kept up, the gold rush would turn into a mass tragedy. Steele knew that he must act.

He called the people to gather around him. A large crowd assembled. Then he raised his booming voice. Knowing that most of his listeners were American, he said: "There are many of your countrymen who have said that the Mounted Police make the laws as they go along, and I am going to do so now for your own good, therefore the directions that I give shall be carried out strictly, and they are these:

"Corporal Dickson, who thoroughly understands this work, will be in charge here and be responsible for the proper management of the passage of the canyon and Whitehorse Rapids. No women or children will be taken in the boats. If they are strong enough to come to the Klondike, they can walk five miles of grassy bank to the foot of the Whitehorse, and there is no danger for them there.

"No boat will be permitted to go through the canyon until the corporal is satisfied that it has sufficient free board to enable it to ride the waves in safety. No boat will be allowed to pass with human beings in it unless it is steered by competent men, and of that the corporal will be the judge.

"There will be a number of pilots selected, whose names will be on the roll in the Mounted Police barracks here, and when a crew needs a man to steer them through the canyon to the foot of the rapids, pilots will be taken in turn from that list. In the event of the men not being able to pay, the corporal will be permitted to arrange that the boats are run without charge. The rate now charged, five dollars for each boat, seems reasonable."

Steele paused to let the crowd digest the details of his message, then added that the penalty for noncompliance would be a hundred-dollar fine.

How many lives he saved by this decisive laying down of the law is beyond speculation. But the fact is that although five persons were drowned the first day, not a single additional life was lost in the seven thousand boats that ran the rapids under this system in the next few weeks.

Most of the gold-rushers were duly grateful. Not all, however. Some protested having to pay the pilotage fee, and an Australian named Frank Dunleavy complained that Corporal Dickson and Constable Fyffe were soliciting fees for themselves. Steele did not believe a word of this—he considered Dunleavy a "professional agitator"—but he went by the book, as he usually did in matters of internal discipline. The evidence was such that it exonerated Dickson immediately, but it was not so cut-and-dried in the case of the constable. He had Fyffe taken under guard to Dawson, where an investigation cleared him of the charge.

Back at Bennett Steele turned his mind to a peculiar problem. Over the winter the summit police posts had collected almost $150,000 in customs fees. He was sitting quietly with Inspector Zack Wood in his headquarters on the evening of June 4 when an order arrived instructing him to deliver the customs revenue to Victoria.

"I'd like to take the gold outside, sir," said Wood. "Let me see it through?"

Steele agreed, and they discussed how to get this fortune safely past Soapy Smith's gang. No protection could be expected from the authorities on the Alaskan side of the boundary; they were all in Smith's pay. So they devised a scheme: It would be logical, they decided, that Wood should be transferred back to the Northwest, since he had closed his office in Skagway. If Smith, through his impressive intelligence system, could be convinced that Wood was simply returning south on personal business, there was a good chance that he could carry the money safely through.

The next day Steele set this ruse in motion by having the word spread in the gossipy camp at Bennett that Wood was leaving the Yukon. After giving the rumour time to circulate, he said goodbye to Wood on the morning of June 9.

The inspector was accompanied by two constables, one of them his orderly. The other was helping out with the "luggage," so it was said. In this was $27,500 in customs money, much of it in the form of gold nuggets. Wood took possession of another $94,000 at the Chilkoot post the next night.

He called from the post to Skagway over the Chilkoot Railroad and Transportation Company's new telephone line and learned that the next Victoria-bound boat, Canadian Pacific's *Tartar*, was not scheduled to dock until five days later. Concerned that a delay would spoil his cover story, he crossed the boundary into American (meaning Soapy Smith's) territory nevertheless. With him were one sergeant and his orderly—and $224,000 stuffed into regulation N.W.M.P. kit bags. There was no sign of the Smith gang on the trail into Dyea. After spending an anxious night in a vulnerable tar paper shack outside the town, they checked into the local hotel.

A sergeant rowed across from Skagway with bad news: The Smith gang seemed to have learned of their mission. He had been followed and gang members had been seen prowling the Dyea streets. Wood summoned the Canadian Pacific agent in Skagway to the hotel, and together they made further plans to outwit the infamous Soapy. They secretly hired a small tugboat and procured a rowboat, which they hid near the Dyea dock.

At 6:30 on the morning of the fourteenth the agent telephoned Wood to report that the *Tartar* had docked in Skagway. The Mounties hastily carried the bags of money to the spot where the rowboat was concealed. They rowed without incident to the hired tugboat, but Soapy's men were watching. As the tug pulled out into the bay, a boat full of gunmen appeared in its wake.

Wood ordered his two men to shoulder their Winchesters and shouted to the men in the boat that they would open fire if they came any closer. The boat veered out of range. The tug anchored in Skagway harbour, and the policemen rowed to the wharf with the money. They had just climbed up on the wharf when a rough-looking mob came charging down it, headed by Soapy Smith himself.

There could be no doubt now that Smith had somehow found out what was in the kit bags. The crowd closed in on the policemen and began to jostle and shove them as they tried to carry the bags to the *Tartar*, which was moored alongside. Then an order rang out from the ship's wheelhouse, and a squad of sailors ran down the gangplank with loaded rifles. They levelled them at the mob. Another squad took up position on the hurricane deck with rifles pointed. At that moment Inspector Wood came face to face with Soapy Smith.

"Why don't you stop in Skagway for a while, Inspector?" the gang king said smilingly. Wood politely declined the invitation, and Smith turned and led the mob off the dock.

The money was delivered without further trouble to a bank in Victoria. Steele and Wood had triumphed over Soapy Smith. Less than a month later, Wood, by then back in the Yukon, was promoted to superintendent, with the military rank of major. Steele was promoted to the military rank of lieutenant colonel, made a member of the new Yukon Territorial Council, and placed in command of all the Mounted Police in the Yukon Territory and British Columbia. Appended to these orders was a vote of thanks to Steele from the governor-in-council in Ottawa for the work he had done since he had landed in Skagway. Steele received these orders on July 7; on July 8 Soapy Smith was killed in a shoot-out on the Skagway dock with the leader of a vigilante group that succeeded in breaking up his gang and chasing it out of town.

25: LION OF THE YUKON

If Dangerous Dan McGrew had really lived in Dawson City instead of only in Robert Service's celebrated poem, he might have been sued for alienation of affections. Certainly he could never have shot it out with the dog-dirty miner over the favours of the lady that's known as Lou, because neither he nor his adversary would have been permitted to carry a gun. If he had tried to do so, the Mounted Police would have taken the weapon away from him. If he had resisted or armed himself a second time, he would have been in for one of the most dreaded experiences Dawson had to offer: an appearance in court in front of Sam Steele.

In Dawson's heyday, the boys really did whoop it up in places like the Malamute Saloon, and ladies like Lou were a conspicuous part of the scenery. Miners fresh from the creeks did stumble out of the night, which all too often was fifty below. There was a real-life piano player called the Rag Time Kid and potential Dangerous Dans by the dozen. Holdup men, crooked gamblers, gunslingers, and con artists—they had all come itching for action in the last great gold rush town.

But this was no Dodge City or Tombstone or Deadwood. This was not their town; it was Sam Steele's. And because it was his town, it was peaceful by any standards. "I am glad to report that in proportion to the population, crime is not very prevalent, and in fact the crime sheets of the Yukon Territory would compare favourably with those of any part of the British Empire," he wrote at the end of that year of years in the Yukon, 1898.

Behind these bland words was a kind of a miracle that was

mainly of Steele's making. The way had been cleared for him to
some extent by his predecessor, Superintendent Charles Constantine. But Steele had taken command in the Yukon just after
its population had swollen to almost forty thousand, including a
mass of camp followers who had arrived to reap the rewards of the
gold diggings without getting their hands dirty. Dawson was the
centre of attraction, with about fourteen thousand people in the
town and working gold claims on the creeks nearby.

Although he had been in charge of the Mounted Police in the
Yukon and British Columbia for several months, Steele did not
arrive in Dawson until early September. Working from his headquarters at Lake Bennett, he had been busy with administrative
work such as handling timber and mining licences while, at the
same time, reorganizing his command to establish eight new outposts located so as to cover every route in and out of the territory
with a fine protective net. His schedule had been interrupted late
in July by a gold rush within a gold rush into the empty country
around Atlin Lake, British Columbia. The first discoveries there
were claimed under Yukon mining law in the mistaken belief that
they lay within territorial bounds. This misunderstanding raised
the threat of trouble among the prospectors in the area because it
was legally possible for newcomers to jump the original claims by
registering them in British Columbia. Steele had to go to the
Atlin country to ascertain whether the area was in the territory or
in the province and deal with the legal conflicts that had arisen.
He stayed on to set up a Mounted Police post there, bringing the
law to yet another corner of the north.

He arrived to find Dawson a "city of chaos." The place had
been built only two years before on a frozen swamp. There was no
drainage system, and the thousands of gold-rushers who camped
on the site had given no thought to sanitation. Floods in the
spring and summer had turned the whole townsite into one vast
sewer. When Steele first saw it, "deposits of every imaginable
kind of filth" lay everywhere. These noxious conditions had
caused a raging epidemic of typhoid fever. Eighty-four people died
from the disease in Dawson that year.

One look around at the saloons, gambling dens, dance halls,
and brothels was enough to bring him to an immediate decision.
The jail accommodation, he ordered, must be increased. Men

were set to work building thirty-four new cells to add to the
twenty-four already in use at the Dawson post, which was called
Fort Herchmer after the N.W.M.P. commissioner. Several other
buildings were constructed at the fort as part of a massive construction program initiated by Steele that saw the completion of
sixty-three new buildings at the force's twenty Yukon posts and
outposts by the fall of 1898.

He instituted a policy of putting prisoners to work cutting
wood, collecting refuse, washing dishes and the like, and shovelling snow in the winter. He calculated that through their work, the
prisoners would each save the government at least five dollars a
day. The Dawson jail compound had no fence, but that hardly
mattered. There was nowhere for an escaped prisoner to go; the
only one who did make a run for it was picked up on the riverbank within a matter of hours.

Steele assumed personal command of the Dawson District in
addition to his general duties. The other district, centred at
Tagish, was under the trusted Zack Wood. Steele's own district
presented a serious problem. The force at his disposal to police
the rip-roaring boomtown of Dawson was thirteen men, including
the sergeant in charge of the town station. Fewer than thirty
others were available to man the outlying detachments and patrol
the mining camps scattered widely over fourteen different gold-
bearing creeks.

These policemen had done a magnificent job of keeping order,
but the situation was precarious. For one thing, former members
of Soapy Smith's gang, which had been smashed by the vigilantes
in Skagway, had somehow slipped through the Mounted Police
net and were seeking to re-establish themselves in Dawson. Much
of the rest of the gold rush capital's population seemed to be "the
sweepings of the slums and the result of a general mail delivery,"
as Superintendent Constantine had so memorably phrased it.
Among them were "a very large number of desperate characters,"
Steele reported. "Many of them have committed murders, 'held
up' trains, stage coaches, and committed burglary and theft in the
United States." He estimated privately that up to half of the denizens of Dawson had at one time been on the wrong side of the
law.

The opening of navigation from the top of Alaska, plus the new

tramway to haul freight up the Chilkoot Pass, meant that a steady
stream of luxury goods, including huge quantities of champagne
and whiskey, was now reaching Dawson. This was the lifeblood of
the multifarious shenanigans that went on night and day in "the
San Francisco of the North."

There was enough gold about for a man with a claim of a
few square feet to recover almost a ton of it over a winter. The
riches of the Klondike creeks were flung about with such abandon
that a pot of $150,000 once changed hands in a two-man poker
game. The instant wealth, the raffish population, the casual vice—
all amounted to a recipe for uncontrollable disorder among the
shacks, tents, saloons, and dance halls. The grossly overworked
and underpaid Mounties of Dawson were just barely holding the
line.

Steele was not a man to be content with holding a line. To him
the only way to secure control was to take the offensive. He went
to his friend William Ogilvie, the great northern surveyor who
had replaced James Walsh as commissioner of the Yukon,* and
asked permission to "borrow" manpower from the Yukon Field
Force. The Field Force was a Canadian Army battalion that had
been stationed at Fort Selkirk, 150 miles upstream from Dawson,
primarily to show the Canadian flag. Steele soon had seventy of
these soldiers under his command at Dawson. He employed them
to guard the gold-choked banks and government buildings, guard
and escort prisoners, and perform other routine duties, freeing his
force of mounties for straight police work.

With his hand thus strengthened, he clamped down hard. He
formed a small squad of undercover detectives "only known to
myself" who checked up on suspicious characters and obtained information on their real names, past histories, and criminal special-

---

* Walsh resigned and left the Yukon in August 1898, leaving a cloud of
scandal behind him. He had been accused of allowing his household cook a
head start when the territorial government lifted a ban on staking claims on
the rich Dominion Creek. The cook later testified that he had agreed to
give Walsh's brother Lewis, who was on the commissioner's staff, a three-
quarter interest in any claims he might stake in return for the capital to
commence mining operations. James Walsh denied all the accusations against
him in a subsequent inquiry, and the matter was dropped. It has been suggested elsewhere that Walsh and Steele had fallen out before the scandal;
this was not so, according to Steele's son Harwood. He says that it was a
matter of regret to his father that his old comrade's reputation had been
stained.

ties. The men of the town patrol, now ably commanded by Inspector Bobby Belcher, dogged the heels of suspected felons
wherever they went. This served a dual purpose: It was salutary
for the rest of the population to observe that the Mounties
haunted the saloons and gambling halls, and the subjects of the
surveillance were usually to be found in such establishments. Just
as Steele had planned, the crooks and all the rest seemed to see a
red coat every time they looked around.

"The way in which these undesirables were kept inactive and
below the surface was nothing short of marvellous; to such an extent were they kept out of sight that many people lived in Dawson without the slightest idea of the reality of the menace," wrote
a gold rush veteran. Steele's strategy was to make life in Dawson
"unattractive" to them. Many took the hint, boarding the steamboats that ran to Alaska and thence to "the outside."

Those who stuck around had a choice: to behave themselves or
be arrested on their first misdemeanour. The police magistrates
often sentenced them to a "blue ticket" to leave the territory
forthwith. This was a serious punishment for gamblers, confidence
men, pimps, and others whose livelihood depended on being on
the scene to extract gold from the accommodating miners. Those
who persisted in staying after they had been ordered to leave were
sentenced to six months' hard labour, usually on the infamous
Dawson woodpile, which was Steele's special pride and joy.

"That wood pile was the talk of the town, and kept fifty or
more toughs of Dawson busy every day," he wrote with no little
satisfaction. It was a useful innovation, for the Mounted Police
and other government buildings used enough fuel over the year to
make a four-by-four-foot stack of wood nearly two miles long. The
wood all had to be sawn into stove lengths by the prisoners, who
were kept at it for ten hours a day. (One imaginative convict, it is
said, got his revenge by spending three months sawing every log
he handled exactly half an inch too long for the stoves.)

In his book *The Yukon Adventure* Percy C. Stevenson graphi-
cally described this unforgettable feature of the Dawson scene:
"In bitterly cold weather, when a kind of mist hung over the
ground, one's thoughts reverted to Dante's Inferno, on passing
this unfortunate legion, sawing, chopping or hauling wood for

Her Majesty, under an escort of Mounted Police, garbed in short buffalo coats and carrying carbines." The frigid hell of the woodpile was presided over by a Corporal Moodie, whose sharp eye and steely grip were the terror of the most hardened men. Steele remarked that he had never known prisoners to be kept in a better state of discipline. A convict assigned to the sanitation patrol, which did the rounds of the cabins daily picking up slop pails and emptying the contents into a waiting cart, considered himself fortunate to have such a relatively soft job.

Steele extended the principle of making crime pay, not for the criminal, but for the law, into the courtroom. The commissioner of the Yukon was supposed to have sufficient funds available to administer the territory for a year, but the horrendously high prices soon used up all the money earmarked for health care. In line with the medical practice of the day invalids were fed champagne at twenty dollars a bottle. Eggs were five dollars a dozen; milk, a dollar a tin. Dawson's two crude public hospitals were choked with typhoid and scurvy victims, and the territorial government had run out of means to feed them. As chairman of the Board of Health, a body that he instituted, Steele used his other offices as police chief and magistrate to set matters straight.

He and the other magistrates dealt with all the "loose characters" who came before them "with the utmost severity." The heavy fines they imposed "furnished a large and useful fund, every cent of which was devoted to the patients in the fever-crowded hospitals," he explained. This unconventional fund-raising campaign gave rise to one of the most popular anecdotes about Steele, though it is probably apocryphal because it has also been told with variations about every tough judge in Canada. Anyway, one day Steele was supposed to have hit a gambler with a $50 fine.

"Fifty dollars? Is that all? I've got that in my vest pocket," said the gambler.

"And sixty days on the woodpile. Have you got *that* in your vest pocket?"

It may be apocryphal, but then it sounds just enough like Sam Steele to be true.

Besides serving as chairman of the health board, he was also chairman of the Board of Licencing Commissioners. This post he also employed to replenish the territorial government's coffers. Every saloon, dance hall, inn, or other drinking place—and there were scores of them—had to buy an expensive licence and abide by the commission's rules. About $90,000 was collected in this way, ultimately saving the territorial government from bankruptcy. The funds voted by Parliament to administer the territory had been exhausted, but the revenue from the fees saw it through.

Liquor licences were issued "in numbers sufficient to meet the needs of the population, with the result that 'dives' and low drinking dens are a thing of the past, never to return," as Steele reported. This realistic policy was part and parcel of his general approach to the phenomenon of the Yukon in the gold rush days: to let human nature take its course under intelligent control. Steele's orderly-room clerk at the time, Christopher Reed, told a story in later years that got to the core of Steele's attitude to the frenetic happenings around him: "The sergeant-major (that best of sergeants-major, Tucker) came in one day and said that he was sure that some of the men were breaking barracks at night, and should he have 'check rounds.' The colonel said 'No! they are young men, they'll never see a mining camp like this again, and so long as they do their duty, it won't hurt them to go a bit large.'"

He let all Dawson "go a bit large." He allowed the gambling halls to operate wide open but told the owners that if he heard any verifiable complaints of sharp practice, he would shut them down. They understood; any customer who claimed, truthfully or otherwise, to have been cheated had his money restored in full before being chucked out onto Front Street. The men of the town patrol kept an eye on the gaming tables, casually strolling in from time to time and looking over the players' shoulders. Three months on the woodpile awaited any individual convicted of "cheating at play."

As time went on, Steele and his men brought the gaudy gold rush mecca under their control to a degree that was amazing. An obscene remark or performance on a stage was enough to have a music hall closed down at once. Steele banned the famed hootchy-kootchy dance that had titillated audiences at the 1893 World's Columbian Exposition in Chicago. An American performer who ventured some disparaging remarks about royalty found that he had committed a grievous offence in Sam Steele country. Steele gave him the choice of a blue ticket to the outside or of changing his material. He left the courtroom to "sin no more."

Sundays in Dawson under Steele's regime would be remembered as long as there was a gold rush veteran left alive. "No one required a time piece" to tell that the hour had passed into the Sabbath. At five minutes to midnight on Saturday the places of entertainment would be going full blast, the ragtime pianos tinkling, the champagne flowing, men crushing together at the faro tables. Yet four minutes later everyone would be out of the doors, bidding a subdued good-night to the Mountie patrolling Front Street. The day would pass in tranquility unless someone broke one of the strict Victorian Sunday laws. Men were arrested for commercial fishing and for sawing wood on the Lord's day. For most part, the only sound to be heard on a Dawson Sunday was the singing of hymns in the churches and on the street by the resident Salvation Army unit. The quiet would prevail until 2:00 A.M. on Monday. Then the fleshpots would fill up as suddenly as they had emptied and within minutes would be going full blast once again.

Steele was a stickler for having chilled boiled water available in the saloons, and heaven help the barkeeper who served a minor. Yet otherwise he permitted them to operate at all hours. He was sufficiently tolerant of human frailties to let dance hall girls like Diamond Tooth Gertie, Sweet Marie, and the Oregon Mare make their fortunes from milching lonely miners. If a man wanted to blow his poke of gold on the waltzes and smiles of these painted ladies, it was his own business. Many the man in mukluks would dance away hundreds of dollars in a single night.

It was a man's own business, too, if he cared to leave his earnings at a faro or roulette table, provided the game was honest. As far as Steele was concerned, "there were worse men than the gamblers of the Klondike. Some of them were the most charitable of men, always ready with money to help the sick or assist a mission, and one often thought what a pity it was to see such naturally fine characters making their living in that manner." He recorded of Silent Sam Bonnifield, the most fabulous gambler of all, that "the sick and poor never went to him in vain."

He recognized that there could be no stopping prostitution, so he acted to keep it under control by moving the prostitutes into red-light districts in Paradise Alley and Lousetown. As long as their business was conducted in an orderly fashion, the sirens of Dawson had nothing to fear from the police. There were a few arrests for soliciting, however. These usually resulted from a girl or her pimp straying outside of the red-light zones or breaking Steele's arbitrary rule against operating before four o'clock in the afternoon.

As the well-known Yukon newspaperman Stroller White remarked, these policies made Dawson a place of sinful gaiety with none of the grimness and terror of Soapy Smith's Skagway. They earned Steele a sort of affectionate respect. Big Sam was regarded as the stern paterfamilias of Dawson City, doing what was right for everybody. Henry Woodside, the editor of the Dawson *Midnight Sun* (later called *Yukon Sun*), called him "the Lion of the Yukon." Christopher Reed, the orderly-room clerk who would become an Anglican archdeacon, wrote: "He would have made a fine rajah if there had been another Sarawak for him. Indeed he was almost that in Dawson. Whatever he said went. His large presence, his big gruff voice, his dominant personality, his sense of honour, fair play and justice, and a little twinkle in his eye, showing his sense of humour, made him 'It' with a large capital I."

If Steele was respected by the civilian population, he was virtually worshipped by the Mounted Policemen who served under him. Christopher Reed's reminiscences of life with Steele in Dawson help to explain why.

"One day," wrote Reed, "a man came into the office and asked to see the C.O. When he got inside he began a long story about a corporal on Dominion Creek so evidently full of spite and lies that the colonel suddenly shouted to me in the outer office, 'Reed! Is the door open?' 'No, sir,' I said. 'Then open it and stand by it,' he called; then, turning to the man, he stood up, pointed to the door and said, 'You're a liar! Go!'"

On another occasion, Reed recalled, a Yukon Field Force officer charged a Mounted Police corporal at an outpost where he had stopped for the night with insolence and insubordination. The officer had ordered the corporal to fetch him some hot water; the corporal had told him to go to hell. Steele heard the evidence of both parties and stiffly reproved the NCO for using such language to an officer. That done, he crisply told the officer to leave. Then he turned to the corporal. "I'm not going to make an entry on your defaulter sheet," he said, "for I'm sure I should have done the same thing myself!"

In the midst of the glitter, sin, and easy wealth of that city of gold, Steele "enthused the whole force with a sense of honour and an *esprit de corps* that was greater than all temptation." The steadfast integrity of the men of the Mounted Police in the Yukon was almost beyond belief. In all his time in Dawson Steele had to deal with only one complaint of police graft. He was told that the harassed constables handling the mountains of mail at the makeshift post office had been accepting bribes to allow men to jump the queue, in which some were forced to stand for many hours. On investigation he found that the policemen had not accepted money during office hours but had been paid by a syndicate of mail-starved miners to stay on at night to speed up the sorting of letters. "I removed all the police from the office and sent them to duty," Steele reported, "and gave orders that on no account was any money to be taken at any time."

"Beyond all praise" was how he described the conduct of the incredibly willing and diligent men who served under him. They built cabins with their own hands; they carried vast sums of gold over the lonely trails and even to the banks in Seattle without losing or misappropriating an ounce. They nursed the sick and injured they found in lonely cabins in the wilds; they helped the paupers who were streaming out of the Yukon after their dreams of gold had exploded. They took into protective custody the many madmen that the shattered dreams, the hardship, and the isolation had produced. Along with their comrades of the Yukon Field Force, they fought fires, twice saving Dawson from destruction. They assessed and collected mining taxes; they sorted and delivered the mail. They went out on epic patrols into the wilderness to look for missing persons. They buried the dead.

In a region where prices were between four and five times higher than in the rest of Canada, the maximum pay for a constable was $1.25 a day, the same amount as a labourer in the mines could earn in an hour. And in a region where any man could make a fortune in gold if only he could find it, they were prohibited from prospecting in their scarce spare time.

If, out of necessity, Steele drove his men hard, he drove himself harder. "My waking hours were at least nineteen," he wrote. "I retired to rest about 2 A.M. or later, rose at six, was out of doors at seven, walked five miles for exercise between that hour and eight, two and a half miles up the Klondike on the ice and back over the mountain, visited every institution under me every day, sat on boards and commissions until midnight, attended to the routine of the Yukon command without an adjutant, and was in the town station at midnight to see how things were going."

Nor was his day over when he returned to his quarters. "Every evening numbers of persons dropped in, often as late as midnight, to see me or to have a chat with others who came every night. Frequently I was unable to be present, but it did not matter; they got on very well until I returned. The party was always cosmopolitan. English, Scotch, Irish, Canadians, Jews, Americans, Norsemen, Danes, Poles, Germans, doctors, lawyers, engineers, soldiers and sailors were among our visitors, and discussed the affairs of the territory and the outside, the amount of pay dirt on their claims, their troubles and intentions, until about 2 A.M., when they usually retired to rest, and in winter I was in my sleeping bag at 3 A.M." It was intensely cold, the temperature sometimes plunging as low as —70° F. But he let the water bucket in his room freeze to the bottom during his scant hours of sleep, "for, had my stove caught fire, I should not have been able to escape, as it was between me and the door."

His days were spent working on police and territorial council matters, hearing cases in court, answering correspondence, and ploughing through the huge stacks of cheques, vouchers, and returns that piled up owing to the fact that the entire government organization in the Yukon was supplied through the Mounted Police system. Yet he found time to visit the mining camps on the creeks, where he was received with the warm hospitality the miners always afforded the Mounted Police. He dealt with a bewildering and bizarre range of problems. One such involved the execution of a prospector who had murdered his partner in 1897 and the three Indian murderers captured in the spring near Bennett (the fourth had died from fever). They were scheduled to be hanged on November 1, All Saint's Day, but the presiding judge in Dawson, Mr. Justice Dugas, had second thoughts about the legality of carrying out an execution on a religious holiday. He postponed the event only hours before it was to have occurred.

On the appointed morning a woman in tears was ushered into Steele's office. She was Faith Fenton, a reporter for the Toronto *Globe*. In an excess of journalistic enterprise, she had written a full and vivid imaginary account of the execution and had sent it off to her paper in the mail that had left Dawson by dog team a few hours earlier. Steele saved her job by sending a police team out after the mail sled, which was intercepted some thirty miles up the river. "The offending report was captured and brought back for future use, much to the relief of the distressed damsel," he recalled wryly. The executions did not take place until the following August.

The mail was added to the manifold burdens of the N.W.M.P. when the contractor responsible for its delivery vanished. Incoming mail had simply been dumped in Skagway to pile up. For a time Steele permitted the outgoing mail to be carried on police patrols on a casual basis, but as winter set in, the mail problem grew serious. It was the responsibility of another government department, but as usual the police were left holding the bag.

Steele organized a fortnightly postal delivery service using police dog trains under instructions to move "at all possible speed" over a trail shortened by cutting across bends and points along the Yukon River. Dog teams and drivers were changed at every detachment along the line. Soon the police had the mail moving night and day, carrying loads of five hundred to seven hundred pounds in appallingly cold and stormy weather. They frequently covered the six hundred miles between Dawson and Skagway in seven days. The men made a kind of sport of it, attempting to beat one another's records from detachment to detachment. A constable from Indian River regularly made his thirty-mile stage in four and a half hours, running behind his team all the way. Zack Wood at Tagish had a team of Eskimo dogs from Labrador which moved so fast that the driver could not keep up with it on foot; he had to ride on top of the mailbags. These particular dogs could travel the fifty-seven miles from Tagish to Bennett in seven hours. They were well known in the Yukon for their reputation of having killed and eaten their driver back in Labrador.

By the end of the winter the mailmen of the Mounted Police had logged 64,012 miles, the equivalent of about two and a half times around the world, in some of the world's worst weather. The communications problem between the Yukon and the outside had been licked. So had many of the other problems that had faced Sam Steele on his arrival in Dawson. He had so tamed the place that, as he reported, "any man, woman or child, may walk at any time of the night to any portion of this large camp with as much personal safety from insult as on Sparks Street, Ottawa."

Few of the tough element remained when the ice broke on the Yukon that spring; of those that did, "no one could form any idea that they were other than law-abiding, respectable citizens." There were a few petty thefts, often committed by men stranded without money in the aftermath of the rush, and the usual cases of nonpayment of wages, gambling, and prostitution common to all mining camps. One prospector was awaiting trial for manslaughter, having shot his partner after the latter had given him a beating. But as the round-the-clock darkness of the subarctic winter lifted in the spring of 1898, Steele could rest easy in the knowledge that he had made Dawson safe from violent crime.

He had different things on his mind. The first was to clean up the physical surroundings of Dawson in order to avert another typhoid epidemic. He ordered the prisoners out on the streets to clear up and burn the refuse and to dig a system of drains. He had written to Ottawa suggesting that Russian authorities in Siberia be consulted about public sanitation methods in far northern conditions, but nothing had come of this. Instead Steele and his fellow members of the health board designed and installed their own system of drainage, sewage and garbage disposal, and a pure water supply. As a result the number of hospital patients in Dawson was reduced to about one tenth the number of the previous spring. The health officer, Dr. Good, said that health conditions were "about as favourable as those in any part of Canada" after these improvements had been made.

Steele might have wished that the other type of corruption in Dawson were so simple to eradicate. Since the beginning of his tour he had been obliged to stand by more or less helplessly while government officials wallowed in graft. He called them "wolves in sheep's clothing, who cheated the decent miner of his hard-earned claims." Too often, however, the offences they committed were obscured by tricky bureaucratic paper work. The ownership of claims was changed by altering names and dates on records. Men who had staked claims were sometimes told that their ground had been closed by government order, only to learn later that the claims had been registered in the names of the officials or their friends. When a claim had been staked legitimately, they would tell the owner that it must be surveyed. In the meantime they would have it staked for themselves.

Given the lack of hard evidence, Steele was unable to do much more than let these white-collar thieves know that he was on to their tricks. Only one official was ever convicted of graft, and he was a minor clerk. Commissioner Ogilvie was powerless to rid his organization of grafters because they operated under the protection of Clifford Sifton, the minister of the interior, who was also chief organizer of the ruling Liberal Party. When the governor-general, Lord Minto, later visited the Yukon, he came to the conclusion that the minister was guilty of "criminal administration." He found that "public opinion of the Minister as expressed in ordinary conversation would be enough to ruin any man."

"I do not think that so much rascality has been done since the country commenced to open up the West," Steele wrote to his father-in-law, Conservative MP Robert Harwood. He said that government officials who had grown rich on ill-gotten gains were keeping bejewelled mistresses and living it up on champagne. An open system of kickbacks flourished in the allocation of Crown timber rights. Crooked officials had gone into league with powerful mining interests devoted to acquiring individual prospector's claims by fair means or foul.

Of all the six members of the territorial council, only Steele and Commissioner Ogilvie were not making money on the side in a questionable manner. Ogilvie complained in vain to Sifton that F. C. Wade, the Crown prosecutor, was occupying "incompatible

positions" by serving as clerk of the court and operating a private
law practice; once, Ogilvie claimed, Wade had even argued a
court case for both sides. In his private capacity, the prosecutor
represented the big mining interests, and he had garnered a fortune from dealing in mining properties. Ogilvie later protested to
Sifton that two other council members, Mr. Justice Dugas and
J. E. Girouard, devoted "too much time to the acquirement of
claims."

Steele had learned that yet another council member, government legal advisor W. H. P. Clement, had openly boasted that he
could fix cases in his capacity as a private lawyer by using his political influence. Steele particularly abominated a man named J. D.
McGregor, a personal friend of Sifton's whom the minister had appointed to the marketable position of inspector of mines. Steele
regarded McGregor as nothing more than a thief; in fact he knew
that McGregor had once been tried for horse stealing. When Sifton attempted to appoint his protégé "issuer of liquor licences," a
post that obviously offered great scope for patronage and plunder,
Steele put his foot down. Backed by influential Dawson citizens,
he weighed in against his fellow council members and succeeded
in having the appointment quashed.

This was tantamount to a declaration of war against Sifton,
who was his ultimate boss; Prime Minister Sir Wilfrid Laurier
delegated to Sifton all responsibility for Mounted Police matters.
To defy the minister further, Steele then refused to give a meat
contract to a Liberal Party hack. These moves gave the grafters
the chance they had been waiting for. They went to work on Sifton, complaining to him about the conduct of the Mounted
Police. McGregor wrote to the minister that the police were interfering in the affairs of other departments, going on to state
brazenly that such duties as collecting mining royalties would be
better left to civilian officials. Steele's actions, he implied, were
motivated by political considerations. It was well known that
Steele was a Conservative Party supporter, yet there he was, practically running the Yukon. Should a Liberal minister of the interior allow a professed Tory to run such an important show?

The attacks on the Mounted Police hit Steele where it hurt. He
was fiercely proud of his men, and he felt that the incredible job

they were doing was not being properly appreciated. He was furious that their conduct should be reproached. He was also angered by the government's obstructive treatment of that "truest and best of men," Commissioner Ogilvie, whose unavailing struggles against the corruption around him had made his life "a bed of thorns."

But to paraphrase the headline of a Dawson newspaper at the time, "wrong was triumphant." A party of government officials, including two of Steele's adversaries on the council, went "on leave" to Ottawa in the spring. It was clear that part of their mission was to get Steele's head. According to no less well-informed a witness than William Ogilvie, they succeeded. The commissioner told the governor-general a year later that Sifton had Steele ousted from the Yukon because of his opposition to patronage and graft.

Steele heard rumours of his impending transfer over the summer, but the axe did not fall officially until September. Sifton personally notified him of his removal in a telegram sent over the newly strung telegraph wire from Dawson to Bennett on the eighth of that month. The minister's message said crisply that Steele's duties in the Yukon were terminated and that he was to report to headquarters in Regina without waiting to hand over his command to his successor. Steele tried to keep the news quiet, but it soon spread out onto the Dawson streets.

There was an instant angry outcry. The people of Dawson knew perfectly well why this incorruptible man was being plucked from their midst. The town's three newspapers, normally aggressive rivals, all blazed indignantly into print. The Liberal *Yukon Sun* urged upon the government "the wisdom of cancelling the order of recalling Lieutenant-Colonel Steele from the Yukon." The opposition Dawson *Daily News* said that the loss to the territory of Steele's going would be almost irreparable. "Lieutenant-Colonel Steele," it noted pointedly, "has proved himself the miner's friend. He has given them all the protection in his power." That outstanding specimen of rough-and-ready frontier journalism, the *Klondike Nugget*, pulled out all the stops: "Without one word of warning which might have led to a national protest Colonel Steele is relegated to obscurity, that not even one pair of keen cold, honest eyes should witness the villainous prostitution of governmental prerogative in turning over to private bodies the public property of this great and growing Arctic commonwealth." It went on to run a seemingly endless list of comparisons between Steele's upright character and that of "political pirates" of the "Sifton gang."

Henry Woodside, a strong Liberal who was editor of the *Sun*, reinforced his editorial declarations with a telegram to Prime Minister Sir Wilfrid Laurier. It could not have been less equivocal: "For the good of government beseech you to suspend order removing Colonel Steele from command here. Will be terrible blunder. . . ." The editor followed it up with a personal letter to the Prime Minister again protesting Steele's removal and calling him "the strongest single factor we have here in reconciling the people to conditions. . . ." Laurier, who, like Macdonald before him, was nominally responsible for the N.W.M.P., washed his hands of the matter. He told Woodside that he knew nothing of any "removal" and referred him to Sifton, who, after all, was the one having Steele removed.

A petition signed by prominent Yukon citizens was dispatched to Ottawa, followed by a meeting on the Saturday night of September 16, when a crowd of five hundred packed the Criterion Theatre to demonstrate their indignation. Many of those attending were miners who had walked in from the creeks several miles away. Klondike Joe Boyle, a magnificent character who would go on to become a top British secret agent in Russia during World War I and later, as Queen Marie's lover, the "uncrowned king of Rumania," was chairman. The aroused throng heard a succession of speakers from both political parties verbally flay the grafters and praise Steele, who was about the only honest man in Dawson not in the crowd. Boyle drafted a memorial to be sent to Ottawa that was passed unanimously. It expressed "the feeling of dissatisfaction of the entire population of this Territory at this, the removal of our most popular and trusted official." It ended bluntly: "It would be a direct injury to the Territory should he be taken away."

Joe Boyle volunteered to circulate the memorial around the creeks and thousands signed it. The list of names was telegraphed to Ottawa at great expense to show how much support there was for the cause.

What about the man in the centre of this storm of protest? Steele had had enough. He was heartsick at the turn of events, and he was tired. No one could dispute his statement that his time in the Yukon was "the most difficult that has ever fallen to the lot of a member of the N.W.M.P." He had not seen his family in more than a year and a half—he had abandoned a plan to have them come to Dawson—and he wanted to resume his family life. He had a statement ready for a deputation of Dawson people who urged him to resist his transfer: "On no account would any influence induce me to remain unless I were ordered and even then it would be against my will."

In any case the government would not be budged. September 26 was set as the day for Steele's departure. The man who had gained a reputation from his work in the Yukon "as wide as the continent of North America," in the words of Commissioner Ogilvie, tried to slip quietly away. But the flamboyant town he had ruled with such a firm yet humane hand was not about to let its hero go without a characteristic flourish. Down they poured to the Mounted Police dock where his steamboat awaited—the gamblers, the dance hall girls, the grizzled prospectors, the ragtime piano players, the whores. The whole fantastic population of the world's greatest gold rush town was there, plus hundreds more who had made the journey from the creeks for miles around. They were there to give him "such an ovation and send-off as no man has ever received from the Klondike gold seekers," in the words of the *Sun*.

The "King of the Klondike," Big Alex McDonald, had been chosen to deliver the parting address and present Steele with a poke of gold nuggets collected from the miners and merchants. All Dawson held its breath as the two men came together on the dock. At that sentimental moment, Big Alex's powers of speech failed him. He thrust the bag of gold at Steele. "Here Sam—here y'are. Poke for you. Goodbye."

The steamboat threw off her lines and started up the river. Steele looked back to see every wharf, boat deck, and point awash with people cheering and waving handkerchiefs and hats. All the steamboats along the waterfront let loose with their whistles. The sound of cheering rolled on and on as the steamboat puffed up the valley of the Yukon. It could still be heard when the boat passed out of sight.*

* Steele's achievements in the Yukon are commemorated today in the 16,644-foot Mount Steele, the sixth highest peak in Canada. A mountain motif has often been used by writers attempting to sum up Steele's appearance and character. John Garvin, editor of the London *Observer*, described him as "that monumental man, as strong and selfless as the Rocky Mountains." Of all the things in Canada named after Sam Steele—parks, schools, Royal Canadian Legion branches, and so on—Mount Steele seems most apt.

26: FIGHTING SAM

There are few sadder classes of men than unemployed officers. On leave after rejoining his family in Montreal, Steele must have felt cast adrift by the country he had served so long and so well. His firm friend Fred White, the N.W.M.P. controller, let him know that he could choose from a number of jobs in the force, but any one of these would be a comedown from his semi-independent command in the Yukon. For all the lustre of his record his career seemed to be coming to a disappointing end when he was still a physically fit forty-seven years of age.

Then, just as the picture looked dimmest, he was launched into a fresh adventure. After years of bickering over the rights of the British Uitlanders in the Boer republics of South Africa, the Transvaal and the Orange Free State, the British and Boers went to war on October 11, 1899. In that age of "ready aye ready" imperialism, a reluctant Canadian government was obliged to send a Canadian contingent to support the British. A shortsighted military establishment in London asked Canada and other parts of the Empire for "dismounted" troops. Canada duly recruited and dispatched an infantry force of 1,000 men.

This could hardly have suited the Boers better. They were splendid horsemen who fought as mounted troops, using their horses to give them the mobility to hit and run. These tactics more than overcame their main disadvantage against the British, a deficit of manpower. Within a few weeks of the war's opening, these rustic burghers had dealt the professional British Army a series of shattering defeats.

It slowly dawned on the imperial general staff that the Boers could best be fought by men like themselves, rugged and resourceful outdoorsmen who could handle horses, shoot well, find their way without maps, and know where to look for cover in rough country. Western Canada was full of just such men. The North-West Mounted Police offered a resident cadre of highly trained and disciplined mounted riflemen. And as it happened, the force could also supply the ideal leader for an expedition of western Canadian horsemen to South Africa: the excellent but temporarily idle Lieutenant Colonel Sam Steele.

Steele volunteered for service in South Africa on the understanding that he would remain an officer in the Mounted Police. In mid-December Major General Edward Hutton, then commanding the Canadian Militia, offered him the position of second-in-command of a regiment to be dominated by the Canadian cavalry, with a minority representation from the force. Steele turned this down on the grounds that the arrangement would be unfair to the N.W.M.P. and that he would be redundant in the command structure. He went back to his hotel room in Ottawa disappointed. But the next day Hutton called him back to make a proposal more to his liking: to command a mounted regiment based on the Mounted Police.

Steele accepted at once. The police organization was responsible for recruiting both the police and civilian (largely ex-police) segments of the new regiment. He routinely contacted Commissioner Herchmer about the recruiting plans, but the commissioner had plans of his own. He wanted to command the unit in South Africa personally. He appealed to Steele to step down in his favour—for the good of the force.

Sam Steele had no reason to love Lawrence Herchmer, but he did love the Mounted Police. The regiment, to be known as the Canadian Mounted Rifles, would in effect be the official Mounted Police contingent in the war. Although Steele may have doubted that it was really in the force's best interests to have its unreasonable commissioner lead it in the field, he put his loyalty ahead of his personal feelings. So, "of my own accord and for reasons of my own," as he phrased it, "I gave up command and was appointed second." He travelled west and worked willingly with Herchmer over the next few weeks to organize the regiment. Two days before he was to embark for South Africa with it from Halifax, events took another unexpected turn.

On January 25, 1900, he received a telegram from Dr. Frederick Borden, the minister of militia, offering him command of an entirely new unit. This was to be a special corps of mounted riflemen for service in South Africa to be raised in western Canada and built around a cadre of officers and NCOs from the Mounted Police. It was to have a strength of roughly five hundred men and six hundred horses; the entire expense of putting it in the field was to be borne personally by Donald Smith, Lord Strathcona, the man who had driven the last spike on the Canadian Pacific Railway and had later travelled with Steele in British Columbia. The former railway financier and governor of the Hudson's Bay Company had become Canadian high commissioner in London. Steele's first official act as the commander of this paper regiment was to name it Strathcona's Horse.

He rushed back to Ottawa to confer with Dr. Borden and General Hutton. The wealthy lord's offer had been received with grateful enthusiasm in the capital, for it extricated the government from a tight spot. Empire-minded English-Canadians were insisting that Canada do more for the mother country in a war that so far was being won by the enemy. Sentiment in French Canada was running against spending Canadian tax money to fight a British colonial campaign. Having Canadians serve in South Africa at private expense looked like a heaven-sent solution to Laurier's quandary. Steele would have the government's cooperation in every way.

He was allowed his pick of volunteers among Mounted Police officers and other ranks who could possibly be spared from duty. He immediately chose his old friend Inspector Bobby Belcher as his second-in-command. He later selected five more officers and twenty-six other ranks, mostly NCOs, from the list of Mounted Policemen who had volunteered for South African service. Among these were several who had been close to him in the past: men like Sergeant Major William Parker, formerly of Steele's Scouts; Inspectors Cartwright and Harper, who had been with him in the Yukon; and Sergeant George Skirving, who as a constable had accompanied him on his first hard climb up the Chilkoot Pass.

The Mounted Police organization was placed at his disposal to do the recruiting. He set the wheels in motion by telegram and caught a train west. The response to the news that the celebrated Sam Steele was forming a corps to go to South Africa was phenomenal. He was besieged by volunteers in western towns and cities and bombarded with telegrams from men in faraway places asking him to hold a place for them until they arrived. Men came long distances by dog sled and snowshoes to put their names down at Mounted Police posts. He had an offer, impossible to accept, from 600 Arizona cowboys who said they would bring their own horses and buy rifles of whatever pattern he chose. Only five days after the opening of recruiting Strathcona's Horse was up to its full complement of 537 all ranks; almost four times that number had come forward. The regiment was fully raised only fifteen days after Steele had received Borden's telegram.

"The men enlisted are composed of the very pick of the cowboy, cowpuncher, ranger, policeman and ex-policeman of the territories and British Columbia," Steele reported. They signed on for a maximum of a year and a minimum of six months. They were a mixed lot, mainly attracted by the adventure of going to war in the hell-for-leather style of Teddy Roosevelt's famous Rough Riders in Cuba. They included the drunken son of the duke of Hertford, an apparent fugitive from the law in the United States, a newspaper reporter, and a man who had made a fortune in the Klondike gold rush. University and military school graduates mingled in the ranks with cowhands who could barely write their own names. Several ex-British Army officers signed on as privates. The War Office in London turned down Steele's recommendation that E. C. Parker of Fort Steele be appointed a captain on the grounds that Parker had once been forced to resign his commission in the Essex Regiment for conduct unbecoming an officer. Parker promptly volunteered to serve as a sergeant. (The Strathconas were considered a British Army unit; unlike other Canadians its officers received their commissions direct from the Queen.)

They came from over a million square miles of territory. Steele had handpicked them for their toughness; most of them were bachelors over thirty years of age. They were inclined to be rowdy, but Steele and his Mounted Police officers knew how to handle rough diamonds. They were, in fact, not unlike the men of the early Mounted Police.

He had the whole motley lot assembled at Lansdowne Park in Ottawa by the middle of February. They bedded down on straw matresses in stables rudely converted to barrack rooms. The horses began to arrive: ranch-trained western mustangs selected by an expert. A fifteen-year-old drummer boy from Toronto, Edward ("Mickey") McCormick, arrived at the park in time to see cowboys still in buckskin clothes breaking the wildest of the horses in corrals while wagonloads of supplies streamed through the gates.

Young McCormick was there under false pretences. He had written to Steele begging to join the regiment and saying that he was sixteen, a qualified trumpeter, and an experienced rider—of which he was none. The regimental sergeant major paraded him before the commanding officer, who asked to see his mother's written permission to leave home. Steele's manner showed clearly that he knew the boy was not so old nor so well qualified as he said he was. He told McCormick that he could join despite this. The sergeant major was marching the lad out when Steele said: "Just a minute, McCormick. Your mother wrote to me and I know she really doesn't want you to come, but you'd leave home anyway. So I'll have to be a father to you as well as your colonel and keep you out of trouble." He later appointed McCormick his mounted orderly, mainly, it seems, so that he could keep an eye on him. It was the gesture of a man who had once lied about his age to get into the Army himself.

Over the next few days the troops were issued their uniforms and equipment. Lord Strathcona had written to Steele to spare no expense in providing for the efficiency of the regiment and the comfort of the men, and Steele had taken him at his word. His western background showed in the way he outfitted the corps with high-horned ranch saddles, lassoes, and a revolver for each man in addition to his Lee-Enfield rifle. Their standard headgear was the stiff-brimmed Stetson hat that Steele had been instrumental in introducing into the Mounted Police.

He put the men to work on a stiff regimen of military training. They were sufficiently well drilled to parade before Governor-General Lord Minto early in March. His lordship was not impressed. He wrote of "the useless ruffians, the halt, the lame and the blind that were piled into Strathcona's Horse." It was hardly the sort of regiment to please an English aristocrat.

They were given tumultuous send-offs in Ottawa, Montreal, and Halifax, from which they embarked for Cape Town on March 17 aboard the Elder Dempster Line's S.S. *Monterey*. Lord Strathcona had chartered the vessel to carry his regiment. Five hundred forty men and 599 horses sailed. It was a miserable voyage: the men of the prairies had never experienced anything quite as horrible as seasickness. An epidemic of pneumonia broke out among the horses, taking the lives of 176 of them. Day after day working parties dumped the carcasses of the animals overboard to waiting sharks attracted by the feast of horseflesh. One trooper engaged in this distasteful duty remarked, "I guess we'll be Strathcona's Foot by the time we get to South Africa."

Steele employed the time on board to give the men weapons training, drill them hard, and tighten up on discipline. Those who had not served with him before got to know the kind of commanding officer he was: a strict disciplinarian who was also quick to forgive. He rode his officers hard; he expected a great deal from them, and he got it. By the time the ship anchored outside of Cape Town on April 10, he was able to congratulate the regiment warmly on its shipboard conduct. As for training, "We could have left for the front at once."

Instead of orders to go to the front, however, he received a cryptic message from Lord Roberts of Kandahar, the field marshal commanding in South Africa: "Bloemfontein. The officer commanding Strathcona's Horse not to be disappointed at being brought here. There is special work for his corps to do for which I have specially selected it." Steele moved his troops into Green Point Camp near Cape Town for further training and manoeuvres. Living under canvas in rainy weather, he waited word from Bobs, as Roberts was called in the British Army, concerning what the Strathconas' "special work" might be.

The answer came after six weeks in the form of top secret sealed orders. Steele was to lead a daring long-range penetration mission deep behind enemy lines. The object was to shorten the war by severing the landlocked Boer republics' only supply line from the outside world, the railway between Pretoria in the Transvaal and Delagoa Bay in Portuguese East Africa (Mozambique).

A key bridge at Komatipoort on the Transvaal side of the border with the Portuguese colony could be reached without violating Portuguese territory via a back-door route through Tongaland and Swaziland. This would, however, entail an extremely hard march of more than two hundred miles as the crow flies over unmapped mountainous terrain. Strathcona's Horse was ordered to move over the mountains to attack the garrison guarding the bridge. Royal Engineers officers attached to them would blow it up.

The Strathconas were to move on the objective in two columns. The first, a force of two hundred under Steele, was to make a secret amphibious landing at Kosi Bay on the coast of Tongaland and cross the rugged Lebomo Mountains on foot, with pack horses carrying its supplies. After Steele's column had dealt with the Komatipoort garrison and destroyed the bridge, the second column, under Major Belcher, was to march over the mountains of Zululand and Swaziland to link up with Steele's party and hold the position against the inevitable Boer counterattack. Belcher was to bring with him sufficient supplies to hold out for several weeks.

Steele's detachment sailed on the *Makool* from Cape Town on May 28. The food served on board to the troops was atrocious. One trooper's diary records: "The colonel ordered a better supply of grub, paying for it himself." They reached Kosi Bay on June 2, to be met there by two British cruisers sent to assist in and cover the landing. Steele went over the preparations for the march with Roger Casement, the British agent who had conceived the operation and who would act as his liaison with the natives.* They were to land on receiving a signal from an agent on the beach who would act as their guide.

On the afternoon of Sunday, May 3, naval parties prepared to string hawsers from the ship to the beach and bring surfboats alongside to carry the equipment and provisions. Steele had his men fitted out with life jackets; they were to swim the pack horses ashore. The animals were strapped up to be lowered into the water. He and Casement scanned the beach, looking for the signal

---

* Later elected to Parliament and knighted, Roger Casement was executed for high treason in 1916 after he had landed in Ireland from a German submarine with the intention of starting an uprising against the British government.

from the guide, but no one appeared. Instead there was an exchange of signals with a naval ship that had just steamed in from the Portuguese East African port of Lourenço Marques: The operation was off.

According to British intelligence, the Boers had learned about the raid and sent a thousand men to ambush Steele's party. It was later learned that the ambush story was false, probably planted by the Boers to get the expedition called off. Steele and his men sailed back down the coast to Durban, where he was apprised of another change of plans. The raid on the bridge was to proceed, but this time it was to be launched by the entire Strathcona's Horse moving on horseback over the mountains of Zululand and Swaziland. They were all set to strike out from their jumping-off point of Eshowe in Zululand on the evening of June 12 when these orders were also cancelled. Misled by false intelligence, the high command had decided once and for all to abandon the operation. The Strathconas were to join General Sir Redvers Buller's Natal Field Force with all possible speed.

They made a fast forced march that much impressed the English generals to reach Buller's main force at Zandspruit on the Natal-Transvaal border on the evening of June 20. It was midnight before they settled down, but they were up at dawn to advance into the Transvaal as part of Major General Lord Dundonald's 3rd Mounted Brigade. A dashing guards officer of forty-two, the twelfth earl of Dundonald was Steele's kind of leader. He believed in mobility and innovation, having invented a light machine gun, a light ambulance, and a light gun carriage drawn by a single horse. In this respect he was the opposite of his top commander, Sir Redvers Buller, who had been superseded as commander in chief by the sixty-seven-year-old Lord Roberts after a succession of British defeats a year earlier. Buller was a hesitant and slow-moving general who could never seem to keep up with the mercurial Boers. Steele, however, liked the personable Buller, as did most of the rank-and-file soldiers. Buller visited the Strathconas on the first day on their march and had a cordial chat with the Canadian colonel about the Red River expedition on which they had both served thirty years before.

The mounted brigade was the spearhead of the 2nd Division, which was advancing along the Natal Railway towards Johannesburg. On June 22 the Strathconas led the way into the large railway centre of Standerton, where the Boers were forced to leave 18 locomotives and 148 railway cars behind. The Canadians were unopposed, but they arrived in time to see a railway bridge blown up by the Boers as they retreated. Buller characteristically called a long halt in the town.

It was not until July 1, 1900, that the Strathconas finally came into contact with the enemy. The Boers fired on them from a hill and from two farmhouses flying white flags. Four Boers were killed, and the rest retreated in the sharp fire fight that followed, but a young cowhand from Pincher Creek had been shot dead and a captain and another private taken prisoner. The engagement was a reminder of the regiment's inexperience. The captured men apparently mistook a party of Boers for friendly troops.

From that day on Steele's men were almost continually in action as they served as scouts and flank guards for Dundonald's column. It was mainly a war of exchanging rifle fire with snipers of the Boer rear guard. The regiment suffered fifteen casualties, three of them fatal, in its first week at the front. That the casualties were not higher was thanks to Steele's constant mother-henning of his brave but sometimes reckless troopers. In his orders of the day he urged them not to be quite so daring. He pointed out the special perils of scouting: "The regt. is cautioned when scouting against crowning the hills too suddenly. It should be done with great care."

Now that men's lives were in danger, he would brook no slackness. He demoted incompetent NCOs and tongue-lashed officers for drifting out of touch while on patrol. He tightened up on discipline generally, once sentencing a trooper to fourteen days' field punishment for stealing some jam. He banned fires on bivouac whenever possible; a cup of tea, he declared, was not worth the risk of death or injury from sniping or shelling. When the Strathconas did come under a barrage from the skilful German-trained Boer artillery, he and Belcher set an example of coolness by retiring behind an anthill and lighting up their pipes.

Dundonald came to think so highly of Steele that he chose him over several more senior regular officers to lead the column when he was away at conferences. The Boers kept threatening the British flanks, involving the brigade in a running cat-and-mouse battle up and down the railway line. In their hot pursuit of the Boers the Strathconas often ran far ahead of their supply wagons, having to camp without food and blankets. Steele was in the saddle from dawn to dark, showing the stamina of a man half his age.

In many ways the Boer War ushered in the twentieth-century style of dirty warfare. The old chivalrous usages were abandoned. The British burned down farms, destroyed crops, and herded women and children into concentration camps. The Boers sometimes employed the white flag as a tactical weapon. Sergeant Parker—the same Parker who had been refused a commission because of his past record—was shot dead at point-blank range as he approached a party of Boers to accept their surrender. A private with him was fatally wounded. The Strathconas learned to deploy in skirmishing order when they approached a farmhouse flying a white flag.

For a week in August the regiment formed the advance guard of Dundonald's column. In this capacity it began to run into major enemy concentrations, complete with heavy guns. Men of Strathcona's Horse were the first to enter Amersfoort after a battle with an entrenched Boer commando unit in the hills nearby. On the ninth they advanced through heavy fire towards Ermelo. Their one-pounder pom-pom gun went into action, killing four of the enemy in a brief engagement. The Canadian horsemen stormed a Boer trench, putting its occupants to flight and taking several prisoners. The next day they entered the town unopposed.

"Tuesday [August 14, 1900] was another interesting day for the regiment," Steele wrote to Lord Strathcona. "About noon Lord Dundonald ordered me to send a squadron and one troop of 'A' [squadron] to go forward and search the town of Carolina. I sent Major Belcher in command. He was fired upon from stone walls close to the town. He advanced the men in skirmishing order, drove the enemy out of position and through the town. The place was held long enough to allow the Provost Marshal to complete the work of searching. The contents of the magazine were blown up before leaving, and a lot of ammunition and two prisoners taken. Three of the men on the right flank arrived in the town after the squadron had withdrawn and were forced to stay there owing to the darkness and the condition of their horses. They pretended to the inhabitants, who were mostly hostile, that they were part of a big force which had surrounded the town. Before leaving in the morning they succeeded in getting a lot of valuable information as to the whereabouts of the enemy, the number of guns in their possession, etc. Our force had been fired upon to cover the withdrawal of a number of wagons belonging to General Prinsloo's train. They learned that a field cornet [a high-ranking Boer officer] had been shot by our men in the afternoon affair."

Towards the end of August the tide of battle had turned in favour of the British, or so it seemed. The main Boer cities had fallen, and besieged British forces in several towns had been relieved. Roberts and Buller worked out a plan to crush the army of the Transvaal commander in chief, General Louis Botha. This was to take the form of a giant pincer movement in the rugged mountains north of the Delagoa Bay railway line.

On the twenty-third the Strathconas took part in the Battle of Bergandahl Farm, from which they miraculously emerged without losses. The battle was indecisive in the tactical sense—most of the Boers slipped through the British cordon—but the proximity of the enemy caused President Paul Kruger of the Transvaal to leave for exile in Holland via Delagoa Bay. Botha fell back towards the mountain stronghold of Lydenburg. He entrenched his troops along a valley, blocking the way.

The Strathconas' role in the next phase of the campaign was to screen the flanks of the advancing Natal Field Force. It was dangerous duty, taking a toll of six wounded and one killed. On August 26, during the attack of Buller's army on Machadorp, the regiment occupied six abandoned Boer trenches and engaged in a sniping duel with the enemy that went on from dawn to 5:00 P.M., when Lord Dundonald sent field and machine guns to their assistance. The Strathconas then withdrew under heavy fire.

It was before Machadorp that Steele came within a few feet of death from an artillery blast. He had ridden up a hill to consult with Dundonald's brigade major, W. R. Birdwood (later to become a field marshal). Birdwood had just finished saying, "Well, colonel, looks like we'll have some fun today," when a Boer shell burst between them. Birdwood was seriously wounded and his horse's head blown off.

On the twenty-eighth a squadron of Strathconas crossed a

mountain and carried the town of Machadorp in the face of heavy artillery fire. Another party raced for the village of Helvetia, arriving minutes behind a patrol from the cavalry division commanded by another future field marshal, Colonel John French.

On September 3 the regiment returned to guarding the right flank of Buller's army. On the march Steele noticed that no piquets had been posted on the high ridge overlooking the Crocodile Valley, through which the main body must pass. It was an example of the kind of negligence that cost the British Army thousands of unnecessary casualties in South Africa. Steele sent a scouting party under Lieutenant Leckie to find out whether the Boers had occupied the heights.

Leckie went up on horseback and sent Sergeant Logan and four men along the ridge to look for signs of enemy activity. The sergeant's party ran into more than a hundred Boers. They blasted one Canadian out of the saddle and surrounded the other four, who had dismounted. The Boers called on them to surrender, but they fired back; they found just enough cover to make a stand. Their bodies were found the next day riddled with bullets; all their ammunition had been expended. Seventeen dead Boers were scattered around the perimeter of the little hollow where they had fought to the last round.

Logan and the others were still holding out when Leckie and the rest of his men also came under fire from the large Boer party. Steele saw what was happening and sent two troops of riders to their relief. They got into a prolonged sniping duel as they attempted to work their way around the Boers, causing them to abandon the ridge in the evening. In the meantime Sergeant John Brothers, the Strathcona who had become rich digging gold in the Klondike, went off with a private to scout the situation in the direction taken by Sergeant Logan. The two became entangled with the Boers, accounting for six enemy dead with their revolvers before they were killed themselves.

Botha continued to fall back on Lydenburg in the days that followed, keeping Buller's army at a distance with long-range gunfire. But another large British force threatened his flank, and he had to give ground. The Strathconas were among the first troops to enter Lydenburg when it was evacuated on September 6. Botha attempted to slip away to the northeast, with Dundonald's mounted brigade hot on the trail behind him. On September 9 a squadron of Strathconas swept down a hill to attack the retreating Boer column, almost capturing one of the enemy's famous Long Tom guns, but they were out of range of the British artillery and had to disengage for lack of support. Botha continued to flee with most of his forces. After moving through the mountains as far as a lonely Boer redoubt called Pilgrim's Rest, Steele and his men were ordered back to Machadorp on October 8.

At this juncture it appeared that the war was virtually over. They camped and relaxed. Visitors appeared; one evening Rudyard Kipling, in his semiofficial capacity as a literary cheerleader for the war, had dinner with Steele and his officers in Steele's tent. Sir Redvers Buller left for England, pausing on the way to tell the assembled regiment, "I have never served with a nobler, braver or more serviceable body of men." Steele was intensely proud of his troops, with good reason. Word had arrived that one of them, Sergeant Arthur Richardson, had been awarded a Victoria Cross for his valour in rescuing a wounded comrade under fire in a battle fought in July by thirty-eight Strathconas attached to another unit. It was the first Victoria Cross to be won by a Canadian in South Africa and only the second ever to be awarded to a Canadian. It added to Steele's satisfaction that Richardson was a member of the North-West Mounted Police.

The regiment moved into a rest area near Pretoria after turning its horses over to Colonel French's cavalry. Steele made plans to take his men home. Then the brilliant Orange Free State general, Christiaan De Wet, showed that the war was very far from over. He turned on the British column that was pursuing him in the southern Transvaal and surrounded it. It was like a lion driving a hunter up a tree.

Steele had been in Pretoria only a few days, enjoying the luxury of the Grand Hotel, when Lord Roberts ordered him to prepare the regiment for further action. A few days later the chief of staff, Lord Kitchener, called Steele to his office and gave him orders to march. Strathcona's Horse was to join a flying column to go to the relief of the surrounded British force of Major General George Barton. They left that day, linking up with a relief force that included the Essex Regiment, half of the Dublin Fusiliers, and two Royal Artillery gun crews. The Strathconas were given the task of screening the column. It was expected to meet heavy resistance in the hills on the way.

They marched in relentless drenching rain and came under gun and rifle fire from the surrounding heights on several occasions. But they arrived outside of Frederickstaad in the early hours of the twenty-fifth, just at the moment when De Wet was putting in an attack on Barton's exhausted troops. They swung into battle, punching through the Boer cordon. But the wily Boer general and his commandos slipped away.

Over the next few days the Canadians cleared the town of Frederickstaad, taking twelve prisoners in a sudden night attack. Then they struck out across the veldt in pursuit of De Wet's main force. On November 10 Steele succeeded in surrounding a large part of the retreating Boer convoy. There was a hot exchange of fire as the Strathconas tried to pin the Boers down long enough for Barton's infantry and artillery to arrive. It failed to get there on time; the Boers burst away, but they were forced to leave without their food supply of 1,200 sheep and at least 600 head of cattle. The following day Steele received a message from General Barton: "I cannot speak too highly of the practical and effective way in which the duty assigned to you and your splendid corps was carried out yesterday, and I have specially mentioned this in my report to the Field Marshal Commanding-in-Chief. I only regret that circumstances prevented my supporting your movements by advancing with the main body. The capture of the stock is most satisfactory. I regret the casualty of one man missing and one wounded." The Strathconas added to their laurels a few days later by capturing forty Boers.

While Steele was at Frederickstaad, Major General Robert Baden-Powell, the hero of the seige of Mafeking, sought him out with an interesting proposition. The future founder of the Boy Scout movement was engaged in organizing the South African Constabulary to keep order in the aftermath of the war; he wanted to model this force on the North-West Mounted Police. He asked Steele if he would consider commanding the S.A.C. in the northern Transvaal. Steele replied that he would join if Sir Wilfrid Laurier would permit him to be seconded from the N.W.M.P. to the S.A.C. after his service with Strathcona's Horse was complete.

On the trail of De Wet Steele got ptomaine poisoning, probably from eating tainted bully beef. He had to be put in an ambulance on the return march to the quiet area of Potchefstroom; he was very ill indeed. His batman, the son of Jack Kerr, the man who was stabbed in the barracks room in Fort Garry so many years before, arranged to hire a room for him at Potchefstroom in the home of a woman whose husband was an officer serving in a Boer commando unit. "I shall never forget her kindness and that of her daughters, whose husbands were also in the field," Steele wrote in his memoirs. "I have never felt worse in my life; but there was nothing that those kind people could do that was left undone to bring me back to health." After a two-week convalescence in which he lost some thirty pounds, Steele was glad enough to grant young Kerr leave to marry a local Boer girl.

He had scarcely recovered when the Strathconas were put back on the trail of De Wet, who had since defeated the British garrison at Dewetsdorp, taking 490 prisoners. De Wet was being chased through the rocky country of the Orange Free State, always keeping one jump ahead of his pursuers and occasionally lashing back with an unexpected attack. On November 29 Steele's regiment joined the "second de Wet hunt" at Bethulie, on the southern border of the Free State. There they became part of a mobile column commanded by Major General Charles Knox, which was supposed to drive De Wet's commandos north against a chain of fixed fortifications. The hard-riding Canadians soon closed in on the enemy.

An entry from their battle diary conveys the character of that gruelling and frustrating campaign: "Marched 4:30 a.m. Williams' column. . . . At 5:30 Williams came in contact with the enemy who was reported to be 13 miles, but in reality was only 3. The usual blundering intelligence. The guns and Mounted Infantry came under rifle fire. Regiment ordered to move along the enemy's right, his left as he retreated, and bring him to a stand. His convoy could be seen about 4 miles off passing through a nek [pass] between high rocky kopjes [hills]. Regiment advanced as fast as possible at least 2 miles in advance of the column and came in contact with the enemy at Meluvtia Farm, severe fire opened upon us which we returned briskly. Bullets whistled through us but we had our usual luck. O.C.* withdrew the reserve and pushed along the enemy's flank turning the right and came into position, which brought the whole of his convoy, and right, under our fire. He was now in such a position that if our guns were pushed forward the whole of his transport animals could have been destroyed and his column headed off. The C.O. sent a message back for a gun or guns. The general would not send them, being under the impression they were needed elsewhere."

Time and time again Steele's troops rode down De Wet, and time and time again the lugubrious infantry and artillery failed to take advantage of the contact. They moved north in a zigzag pattern up the rocky spine of the Orange Free State. This was their hardest campaign yet. Reveille was at 3:00 A.M., rations were short, horses tired, the weather wet and bitterly cold after sundown. De Wet's rear guard sniped at them daily. But they kept up the pressure, forcing the Boers to leave a tribute of sorely missed guns, stores, and ammunition behind.

The military skills of the Mounties and cowboys of a few months before had been sharpened to a fine edge by continual combat. An entry in the regimental battle diary about a withdrawal in the face of a Boer counterattack shows a picture of precision and poise: "Threw two troops across the bridge of the Vet River. . . . The pom pom [a small artillery piece] did excellent work here, getting the enemy's range at once with ease. The enemy's fire very hot, it is marvellous that we got off so lightly with bullets whistling through our ranks. Before arriving at the bridge the supports commenced to dismount and to open fire on the enemy, but the O.C. would not permit it, the rear being forced to hold their ground until the supports passed the bridge at a rapid pace. The support and pom pom from the other side of the river opened a heavy fire on the enemy as soon as our firing line unmasked them; as they dashed over the bridge all officers retired last to encourage the men. Two troops and the pom pom were left to hold the bridge while the remainder resumed the march. The enemy lost considerably, and were in dread of the rifle and pom pom fire."

By this time Strathcona's Horse had become something of a

---

* Steele; he is variously referred to as "O.C." and "C.O." in regimental diaries.

legend. It was said that they exacted six Boer casualties for every one of their own. "Of all the regiments, British or Colonial, regular or irregular, Strathcona's Horse among the Boers were the most dreaded, and, strange to say, the most respected," wrote a London *Daily Express* correspondent. Tales were told of their ferocity. They were said to have lynched Boer prisoners, and when a British staff officer remonstrated, they offered to lynch him, too. The Boers called them the "Big Stirrups"; the British called them "The Headhunters." Steele was referred to in the British press as "Fighting Sam," and "the world's greatest scout."

The Strathconas' penchant for scrapping with the Boers at close quarters did not always endear them to their British general officers. The generals regarded the proper function of scouts as finding the enemy and sending back word so that superior forces could move up to ensure victory. This was all very well in theory, but the generals themselves usually reacted so slowly that the Boers would have got away scot-free if the Strathconas had not opened fire. Often they came too close to the enemy to avoid clashes. In one such case in December 1900 two troopers crested a hill and came face to face with eight Boers who had climbed up the other side of it. They returned the Boer's rifle fire with their revolvers. One Canadian was killed and the other badly wounded. They killed three and wounded two Boers.

The second De Wet hunt lasted five weeks, carrying the regiment from the far south to the far north of the Orange Free State. Steele noted that they had not paused long enough in all that time for a change of underwear. After De Wet had slipped through the fixed defences to the north, Steele reminded the high command by mail that the Strathconas were coming close to the end of their one-year term of service. He pointed out that many of them were absent from their ranches and farms at considerable expense.

He received no reply to this, so he followed it up with a telegram. Early in January, their uniforms in tatters and their horses on their last legs, they got word to move to another front.

The regimental diary recorded: "Received orders to entrain for Blandsfontein but decided not to go until it is decided what action is to be taken in regard to the letter submitted to headquarters by the O.C. pointing out the terms of service and the strong desire on the part of the men owing to urgent private and other important reasons to return to Canada." This minor mutiny had the desired effect. Kitchener, who had succeeded Roberts as commander in chief, ordered the regiment home the same day.

Baden-Powell called on Steele before their departure to complete arrangements for him to join the South African Constabulary. Kitchener inspected the regiment, telling them that they would be pleasantly surprised if they knew how many generals all over the country had asked for Strathcona's Horse. Lord Strathcona had arranged for them to return to Canada via England. They sailed from Cape Town on January 21 after being outfitted with new uniforms to replace the clothing worn ragged in their hard campaigning. Steele was notified that he was to be made a Companion of the Order of the Bath and a member of the Victorian Order, Fourth Class. He was to receive the latter honour in a parade before the Queen in London. Steele looked forward to at last seeing the sovereign in whose name he had served in so many places, but Queen Victoria died the day after they embarked.

"RETURNING HEROS. ARRIVAL OF STRATHCONA'S HORSE IN LONDON," read the headline in the Manchester *Courier*. On February 15 Steele paraded them before a host of dignitaries and a cheering crowd of onlookers inside the grounds of Buckingham Palace, which he found rather cramped. There the new king, Edward VII, presented each man with the South African War Medal—they were the first troops to receive this award—and gave the regiment its battle colours. Then he pinned the Victorian Order on Steele's chest. The King and the Canadian colonel exchanged complimentary speeches, Steele called for "three hearty Canadian cheers," and they marched back to Kensington Palace through streets lined with adoring Londoners. The event was covered in glowing terms and at great length in the British press.

For the next few days Sam Steele was the toast of London. Newspapers and magazines vied for interviews with the colourful man who so perfectly fitted the picture of the imperial hero of the day. The journalists, however, found him frustratingly self-effacing. The most he would say to the suggestion that the Strathconas had beaten the Boers at their own game was, "Well, I don't think they ever got one of our horses." His reticence did not stop the press from singing his praises. Some reporters turned to such sources as Lord Dundonald and General Strange, then living near London, to fill out their accounts of what a great man Sam Steele was. Others made up stories about Fighting Sam from whole cloth. The *Daily Mail* wrote: "Thirty years ago in the remote North West men already swore by Sam Steele and told the stranger that Steele was 'chock full of sand,' a westernism for a man who knows no fear." The problem of having such an uncommunicative hero to celebrate was overcome by one writer who gushed: "Colonel Steele is the perfect frontiersman—a pioneer, and therefore a man of initiative; he is thoughtful and reflective because he deals so much with Nature, the great educator." There was a touch of asperity at Steele's reticence in the words of another: "Colonel Steele never has anything to say about himself."

Enjoying the luxury of the Royal Palace Hotel in Kensington, Steele was propelled into a round of social engagements. He lunched with Princess Louise and the duke of Argyll; he dined with Lord Roberts, the lord mayor of London, Winston Churchill, and Joseph Chamberlain, who was then the most powerful politician in the land. At a dinner held by the duke and duchess of Abercorn he was delighted when a major general told him that the admirable bearing of the men of the Strathconas was "the talk of all the clubs." Steele attended so many functions that he was rarely in bed before 3:00 A.M. He enjoyed it all hugely, especially when he got a chance to show off his trim, sun-baked troopers. At a "magnificent banquet, modestly called a luncheon" given for the entire regiment by Lord Strathcona, he looked down at the rows of his men seated at the tables. "I felt that any country would be proud of them," he recalled.

They sailed from Liverpool on February 26 after that city had tendered them a gala civic reception and luncheon. The weather was foul in the North Atlantic; when their ship docked at Halifax on March 9, it was six days overdue. Anxious relatives and friends, "including my dear wife," rushed aboard as soon as the gangways were lowered. The trip to Montreal on a special train the next day was a triumphal progress, with cheering crowds at every station on the way. A huge throng awaited them at Montreal's Bonaventure Station. "Loud cheers were raised, Colonel Steele being greeted with especial heartiness," said the Reuters news agency account of the event.

In interviews with Canadian newspapers Steele lost no time in correcting earlier reports that the Strathconas had misbehaved in South Africa. He insisted that their conduct had been perfect; this was subsequently confirmed by Lord Esher's commission on the South African war. The commission, called to investigate the disappointing British performance in the conflict, also passed judgment on Steele personally. "There was no better commander than the rough-riding colonel from Canada," its report declared.

27: BACK TO AFRICA

Times had changed in the Mounted Police in the year that Steele had been away from Canada. Lawrence Herchmer was no longer commissioner; true to form, that difficult man had alienated both his junior and senior officers in South Africa and had been relieved of his military command. He then stormed back to Ottawa to fight his ouster on the political level. His campaign for reinstatement so exasperated Sir Wilfrid Laurier that the prime minister fired him from the police commissionership as well.

Herchmer was succeeded in August 1900 by Aylesworth Bowen Perry, whose credentials included membership in an extremely prominent Canadian family. "There has been less political influence and interference in advancing Major Perry than is usual on such occasions," commented the *Canadian Magazine*. But that astringent inside observer of the force, Superintendent Burton Deane, knew better. "On his return to Canada [Herchmer] found that his subordinate had served him in the same manner as he had Colonel Irvine, and had gained the Commissionership of the Mounted Police by the exercise of political influence," Deane wrote. It was commonly believed, even by Perry himself, that he had been appointed to preside over the disbandment of the force as soon as provincial status was granted to Alberta and Saskatchewan, which would form their own provincial police.

In any case the new order held no place for Sam Steele, who was qualified to head the force in every respect but his politics. His application to Prime Minister Laurier for a five-year leave of absence from the N.W.M.P. struck a plaintive note. He said that his appointment in the South African Constabulary as a full colonel would allow him to save a little money since at the moment he had "no prospects" in Canada. Steele was by far the best-known and most popular officer in the force, and the government had suffered political embarrassment in bypassing him. It was perhaps with some relief that Laurier let him go.

He arrived back in South Africa in June 1901 to find the war that everyone had expected to end months earlier still proceeding briskly. Only a few days before a Boer commando unit had routed a superior British force at Vlakfontein. The South African Constabulary, with an authorized strength of 10,000 (including 1,500 newly arrived Canadians) was to be employed as a military formation until the hostilities ended. Baden-Powell, who had worked himself into a state of exhaustion, was on sick leave in England. Steele was ordered to report directly to Lord Kitchener, the military commander in chief.

The man known as "K" instructed him to push a S.A.C. force of about 600 men along the Rustenburg road near Pretoria to clear the country of Boer guerillas. The sector assigned to Steele was a favourite resort of Boers operating against the British lines of communications in small, hard-hitting bands. They raided army supply columns and periodically blew up sections of the Pretoria-Pietersburg railway line. Kitchener's technique for dealing with such raiders was to have British forces sally forth from fixed fortifications and sweep an area until all the Boers in it were killed or captured. It was a good plan in theory; in fact the Boers more often than not were able to slip past his fortifications and live to fight another day.

Steele established a command post on a mountaintop northwest of Pretoria to direct the operations of a chain of blockhouses manned by his troops over a thirty-mile area. He communicated with them by heliograph and bull's-eye lamp. They commenced to clear the country of Boers. It was a ponderous and tiresome form of warfare. During the next few months, however, they accounted for their share of the S.A.C.'s record of ninety-three Boers killed, 117 wounded, and 115 captured in this phase of the South African campaign.

The front eventually quieted down enough for him to move to Pretoria and there establish the permanent headquarters for his B

Division. Kitchener arranged for him to use the pleasant, modest residence of exiled Transvaal President Paul Kruger on Church Street as his officers' quarters and set up his divisional office in Kruger's son-in-law's house next door. Baden-Powell came back from England at the end of 1901. He and Steele worked together on plans to convert the S.A.C. from a military to a police and peace-keeping organization. Steele set out to train the officers and recruits along the lines of the N.W.M.P.

The men were very much like the early Mounties: well-educated young fellows with a taste for adventure and some military experience, willing and able to take hardship. They would have to operate in the same way as their Canadian counterparts, scattered about in small outposts and performing a variety of duties beyond the scope of normal police work. As in the Mounties, every man would have to take on responsibilities far beyond those imposed on a conventional police constable. Steele drew on his experience to train them in a broad array of duties that they might be called upon to perform. He gave them a taste of standard police work by having them do a stint with the Pretoria police department. He had them instructed in the Afrikaans language, making them communicate in it among themselves as part of their daily routine. In a short time he had a body of men under his command who could very well have been North-West Mounted Policemen. They even looked like Mounties in their flat-brimmed Stetson hats.*

In the meantime Kitchener continued to bludgeon and starve the Boers into submission. He used strong mobile forces to drive the remaining commandos into the teeth of a vast system of blockhouses crisscrossing the land. He ordered crops and farm-houses burned and had the wives and children of Boer soldiers imprisoned in concentration camps. Unable to sustain themselves any longer, the Boers sued for peace in April 1902.

Late in May they surrendered their armies and relinquished their independence in return for certain guarantees from the British. Among these was that they would be protected from the Kaffirs (Bantu) who had acquired arms during the war either from their British allies or from looting. The natives had lately

---

* When Baden-Powell formed the Boy Scouts a few years later, he modelled the uniform on that of the S.A.C.

massacred fifty-six Boer burghers. The Boers, who would be
disarmed as part of the peace settlement, had good reason to fear
that the Kaffirs would try to wipe them out in their defenceless
state.

Kitchener's policy of devastation and depopulation had ravaged
the landscape and embittered the Boer population. The difficult
and sensitive work of rehabilitation would fall mainly on the
S.A.C. Steele was to have its most important divisional command,
that of the northern Transvaal. Baden-Powell ran over some of
the potential sources of trouble with him. The Boers themselves
were bitterly divided between those who had surrendered during
the war and those who had fought to the finish. The natives were
eager to loot all they could. "White adventurers and bad characters of various nationalities"—renegades—were taking advantage
of the unsettled conditions to grab land and steal livestock. To
add to all this, starvation threatened. A plague of locusts was
steadily destroying the scant crops that had survived the war.

Steele's division was brought up to its full strength of one thousand. Among them were one troop of one hundred Canadian cowboys and ex-Mounted Policemen, one hundred Australian bush
rangers, and one hundred young Boers who had fought against the
British throughout the war. They took to the field to "cover the
whole face of the country," as Baden-Powell put it, setting up
outposts placed so that every farm in the whole vast district could
be visited at least once a week.

Steele's command contained a larger Kaffir population than the
rest of the former republics put together. Some three hundred
thousand natives were scattered among the jungles, mountains,
and plains. Tens of thousands of them possessed firearms in addition to their traditional weapons. They presented a clear menace
to the defenceless Boer burghers and their families returning to
their vacant farms on the lonely veldt.

Steele recommended that all the Kaffirs be disarmed and that
the government compensate them for their weapons. They were
in a dangerous frame of mind. He had difficulty in explaining to
the chiefs he met that the Boers were no longer the enemy. Now
that the Boers had been beaten, the natives reasoned, the country
belonged to them. They assumed that the victorious British
would at least proceed to punish the vanquished. They could not

see why the Boers should not remain fair game or why their farms should not be looted as a natural sequel to the war.

As a dedicated empire builder with the common mentality of his kind, Steele stood squarely on the side of white supremacy. "I gave orders to my troop commanders and senior captains that they were to insist on the natives treating the Dutch with respect," he wrote. He drew unfavourable comparisons between the Kaffirs and the Canadian Indians; he considered the Africans lazy, untruthful, and difficult to manage. Yet his attitude was ambivalent: once when he came across a renegade Englishman flogging a native, he strode forward and angrily swept the whip out of the man's hand.

He was duly appreciative of the services of the S.A.C.'s black constables in keeping order among the natives. Every outpost had at least one of these men on the strength. Most of them were Zulus, whose reputation for courage and ferocity made them objects of respect among the other Kaffirs. They worked wonders during the tense period when the Kaffirs were ready to go out gunning for the Boers.

Steele saw that it was important for the S.A.C. to win over both the Boers and the Kaffirs. He was ruthless in disposing of bad characters in the ranks. In the rest he tried to instil a code of unexceptionable behaviour to back up their authority as he had in the Mounted Police, and he succeeded. "The natives, like the Boers, respected the constabulary, whose record—in the important matter of the treatment of the women, for example—was absolutely clean," he said in a later interview. "All the members behaved like true gentlemen, and the respect felt for them greatly added to their efficiency."

His expertise in frontier police work came into play shortly after the armistice. A gold rush began to surge into the Lataba hills. "Colonel Steele . . . forestalled this rush by establishing a police post on the spot, with a registration office and rules drawn up for regulating the rush when it came a few days later," Baden-Powell wrote. "Shortly afterwards came an urgent request from the high commissioner that we were to send police to the spot; and when it was found that we had already made all arrangements in anticipation and on a businesslike footing, we received the very cordial thanks of the mining department."

It was, alas, all too rare that the S.A.C. received any sort of rec-

ognition from the colonial bureaucrats who now ruled South
Africa. Steele's recommendation that the natives be disarmed lan-
guished in a pigeonhole while they murdered and robbed the
whites. Fearing a bloodbath at any time, he appealed to Baden-
Powell to put pressure on the government to move on this matter.
The Kaffirs were finally disarmed in September 1902; the men of
the S.A.C. took their weapons and paid them off in a show of tact
that would have done credit to North-West Mounted Policemen.
Almost twenty thousand firearms were surrendered to Steele's division alone.

The delay concerning the disarming recommendation was only
the first of the sore points to erupt in Steele's relations with the
fussy colonial administration. He sought in vain to have senior
constabulary officers appointed justices of the peace to enable
them to try petty offences on the spot. Under the system then in
effect policemen had to escort prisoners and witnesses as far as
sixty miles to appear before one of the district's eight magistrates.
Steele and Baden-Powell got together to press his recommendation on the Colonial Law Department. The system was ul-
timately changed, but it cost him a great deal of time and trouble
to win his point.

The irritations proliferated in the African sun. The district
magistrates acted as if they ran the police force. This raised the
hackles of officers like Captains Scarth and Jarvis who had come
from the N.W.M.P. and were accustomed to Canadian ways. Dis-
eased cattle imported from Portuguese East Africa and Rhodesia
were causing terrible epidemics. Steele had his own men do the
rounds of Boer farmers to show them how to detect the diseases
by taking blood smears and the like. But when his border patrols
tried to stop cattle from entering the Transvaal they were over-
ruled by civilian officials who cared only for the fact that the
relevant import permits were in order. Government Game Department officials objected to the presence of antismuggling patrols in game preserves. Others railed against the force's paramili-
tary character, claiming that it should be more responsive to civil
authority. For his part Steele filed a complaint that some civil servants were setting back the cause of reconciliation by treating the
Boers with contempt.

For all that, he was happy enough in South Africa, happier still when his wife and children came to join him in October 1902. They took a large, pleasant house in Pretoria, where his little son Harwood amused himself with a wooden sword and paper hat, drilling the Kaffir servants as a home guard. On the whole Steele found his work agreeable, and he was a past master at it. It took him out on the trail on horseback on frequent inspection tours, an activity he had always preferred to an office routine. Baden-Powell sometimes accompanied him. These two hearty men thoroughly enjoyed each other's company. Baden-Powell considered Steele a "great character" and relished the stories of the Canadian frontier that Steele told around the campfire. When the pair visited a jungle outpost manned by several ex-Mounties, Steele noted with approval that the Canadians found the S.A.C. chief "a man after their own hearts."

Early in 1903 he made a marathon tour of his division. He found it "as fine and respectable body of men as anyone could hope to command." He was pleased to see that, like the Mounted Police of old, they were regarded as a source of help and advice by local inhabitants. "They knew the country so well that they could take me over any by-path, trail or mountain to any place in the district," he proudly wrote. He talked personally to every man in his command and inspected everything down to the last horseshoe. He covered some 1,800 miles on horseback on this trip. For a man in his fifties he was in astonishing physical condition. He often had to pause to give a rest to younger officers who could not keep up with him on the trail.

The good work of the constabulary changed the attitude of the Boers from one of fearful suspicion to one of trust towards their former enemies. There was a warm welcome and coffee and cake for Steele at every farmhouse where he stopped. He also visited Kaffir villages and parleyed with their chiefs; they, too, were friendly towards the constabulary. In one he was cordially introduced to the chief's eleven wives, aged eighteen and up.

The work went on. A census was taken. Rumours had spread that this was a plot to get all the Boers in their homes at one time so that the natives could massacre them; some hid in the hills the evening the S.A.C. census takers came. Later another story spread of a native uprising. The S.A.C. knew the natives so well by then that Steele could instantly dismiss this as absurd.

By the end of 1904 the spirit of reconciliation had advanced to
the extent that a state funeral in all but name could be held in
Pretoria for ex-President Kruger, who had died in exile in Holland. Steele commanded an honour guard of two hundred men at
the event. Political autonomy for South Africa within the British
Empire was fast approaching. The S.A.C. prepared voters' lists.
Steele impatiently brushed aside reports that meetings of the Boer
Het Volk Party were being held in preparation for a rebellion. He
knew enough about the mood of the Boers to conclude that they
were merely getting ready for the coming election campaign.

Just as the country was settling down, however, a new source of
trouble emerged. The mine owners of Johannesburg, short of
labour, began to import coolies from China in June 1904. Some
35,000 Chinese had come to the Transvaal under three-year inden-
tures by the middle of 1905, and their numbers were constantly
rising. Among them were many who had served in the marauding
armies of Chinese warlords. They continued to practice their banditry in the South African mining region known as the Rand.

Even without their depredations the importation of the Chinese was bound to bring problems. Boers saw them as a threat to
white domination of South Africa, especially when combined with
the thousands of people from India who had settled there. English radicals, on the other hand, charged that the British government was sanctioning slave labour in South Africa. This became a
rallying cry for the opposition Liberal Party in Great Britain.
From his vantage point Steele wished that the "slaves" were a
good deal less free.

The camps where they were quartered were not fenced in, and
before long large parties of them deserted to hide out in the hills
and raid Boer farms and native villages. They murdered or
maimed anyone who resisted them, black or white. Steele found
that one cause of the problem was the Chinese passion for gambling: "It seemed to be a religion with them that money must be
obtained somehow to pay their gambling losses or death at the
hands of the winners would be their portion." Since the roll call
at the camps was once a week, it was an easy matter for them to
spend several days and nights out on raiding parties and reappear
in camp when the roll call was taken. This made them very
difficult to catch.

At first Steele treated the banditry as an ordinary police matter, but it was clear that these were no ordinary gangs of criminals. They moved in large and well-organized bodies and employed infantry tactics in their raids. They were uncannily stealthy, with the ability to slip into houses at night without arousing the occupants. Their methods were shockingly violent: They used dynamite stolen from the mines to blow up houses with families in them and cull the debris for loot. They broke the bones of people who put up a fight. By September 1905 Steele realized that special measures were needed to meet this special menace. He expanded the number of police outposts to intercept Chinese bands moving into the Boer farm country and to patrol the routes they were likely to take.

Panic flourished at the very thought of these terrifying marauders. The press sensationalized the situation, estimating the strength of the roving bands at several thousand. Towards the end of 1905 Boer families with homes on the fringes of the Rand began moving out of range, but the range of the bands expanded accordingly. When Steele's patrols picked up parties of Chinese in the far northern hills, their leaders explained innocently that they were returning to China by an overland route.

The political uproar raised by the importation of the Chinese helped to end the career of the British high commissioner in South Africa, Lord Milner. On his way back to England Milner praised the South African Constabulary: "So complete has been its success in preventing trouble that people, who do not know what I know, have quite forgotten the ever-present sources of trouble in a country peopled such as this." The Liberal Party swept into power in Great Britain in January 1906 after a campaign that dwelt heavily on the theme of Chinese slave labour in the Rand.

The political winds had also shifted in South Africa. Boer politicians were demanding that the S.A.C. be replaced by a locally recruited force. A royal commission was appointed to investigate it. The constabulary emerged from the enquiry with a better reputation than ever; still, soon afterwards its strength was drastically reduced.

Once again Steele found himself being played as a political pawn. His division was to be absorbed into another. He was

offered command of the police in the former Orange Free State
while the man he was to replace, unaware of this, was absent on
leave. He refused the appointment with some indignation. Instead he was made inspecting staff officer at the headquarters in
Johannesburg, effectively second in command of the constabulary.
He prepared to settle down in this unexciting position until he
was due to return to Canada early in 1906.

He was ready to leave when the new high commissioner, Lord
Selbourne, asked him to take on a special assignment. This was to
plan and take measures expressly aimed at stopping the Chinese
raids. He went to work on a set of recommendations that dealt
mainly with confining the Chinese in mining company compounds unless they had a pass for a specific purpose and destination. He proposed that a roll call be conducted daily and that the
compounds be organized so that everyone would have to file out
through the same gate. He said telephones should be installed between the compounds and police posts so that absences uncovered
in the roll calls could be promptly reported. The mine owners
balked at the expense of this program, and most of his recommendations were turned down.

He made the best of what he had, establishing a cordon of special outposts in a three-hundred-mile radius. Each was located
within about ten miles of a mine. This meant that raiders operating out of the mining compounds could not reach the farmhouse
area and return to the compounds without running the risk of in-
terception by round-the-clock patrols. The patrols frequently
scoured the fields, orchards, and plantations where the Chinese
concealed themselves. The S.A.C. kept in close touch with local
farmers and merchants, who reported the presence of any Chinese.

Steele further employed mobile troops to sweep the countryside
for the deserters from the mines who lived off the land. Most of
these rangers had been rounded up by the middle of March 1906.
Steele sent word to the Boer families who had fled from their
homes that they could return and would be protected. It was not
easy, however, to convince people that the menace had abated.
"The rural population, and even the Kaffirs, were in a state of
alarm that would not have existed in war time," he observed.

He knew this for a fact because he personally visited at least eight hundred farmhouses throughout the district, recording the names of the occupants, advising them on security precautions, and issuing firearms in cases of extraordinary vulnerability. He stayed overnight in police outposts, hitting the trail at five or six o'clock in the morning, sometimes riding as far as sixty miles a day. From these tours he concluded that every farmer should be properly armed, and that isolated homesteads should be guarded by S.A.C. men overnight.

The intensive policing had some effect, but there was no hope that the raids could be eliminated until tighter security measures were taken at the mining compounds. He estimated that at least 20 per cent of all the coolies were absent from the mines at any given time. And their numbers grew constantly with the postwar increase in mining production. Almost fifty thousand Chinese, all males, had been imported into the Rand by mid-1906.

The banditry persisted. There was a particularly gruesome incident on the outskirts of Johannesburg in which a large party of Chinese broke the limbs of several people who resisted them. Steele eventually received permission to set up more outposts and send men to guard isolated farms and to arm Boer farmers in isolated places with shotguns. A daily roll call was started at the mines, although the camps were still not fenced.

He had now lost most of his troops, who had been sent to patrol the native regions in connection with an uprising in neighbouring Natal. He asked if he could recruit former Boer soldiers to fill the gap; he soon had three hundred of his former enemies under his command. He posted them in a chain of outposts among which he moved constantly, instructing them in the S.A.C. system. They took to the work willingly, intercepting several parties of Chinese.

His insistence that the root of the problem was in the mining camps finally bore fruit in the form of a meeting with the Johannesburg Chamber of Mines at which he and the lieutenant governor of the Transvaal argued the mine owners into erecting enclosed compounds. They also agreed to have one central gate for each and to have policemen on the premises to issue passes to the Chinese.

The new measures brought the results Steele had predicted. Soon the Chinese wanderings had been curbed, and almost every deserter was either on his way back to China or in prison. Steele decided that his work in South Africa was ended. He sent in his resignation and went on a final inspection tour.

At one Boer station the men turned out in their Sunday best. The Boer officer, who had led a commando unit at the siege of Ladysmith, addressed Steele formally. He praised him for his work in reconciling the British and Boers. If all concerned were like Steele, he said, "there would not be an enemy of the King in South Africa." Steele later received the official thanks of the South African government for his "marvellously good work" from the high commissioner, Lord Selbourne, but the tribute from the Boers impressed him more.

He did not return to Canada directly. The Steele family spent the next eight months in England while he worked as acting adjutant general to the inspector general of cavalry for the British Army, his friend Robert Baden-Powell. In this capacity he gathered experience and studied military science in preparation for yet another troubleshooting assignment: to build up the negligible military strength of western Canada for the coming war with Germany. He had no doubt whatever that this cataclysmic event was only a few years away.

28: THE LAST BATTLE

He was like an old war-horse when the guns began to roar in
Europe. That fateful summer of 1914 found him in Winnipeg in
command of Military District Number 10, which stretched from
the eastern boundary of Alberta to the head of the Great Lakes.
In the past few years he had done a prodigious job of
strengthening Canada's militia forces; enlistments in his district
had increased sixfold. Out of a handful of local companies he had
built a small army of three brigades with all the attached units, in-
corporating more than six thousand men. He had trained them as
well as it was possible to train part-time soldiers lacking every kind
of equipment. Now that the time had come for Canada's "citizen
army" to take the field, Steele believed that his place was at its
head.

He was sixty-three years old, but his service record showed his
age at sixty-five because of the two years he had added when he
first enlisted. He had lost little of his legendary stamina; he had
never slowed down. In addition to his work as commanding officer
of a vast military district and of a regular cavalry regiment—the
Lord Strathcona's Horse (Royal Canadians), which he personally
had named—he was involved in a staggering variety of voluntary
activities. At one time or another he had been president of the
Winnipeg Canadian Club, the Canadian South African Veterans'
Association, a branch of the Quebec Battlefields Association, and
the Great Ibex and Slocan Mining Company. He was an adminis-
trator of the vast Strathcona charitable trust and Manitoba commissioner of Baden-Powell's Boy Scouts. He was active in an infor-

mal organization that had arranged for the settlement of thousands of British ex-servicemen in western Canada. He was honorary aide-de-camp to the governor-general. He frequently made after-dinner speeches and attended various regimental and Mounted Police reunions. On top of all this he had written a 428-page book of memoirs, and he kept up a running correspondence with many friends.

Small wonder he felt perfectly fit to lead the Expeditionary Force that Canada was sending to Europe. According to one newspaper his appointment was "more than probable"; it had been said of him that his name was worth a regiment, and it now seemed to be worth an army division at least. He was the best-known and most respected soldier in Canada. He looked like the very man to inspire young Canadians to enlist and to infuse them with high morale when they got to the front.

No lesser a military man than Lord Roberts had inquired whether Steele would be leading the Canadians overseas. But the Canadian minister of militia and defence, Colonel Sam Hughes, replied that Steele was too old for the job—this to Roberts, who had assumed command in South Africa when he was sixty-seven years old. Hughes went on to write that Steele lacked "the faculty of thinking and acting rapidly when the occasion might demand it," which, of course, was utter nonsense because Steele's whole record proclaimed the contrary. It can only be assumed that Hughes, a very strange individual indeed, was taking out some sort of personal grudge against Steele that was occupying his mind at the time.

The minister of militia was erratic to a degree that bordered on insanity. Before long he was heaping praise on Steele for the speed and decision he had shown in mobilizing the western militia forces: more than 5,500 partially trained men from Steele's command were ready to sail with the 1st Canadian Division within seven weeks of the outbreak of war. In December 1914 Hughes promoted Steele to major general, the highest rank then held by a Canadian. With the promotion came the office of inspector general in charge of training all the land forces from the Great Lakes to the Pacific. The appointment was extremely popular in the West, where people looked upon Steele as their own local hero.

He was flooded with congratulatory messages when it was announced.

The plan at the time was for him to continue in his training function for the duration of the war, which was generally expected to be a short one. He went along with the scheme, but he had other plans based on his conviction that "we're in for a long war." He believed that Canada's ultimate contribution to the Allied effort would have to be much greater than the 31,000 men in the 1st Division. His views were confirmed only a few weeks after his western appointment, when the government began to mobilize a second division to go overseas. Hughes then completed his about-face on the subject of Steele's fitness and ability. He asked Steele to take command of the division about to be formed.

Steele jumped at it; this was exactly what he wanted. He was in high spirits as he went about the preliminary planning for the mobilization of 25,000 men. He had recently suffered a bad fall from a skittish horse and broken his left shoulder, but he brushed aside the discomfort. He was reassured by the comments of the doctors who treated him that "I am the strongest they have had in the hospital in years, heart sound and that I took the chloroform like a youngster." The warm public reception of his memoirs, *Forty Years in Canada*, added to his elation. Within a few weeks of its publication early in 1914 the first edition of the book sold at least a thousand copies in Canada and two thousand in England. He was pleased by the complimentary letters it had drawn.

He had no misgivings whatever about his ability to raise and train an army division and to lead it in battle in the greatest war in history. In fact he longed for this as the crowning achievement of his incredible career. A friend observed, "His anxiety to get into active work and be given a command was almost painful to see. He chafed continually at the feeling that he, fit and able, a soldier by breeding, training and experience, was being passed over and not given the opportunity to give that service to his country which he felt competent to give."

Now the prize was in his grasp; only the formalities remained to be taken care of. The Canadian forces overseas came under British command for operational purposes, and Steele was formally an officer in the British Army, so that his appointment would have to be approved by Lord Kitchener, the secretary of state for war. "K" had once worked closely with Steele and had often expressed his high regard for him. Nevertheless the War Office chief was a traditional British general who believed it necessary that a divisional commander be a staff college graduate, a veteran of many campaigns, and if at all possible, an upper-class Englishman. He further believed that Britain was now fighting "a young man's war."

On March 20, 1915, Sam Hughes cabled to Kitchener: "I purpose appointing Major-General Sam Steele to command Second Canadian Overseas Division. He is splendid organizer and disciplinarian. Do you object?" Kitchener's reply came as a surprise: "I am sorry that in the present state of warfare on the continent, it would not be possible to place General Steele in command of a division. Very experienced commanders are necessary in such positions to do justice to the troops under their command."

Hughes had not been impressed with the quality of the generals appointed on Kitchener's say-so to command Canadian troops, and he was seething over the wretched facilities provided by the War Office on Salisbury Plain for the first division. His asperity showed in his response to Kitchener: "Regret your views re Steele. . . . My opinion based on years of experience in war and manoeuvres convinces me that Steele and my brother, Colonel John Hughes, each as qualified as any officer in British service." He went on to suggest that Steele take the division to England and that a commander satisfactory to Kitchener be named later. "I have no objection to General Steele coming here in charge of contingent, if it is clearly understood by General Steele that when the contingent takes the field as a division other arrangements will have to be made," Kitchener replied.

Hughes's temper snapped: "Am somewhat surprised at your 3833 cypher April 1st. Am not in the habit of deceiving and General Steele will certainly know the exact situation. Am not dictating, merely reviewing. I know many of your major generals; some good and capable but many absolutely reverse, far inferior for administration in office or capability in the field to Steele or a dozen other of my officers. Have calmly and loyally remained aloof from interference with Salisbury horror and disintegration of First Canadians, but please do not ask that too much be borne. Claim no authority to manage force in the field but under Army Act Canada has absolute authority in respect to appointments."

It did no good; Steele's cause was lost, at least temporarily. He would raise, organize, and lead the division to England, but he would not be allowed to lead it at the front. It was a disconcerting blow, but not enough to set back a man like Steele. He still had his old-fashioned conception of duty to succour him; he would always do his best in any position he might occupy. Besides, he might yet get his combat command; it had transpired often enough in the past that his fortunes had brightened unexpectedly at the darkest times.

His performance in the next few weeks dispelled any question about his ability to command a large-scale formation. He organized a complete division of 25,000 men with all its valid accoutrements—signals, hospitals and ambulances, kitchens, engineers, and so on. All that was missing was a portion of the artillery because the 1st Division had taken practically all the serviceable guns available in Canada. Steele's new division came from every corner of the second-largest national land mass in the world. Units were sprinkled across the country because of a lack of camp space. He spent night after night in railway sleeping cars moving from one unit headquarters to another. He had the whole amorphous mass ready to go abroad within two months.

Included in it was an enduring Canadian institution that he had helped to found, the French-speaking 22nd Battalion. Early in 1914 he had met with several French-Canadian officers in Montreal to discuss the prospect of forming a unit that would function in French. Steele had always admired the cheerful gallantry of French-Canadians while serving with French-speaking units at the beginning of his army career and in the Northwest rebellion. He believed that they would be more effective if formed into bodies speaking their own language; besides, it was only fair to the men. But there was prejudiced opposition to this scheme in Parliament and the military establishment. Those who wanted the French throughout Canada assimilated into the English-speaking majority were only too glad to see French-speaking soldiers serving in the English-speaking ranks. A delegation of prominent Quebecers took up the cause of the French battalion with the government. The predecessor of today's Van Doos was raised.

Hughes was determined not to repeat the frightful experience of the 1st Division on Salisbury Plain, where the men were ill sheltered and provisioned and usually up to their knees in muddy water. As a result all the Canadians in England were to be concentrated at Shorncliffe in Kent, a somewhat more comfortable, though far from ideal, camp. Steele arrived there in the last week of May 1915; much of his headquarters staff was already on the scene and working. Unlike the 1st Division, which had sailed from Canada en masse, the 2nd came to England in drafts over a period of about a month. Steele rushed them into training one by one as soon as they got to Shorncliffe. The commander of the Canadian Expeditionary Force had suggested that the 2nd Division could train more easily in France than in England, but Steele had rejected this on the grounds that it would delay the outfitting of his division, whose equipment was being carried on ships with various estimated times of arrival. He probably also had an ulterior motive. He had not given up hope of being sent to the front. At a meeting with Kitchener in June it was agreed that Steele would remain in command of the 2nd Division at least until it had completed the first phase of its training, and no successor had yet been named to take over the command.

He came up with an impressive syllabus to prepare his men for the kind of fighting they would have to do in France and Belgium. In his sixties he was still as innovative as ever. He readily perceived that the war in the trenches was making radical new demands on the average soldier. He decreed that no man would be permitted to go to the front until he had achieved a high minimum score on the rifle range and proven himself proficient at rapid fire. He instituted tactical training on the company level with the emphasis on constructing, defending, and attacking trenches. He had lectures on trench warfare given by Canadian and British officers who had served at the front. One of his first acts as divisional commander was to go to France for a week. There he met with the top British commander, General Sir John French, whom he had last seen when their respective commands had converged in South Africa. He visited the frontline trenches, where, he reported, "all the Canadians were glad to see me." As a result of this tour he devised a system whereby his staff officers and battalion commanders would do a short stint in the trenches with 1st Division units. He also arranged to have officers and NCOs sent to courses at the schools being established in England to teach the ghastly new arts of war.

The countryside around Shorncliffe was soon coated with more than five thousand tents housing the Canadians, in addition to hundreds of hutments. The training went forward in fine, clear weather. Steele escalated it steadily from the company to the battalion to the brigade level; by July he had the complete division maneouvring as a coordinated whole. He was always most content when he was busiest, and he was very busy. He spent his evenings moving along the tent lines and barracks, having a brief chat with every soldier he encountered. He was settled in good quarters, and he had a touch of home about him in the person of one of his aides, his eighteen-year-old son Harwood. The youth had just completed a book of verses in the Kiplingesque manner that Steele liked; Harwood's style was "stripped for action," the proud father wrote in a letter home.*

Yet all through these crowded weeks the question preyed on his mind: Would he get a fighting command after all? He and his friends lobbied for it in London and Ottawa. He let it be known that he was not sixty-six, as his service record said he was, but sixty-four. He knew that Hughes and Kitchener were locked in another dispute over who would lead the 2nd Division at the front. The war secretary had offered the Canadian Government the choice of any unemployed general on the British Army active list, but Hughes insisted that the commander be a Canadian. All the Canadian officers who even vaguely qualified for the command were engaged in the actual fighting as brigade commanders with the 1st Division. None of them had Steele's prestige or seniority. He doggedly suggested that it was only logical that he should remain in command of the division when it took the field.

Late in July, however, Kitchener finally put aside his objections to having a non-staff college man in command of a division and agreed to the appointment of R. E. W. Turner, a Canadian Boer War Victoria Cross winner commanding a brigade in France, to

---

* The late Harwood Robert Elmes Steele, to whom the author is indebted for many of the details in this book, went on to win the Military Cross in France and ended the war as a captain. He later became a noted author and historian. He served as a lieutenant colonel in the British Fourteenth Army in India and Burma in the Second World War.

take over the 2nd Division. Steele was notified that Turner would officially succeed him on August 17.

At the time of the transfer Steele was working on a scheme to make the Canadian Corps the most powerful striking force in the Allied armies. This involved adding an extra brigade to each division, bringing them up to five brigades, and forming a strong backstop of well-trained reserve brigades in Great Britain. His recommendation for the five-brigade divisions was never adopted, but his general idea of extraordinary hitting power for the Canadians prevailed throughout the conflict. The strong reserve brigades were created. This was one of the reasons why the Canadian Corps became such a superb fighting machine later in the war.

Steele presented this plan only the day before he handed over command of the 2nd Division to Turner. In the meantime he had kept an appointment with Kitchener at the War Office. "K" spoke soothingly of Steele's unique position as a Canadian who held a senior rank in the British Army and had experience in handling both British and Canadian troops. He offered Steele command of the southeastern district of England. In this capacity he would wear his hat as a British officer, with all the British as well as Canadian troops in the district under his command. During an interview with Sam Hughes, who was then visiting London, an extra responsibility was added. "Please inform Militia Council that Major-General Steele is promoted to command South-Eastern District including all Canadians in England," Hughes cabled to Ottawa.

The phrase "all Canadians in England" became a fountainhead of confusion over the next few months. The trouble was that at least two other officers also believed that *they* were in charge of all Canadians in England—or that they should be. The first of these was Brigadier General John Carson, a mining promoter and militia colonel from Montreal who had come to England early in the war as "Special Representative" of the Department of Militia and Defence. The portly, florid Carson was a close friend of Sam Hughes. Operating out of a suite in the plush Hotel Cecil in London, Carson grandly proclaimed himself "Vice-Minister of the Department of Militia and Defence in the British Isles and at the Seat of War." No such title officially existed. On the announcement of Steele's appointment Carson wrote to him to claim: "My position is that of control as the Minister's direct representative of all our troops in England, whoever they are and wherever they may be."

The other contender was Brigadier General J. C. MacDougall, who was styled "General Officer Commanding Canadian Troops in the United Kingdom." MacDougall had been in this position before Steele arrived. He had since reverted to commanding the Canadian Training Division at Shorncliffe, but his title had not been altered. Title or no title, he clearly came under Steele's command. But MacDougall or his friends spread the story that his original appointment had been confirmed by government order-in-council and could not be changed unless the order was revoked. Steele believed this falsehood. It was only one of the rumours that circulated in the political infighting over the command of Canadians in England. Another, more vicious one was that Steele was incurably ill.

Caught between the claims of Carson and MacDougall, Steele compromised by agreeing to exercise his authority over Canadian divisions in England only by going through the respective divisional commanders. He also agreed that all matters of training should be left up to them. MacDougall was further placated by having his training mandate extended to all Canadians in England, not just to his training division. Everything seemed to be straightened out: Carson would act as Ottawa's representative on policy, MacDougall would look after training, and Steele would be in overall command.

He had plenty to occupy his mind without bothering with day-to-day matters of training. His wife and two daughters had arrived, and the family had moved into a house in Folkestone, near the camp, which became a haven for Canadian soldiers of all ranks. It was characteristic of the general who had once been in the ranks himself to pay close attention to the feelings of private soldiers. He had always placed the highest value on good morale. He stressed that every Canadian in England was a representative of his country and should do nothing to harm its reputation. In this way he achieved a remarkable degree of discipline among men from a strongly individualistic society. A study that he ordered conducted showed that out of 42,000 men in his command, the proportion of drunkenness never went above 7 in 1,000. "That would be equivalent to seven drunken men in a town of 3,500, reckoning on the probable proportion of able-bodied men," he told a reporter, "or, say, sixteen in a town of 10,000. In fact I never saw a soberer lot of men."

He innovated on the human side of war by developing a complex system to ensure that the Canadian Corps would retain its territorial character. He arranged it so that men from the same geographic areas would be trained together in reserve battalions at Shorncliffe and then sent as reinforcements for battalions from their own areas in the front lines. Thus a man from, say, New Brunswick could be reasonably sure that he would be serving with other men from New Brunswick. The close camaraderie engendered by this scheme was one source of the admirable fighting spirit of Canadian troops in that most discouraging of wars.

He visited the front several times in his efforts to make sure that the Canadians under his command would be as well prepared as possible to go into action. He organized a scheme for junior officers to spend short tours in the trenches before leading their own men into the line. Although Canadian casualties in the First World War were shockingly high, they were not so high as in the other armies considering the intensity of the fighting the Canadians encountered as Allied storm troops. For this a good deal of the credit was owed to the careful conditioning they received in England under Steele.

He succeeded in making a go of his invidious relationship with General MacDougall and his training division. One of its officers, Colonel Wilfrid Bovey, wrote: "The division had its own G.O.C. [MacDougall], but as it was in a British Army area, it had a senior and supervisory G.O.C. [Steele]. Glad we were of his uncompromising support."

The devious Carson, however, was not content to let him get on with his work. Carson repeatedly tried to nudge Steele out of command of Canadians in England so that he could take it over himself. One of his gambits was to try to have Steele raised to the status of a grand old man. In November 1915 he recommended to his friend Hughes that the semihonorary position of "Inspector-General of Canadian Forces in the United Kingdom" be created expressly for Steele. He approached the subject of this proposal in ingratiating terms: "You are, and I say it without trying to throw bouquets, a master hand at matters of inspection and the handling of men." To Hughes, on the other hand, he referred to Steele as "a fifth wheel to the coach in any case." As part of the package Steele was offered a knighthood through the good offices of Sir Max Aitken, the future Lord Beaverbrook, who had taken time out from building his publishing empire to act as an advisor to the militia department. A sincere friend and admirer of Steele's, Aitken tried to talk the older man into taking this honour. Steele replied that it would be a more effective policy to knight a Canadian officer serving at the front.

Neither he nor Hughes would go along with Carson's inspector general scheme. Steele pointed out that he was filling this phantom office anyhow; as part of his duties at Shorncliffe he was constantly inspecting Canadian troops. Everyone settled back into position until a new complication arose in December. Up until that time virtually all the Canadians in the United Kingdom, some forty thousand of them, had been stationed at Shorncliffe and therefore automatically came under Steele's authority. But then, with no advance notice from Ottawa, a batch of a thousand Canadians arrived at a camp at Bramshot, outside of Steele's district. He was startled to learn that this draft of men was the nucleus of another Canadian training division beyond the reach of his command.

The new division, however, came under MacDougall's authority because it had been clearly set out that MacDougall was in charge of all training of Canadians in the United Kingdom. It was a ludicrous state of affairs: MacDougall was answerable to Steele in one place, but not in another. Steele remonstrated to Carson as the government representative on the scene, and Carson proceeded to muddy the waters further. He asked the War Office if it would be possible to add that part of the Bramshot command occupied by the Canadians to Steele's command in Shorncliffe. The War Office promptly informed the British general in charge of Bramshot that Steele would be "entirely responsible for the training of Canadians under your command." MacDougall cried foul. *He* was in charge of training. Thereupon Carson contacted the War Office to explain that MacDougall was "in command of all Canadian troops in England, under the supervision, however, of Major-General Steele." Asked to elaborate on this extraordinary arrangement, Carson added that MacDougall was responsible for the training and discipline of all Canadian troops in England. It was Steele's turn to cry foul. If this were the case, he said, he would be unable to exercise any authority whatever over these matters. MacDougall was responsible for training under Steele's general supervision, but he certainly was not responsible for discipline; that was Steele's job.

Carson juggled further with the semantics in a way that left both Steele and MacDougall dissatisfied and the War Office thoroughly bewildered. The rivalry between the Canadian commanders continued, and Carson continued his intrigues. Soon the commander of the Canadian Corps on the Continent complained about the confusion of having to deal with four different generals on broadly similar matters: Steele, Carson, MacDougall, and Lord Brooke, the commander of the new training division at Bramshot. Not only did the militia department communicate indiscriminately with all four generals, but it communicated directly with the War Office as well. The War Office suggested a straightforward solution: that all military matters concerning Canadians in England be channelled through Steele as the senior officer. This sensible plan got nowhere because Carson insisted on acting as a go-between among the Canadian generals, the generals and the militia department, the militia department and the War Office, and so forth. Carson, after all, owed his unique power to the confusion, largely of his own creation, that reigned.

Never a good political game player, Steele played this one apathetically because the position he had to defend had never satisfied him in the first place. He still cherished his ambition to lead a Canadian division at the front. "It became an obsession with him and it made him very unhappy," said his son Harwood. His indifference to the infighting around him was partly responsible for his exclusion from an informal committee formed in March 1916 to take charge of Canadian military matters in Britain. Through this body Hughes proposed bringing in a brigade commander from France, David Watson, to replace Steele in command of the Canadians in England. Watson insisted on disposing of Steele and MacDougall entirely as a condition of this appointment. The plan was abandoned when Sir Max Aitken, as chairman of the council, objected to Watson's terms.

Aitken's committee was dissolved, to be succeeded in September by an "Acting Sub-Militia Council" organized by Hughes in direct defiance of instructions issued by Prime Minister Borden to establish an overseas ministry to handle all military matters. Steele was made a member this time around.

Hughes was now in deep trouble in Ottawa. Borden demanded to know why his instructions to form an overseas ministry had been ignored. It was a naïve question. The ministry would have been headed by the Canadian high commissioner in London, Sir George Perley, and Hughes had no intention of letting Perley run the show overseas. He fought a delaying action. Finally, though, his unstable temper got the better of him. Early in November he wrote a violently worded memo which, in effect, called Borden a liar. Borden reached the end of his amazing patience with Hughes and fired him. Sir George Perley was then appointed minister of overseas forces, with full control over all military matters in the United Kingdom.

Perley's first priority was to untangle the command situation in England. He requested the submilitia council to continue functioning until he had carried out the reorganization of the command. Steele knew that Perley would opt for a new broom in preference to any of the former contenders for the command of Canadians in England. At the council's first meeting with the new minister Steele came up with a plan born of desperation: that he be appointed inspector general, the semihonorary position he had previously turned down.

He played his cards wrong by suggesting at the same time that Carson be appointed deputy minister to Perley. The high commissioner-cum-overseas minister had suffered grievously from Carson going over his head in the past. Perley wanted nothing to do with either Carson or Steele, although he had no cause to resent Steele as he did Carson. He wrote to Borden recommending that Steele be returned to Canada, where he would be "most useful" in recruiting work, particularly in the West.

The axe fell on December 1, 1916, when General Turner, who earlier had replaced Steele in the 2nd Division, was confirmed as general officer commanding Canadian Forces in the British Isles. Steele's Canadian command was terminated, but he was not finished as far as the British War Office was concerned. The commander in chief of home forces, Sir John French, could see no reason why Steele should not remain as general officer commanding the southeastern district of England. French and his colleagues at the War Office retained a high regard for Steele as an efficient leader of men.

The British appreciated him much more than his own compatriots. The Canadian overseas ministry launched a campaign to get him entirely out of the way because he still exercised control over the Canadians in Shorncliffe as part of his British Army command. The new authorities rudely urged him to retire, using his pension rights as a lever. They pointed out that he could not expect a pension as a member of the Canadian Expeditionary Force if he ended his career in the British, as opposed to the Canadian, service. It was a cruel game to play with a man who had given so much of his life to the service of Canada.

Steele hung on with the support of the War Office. The Canadian authorities persisted in treating him shabbily, bypassing him wherever they could. When the King's honours list was drawn up for 1918, the Canadian government recommended the clerk of the Privy Council and the lieutenant governor of British Columbia for knighthoods. It was left to the British Home Forces Command to put Steele's name forward for a knight commandership in the Order of the Bath in recognition of his services. It hurt him that the initiative had not come from his own country. Sir John French had to talk him into accepting the honour. Perhaps Steele did so in the hope that it would help his cause.

The knighthood was hailed with unconscious irony in the Canadian press as "a well-deserved honour to one of Canada's foremost sons," while in the background the Canadian Overseas Ministry was doing all in his power to get rid of him. Faced with the reluctance of the War Office to go along with their plan to have him removed from the Shorncliffe command, the Canadian authorities kept up the pressure. Rather than displease an ally, the British finally gave in.

Steele was placed on the retired list as of July 1, 1918, a day on which Canadians celebrated the fifty-first birthday of the nation Steele had done so much to develop. Thus a career of wholehearted service spanning forty-eight years came to a saddening end.

He could have looked back on the past few years with great gratification had he been in the mood to do so. His former command in western Canada had made an enormous contribution to the Canadian Corps, which was then in the process of forging the Canadian nationality in the crucible of war. After their experiences in the trenches, the men of the northern half of North America would no longer look upon themselves as Nova Scotians or Manitobans or British Columbians; they were all Canadians together. Above all else it was pride in themselves that made the Canadians the most effective fighters on the western front, and Sam Steele had done much to build that pride.

But he was in no mood to salvage comfort from his recent achievements. He was full of bitterness at the way he had been used. It weighed on his mind; his health was affected. The family moved from Folkestone to a quiet private home in the London suburb of Putney, where the magnificently strong man who had so often endured appalling hardships had difficulty in shaking off a cold.

He had never been a man to be kept down for long, however. His spirits soon rallied, and at the age of sixty-seven, he began to make enthusiastic plans for his return to Canada. He had been offered directorships in several Canadian companies, and he saw an active life ahead of him as a semiretired civilian. He wished to return to the West, the scene of his greatest happiness. He wrote to his friend George Hope Johnston in Calgary asking him to look for a house for his family there.

On November 11 the war ended with the German Army reeling back before the Canadian Corps at Mons in Belgium. The Steeles celebrated the event quietly at home, his contribution to the victory forgotten in the nasty imbroglio over the Canadian command in the United Kingdom. There would be no transportation back to Canada for some time for a retired general and his family. All the available space on shipboard would be filled by returning frontline troops.

A Canadian member of Parliament said that Sam Steele died of a broken heart, but that could not be so; his spirit could never have been defeated. Instead, the life of the man who seemed al-

ways to be on the scene of historic events was carried off in yet another historic event: the great influenza epidemic of 1918–19.

"I cannot think of him dying in Putney—Putney, that jerry-
built fabric of so-called civilization where only the river sees the
stars in their nightly course," wrote E. B. Obsorne of the London
Morning Post. "He was one of the conquerers of the western wilderness, and he should have passed away and mingled his valiant
dust with the lost riders of the plains." But die in Putney he did,
in the early hours of January 30, 1919.

Fortunately there were still enough Canadians left awaiting
repatriation in the heart of the Empire to render their splendid
countryman the parting honours he deserved. His funeral procession two days later was like a pageant of his life and times. His
body lay in a coffin covered with the Union Jack, the flag he had
served from the trackless plains of the Old West to the frozen
Klondike to the African jungle to the muddy trenches of
Flanders. It was carried on a gun carriage, bringing back memories
of young Sergeant Steele sharpening up his artillery battery near
the beginning of a career that saw him rise from private to general
officer rank. Behind the clattering carriage came the emissaries of
his greatest devotion, a troop of red-coated Mounted Policemen
from the contingent of the force that had served at the front. And
behind them, in khaki uniforms and flat-brimmed Stetson hats,
rode a troop of Lord Strathcona's Horse, which had won lasting
glory in its desperate charge at Monreuil Wood in 1918 to deflect
the thrust of the last German offensive. Then file upon file of
men from the 2nd Canadian Division marched by, the infantrymen, gunners, signallers, cooks, dentists, and paymasters of the
vast, complex fighting machine that he had built and sent off to
war.

Hundreds of top-hatted and brass-hatted dignitaries were in the
procession, which was only appropriate because Sam Steele had
known so many of the high and mighty and famous from Sitting
Bull to the King of England. There were dukes and earls, cabinet
ministers and generals, but the spirit of Sam Steele seemed to
dwell less with them than with those hard, proud, victorious
young Canadian soldiers as they marched along.

The service was preached by a friend of Steele's from Winnipeg, one of a legion of friends: Major the Reverend C. W. Gor-

don, known to the world by his pen name of Ralph Connor. Gordon, who had used Steele as a model for characters in his best-selling novels of the Canadian frontier, said exactly what the man they had come to mourn would have wanted him to say: "It was denied to him to share the fate of the soldier heros who were fighting in the front line, and this never ceased to be a great grief to him that he was considered too old to take such an active part; but nevertheless he did give his services, and when he died, he died in the service of his country, as much as any soldier in Flanders." It stretched a point, but it was essentially valid. No one had ever served a country more.

Steele had left a request to be buried in Winnipeg, where it all began. His body did not arrive there until almost six months later, in the middle of the Winnipeg general strike of 1919. Riots were raging on Main Street. Several of the Mounted Policemen called in to restore order were badly beaten up. Rescuers dragged them to safety in nearby buildings. One young constable named McQueen was taken unconscious into an undertaking parlour, where he was laid out on a slab in the back room. There beside him, in the still majesty of death, lay the embodiment of all that was great about the Mounted Police—the body of Sam Steele.

The rioting went on into the evening. The strike was still in progress the next morning, when the largest funeral western Canada had ever seen was held. It brought a lull in the violence. Strikers with bare bowed heads lined the streets as Steele's cortege passed by. Mounted Policemen rode behind the riderless black horse with Steele's boots reversed in the stirrups. The strikers who had battled these men in hatred the day before did not so much as raise a voice against them. Even after his death, Sam Steele was on the stage of Canadian history—and fulfilling his destiny of bringing order to a disorderly world.

NOTES ON SOURCES

Much of the foregoing narrative was based on Samuel Benfield Steele's autobiography, *Forty Years in Canada*, first published in 1914. Unfortunately Steele by no means did justice to himself in his own book; his writing is self-effacing, facetious, discursive, and excruciatingly sketchy, and his memory often seems to have played him false. He tends to dwell at length on the injustices suffered by his colleagues in the N.W.M.P. but hides the facts about himself in such important instances as his ill treatment by Commissioner Herchmer and his removal from the Yukon. *Forty Years in Canada* is so maddeningly incomplete, as a matter of fact, that it excites a desire to know more about the man who wrote it; that is what led me into researching and writing this book.

Two other main sources of material have been used: the meticulous reports and records of the N.W.M.P. at the time and John Peter Turner's exhaustive two-volume history, *The North-West Mounted Police, 1873–1893*. In the interest of maintaining the narrative flow the other sources used are cited in the course of the text, rather than annotated, when of sufficient significance. Many of the details herein come from the personal reminiscences and papers of Steele's son, Lieutenant Colonel Harwood E. Steele, himself a historian. Colonel Steele was kind enough to read and comment on most of the manuscript before his death in the summer of 1978.

—R.S.

BIBLIOGRAPHY

Anderson, Frank R.
  The Dead and Dying Ghost Towns of South West Alberta. Alder-
    grove, B.C.: Pioneer Press, 1973.

———.
  The Riel Rebellion, 1885. Aldergrove, B.C.: Pioneer Press, 1977.
Atkin, Ronald.
  *Maintain the Right: The Early History of the North-West Mounted
    Police, 1873–1900.* London: Macmillan London, 1973.
Baden-Powell of Gilwell, Baron.
  Lessons of a Lifetime. New York: Holt, Rinehart & Winston, 1933.
Berton, Pierre.
  Klondike. rev. ed. Toronto: McClelland & Stewart, 1973.

———.
  The Last Spike. Toronto: McClelland & Stewart, 1971.

———.
  The Wild Frontier. Toronto: McClelland & Stewart, 1978.
Black, Martha M. (as told to Elizabeth Bailey Price).
  My Seventy Years. Toronto: Thomas Nelson & Sons, 1938.
Bridle, Augustus.
  Sons of Canada. Toronto: J. M. Dent & Sons, 1916.
Brown, Lorne, and Brown, Caroline.
  An Unauthorized History of the RCMP. Toronto: James Lewis &
    Samuel, 1973.
Cameron, William Bleasdell.
  "The Trailing of Bad-Young-Man," *Scarlet and Gold,* 1943, pp.
    90–95.
Chambers, Ernest J.
  The Royal North-West Mounted Police: A Corps History. Mon-
    treal: Mortimer Press, 1906.
Deane, R. Burton.
  Mounted Police Life in Canada: A Record of Thirty-One Years'

Service. London: Cassell, 1916. Facsimile edition. Toronto: Coles
Publishing, 1973.
Dempsey, Hugh A.
Jerry Potts, Plainsman. Calgary: Glenbow-Alberta Institute, 1966.
Dempsey, Hugh A., ed.
Men in Scarlet. Calgary: Historical Society of Alberta, with McClel-
land and Stewart, 1974.

————.
William Parker, Mounted Policeman. Edmonton: Hurtig Publishers,
1974.
Denny, Sir Cecil E.
The Law Marches West. Toronto: Dent & Sons, 1939.
Donkin, John G.
*Trooper and Redskin in the Far North-West: Recollections of Life
in the North-West Mounted Police, 1884–1888*. London: Samp-
son Low, 1889. Facsimile edition. Toronto: Coles Publishing,
1973.
Douthwaite, L. Charles.
The Royal Canadian Mounted Police. London: Blackie & Son,
1939.
Duguid, A. F.
Official History of the Canadian Forces in the Great War. Ottawa:
King's Printer, 1924.
Evans, R. G.
Murder on the Plains. Aldergrove, B.C.: Pioneer Press, 1968.
Evans, W. Sanford.
The Canadian Contingents and Canadian Imperialism. London:
Unwin Brothers, 1901.
Fetherstonhaugh, R. C.
The Royal Canadian Mounted Police. New York: Garden City Pub-
lishing Co., 1940.
Fort Macleod Historical Association.
Fort Macleod. Lethbridge: Fort Macleod Historical Association,
1958.
Fraser, W. B.
Always a Strathcona. Calgary: Comprint Publishing, 1976.
Fryer, Harold.
"Steele of the North-West Mounted," *B.C. Outdoors*, January-
February, 1975, pp. 12–17.

————.
Stops of Interest in Alberta: Wildrose Country. Aldergrove, B.C.:
Pioneer Press, n.d.
Harvison, Clifford W.
The Horsemen. Toronto: McClelland & Stewart, 1967.
Haydon, A. L.
The Riders of the Plains: A Record of the Royal North-West

Mounted Police of Canada, 1873–1910. Facsimile edition. Edmonton: Hurtig Publishers, 1971.

Hayes, E. A. (as told to L. W. Checkley).
"Steele's Scouts—1885," Calgary *Herald*, 1935.

Hillcourt, William.
Baden-Powell: The Two Lives of a Hero. New York: G. P. Putnam's Sons, 1964.

Hunton, A. Cherry, and Godsell, Phillip H.
The Yukon. Toronto: Ryerson, 1954.

Hogarth, Paul.
Artists on Horseback. Toronto: General Publishing, 1972.

Horrall, S. W.
The Pictorial History of the Royal Canadian Mounted Police. Toronto: McGraw Hill-Ryerson, 1973.

Howard, Cpl. G. S.
"Soapy Smith, Bad Man of Skagway," *Scarlet and Gold*, 1943, pp. 27–40.

Johnston, George Hope.
"Maj-Gen Sam Steele—An Appreciation," Calgary *Herald*, 1919.

Kelly, Nora, and Kelly, William.
The Royal Canadian Mounted Police: A Century of History. Edmonton: Hurtig Publishers, 1973.

Kemp, Vernon A. M.
Scarlet and Stetson: The Royal North-West Mounted Police on the Prairies. Toronto: Ryerson, 1964.

Kruger, Rayne.
Good-Bye Dolly Gray. London: Cassell, 1959.

Longstreth, T. Morris.
In Scarlet and Plain Clothes. Toronto: Macmillan Company of Canada, 1933.

————.
The Silent Force. New York: Century, 1927.

MacBeth, R. G.
The Making of the Canadian West. Toronto: William Briggs, 1898. Facsimile edition. Toronto: Coles Publishing, 1973.

————.
Policing the Plains: Being a Real-life Record of the Famous Royal North-West Mounted Police. London: Hodder, 1921.

————.
The Romance of the Canadian Pacific Railway. Toronto: Ryerson, 1924.

MacEwen, Grant.
Sitting Bull: The Years in Canada. Edmonton: Hurtig Publishers, 1973.

Macleod, R. C.
The North-West Mounted Police and Law Enforcement, 1873–1905. Toronto: University of Toronto Press, 1976.

Marquis, T. G.
   Canada's Sons on the Kopje and Veldt. Toronto: Canada's Sons
      Publishing, 1900.
Mitchell, J. B.
   "Sir Sam Steele, Major-General," *Scarlet and Gold*, 1919, pp.
      23–25.
Morrison, David R.
   The Politics of the Yukon Territory, 1898–1909. Toronto: Univer-
      sity of Toronto Press, 1968.
Morton, Desmond.
   The Last War Drum. Toronto: Hakkert, 1972.
Nicholson, G. W. L.
   The Canadian Expeditionary Force, 1914–1919. Ottawa: Queen's
      Printer, 1962.
Orillia Historical Society.
   A Medonte Pioneer and His Famous Son. Orillia, Ont.: Orillia
      Historical Society, 1954.
Osborne, E. B.
   "A Famous Pioneer," Calgary *Albertan*, 9 April 1919.
Phillips, Alan.
   The Living Legend. Boston: Little, Brown & Company, 1957.
Reed, Christopher.
   "Colonel Sam Steele in the Yukon," *Scarlet and Gold*, 1921.
Reynolds, E. E.
   Baden-Powell: A Biography. London: Oxford University Press, 1943.
Stanley, George F. G.
   The Birth of Western Canada. Toronto: University of Toronto
      Press, 1936.
———.
   Canada's Soldiers: The Military History of an Unmilitary People.
      Toronto: Macmillan & Company of Canada, 1974.
Steele, Harwood.
   Policing the Arctic. Toronto: Ryerson, 1925.
———.
   The Marching Call. Toronto: Thomas Nelson & Sons, 1951.
Steele, S. B.
   Forty Years in Canada. New York: Dodd, Mead & Company, 1915.
Stevenson, Percy C.
   The Yukon Adventure. New York: Yorktown Press, 1932.
Strange, T. B.
   Gunner Jingo's Jubilee. London: Remington, 1893.
Swettenham, John.
   To Seize the Victory. Toronto: Ryerson, 1965.
Times (London).
   Times History of the War in South Africa, 1899–1903. London:
      Low, 1907.

Turner, John Peter.
  The North-West Mounted Police, 1873–1893. Ottawa: King's
  Printer, 1950.
Wallace, W. S.
  The Dictionary of Canadian Biography. Toronto: Macmillan &
  Company of Canada, 1945.
Wilson, Mrs. W. E.
  The Steele Family. Toronto: Ontario Historical Society, 1940.
Wright, J. F. C.
  Saskatchewan: The History of a Province. Toronto: McClelland &
  Stewart, 1955.
Young, Delbert.
  The Mounties. Toronto: Hodder, 1968.

DOCUMENTARY SOURCES

Archives, Lord Strathcona Horse (Royal Canadian) Museum, Calgary.
Clarke, S. J.
    S. J. Clarke and is (sic) trip to the Rocky Mountains, 1876   Glen-
        bow-Alberta Institute, Calgary
Hicks, Joseph.
    Reminiscences of the Riel Rebellion (memoir)   Glenbow-Alberta
        Institute, Calgary
Indian Affairs Department.
    Records   Public Archives of Canada, Ottawa
Lord Strathcona's Horse.
    Papers on formation and official diary by S. B. Steele
    Orders of the day, 1899–1900   Glenbow-Alberta Institute, Calgary
Macleod, James F.
    Papers   Glenbow-Alberta Institute, Calgary
North-West Mounted Police.
    Letters and documents   Glenbow-Alberta Institute, Calgary
    Reports of Commissioners, 1873–1899
    Reports and Records, 1885–1899   Public Archives of Canada, Ot-
        tawa
Rice-Jones, I. E. C.
    A Diary of "Strathcona's Horse"   Lord Strathcona Horse (Royal
        Canadian) Museum, Calgary
Royal Canadian Mounted Police.
    Records and Reports   Public Archives of Canada, Ottawa
Sanders, Gilbert E.
    Papers   Glenbow-Alberta Institute, Calgary
Steele, S. B.
    Papers and letters   Glenbow-Alberta Institute, Calgary
Walsh, James Morrow.
    Papers   Public Archives of Manitoba, Winnipeg
Williams, Milton.

An Account of a Trip with General T. B. Strange's Forces during the Riel Rebellion, 1885 (memoir)   Glenbow-Alberta Institute, Calgary
Wilson, Thomas E.
Correspondence   Glenbow-Alberta Institute, Calgary

Newspapers and Periodicals

Calgary *Albertan*
Calgary *Herald*
The Canadian Magazine
Edmonton *Journal*
Farmer's Weekly Telegraph
RCMP *Quarterly*
Saskatchewan History
Scarlet and Gold
Winnipeg *Free Press*
Winnipeg *News-Telegram*
Yukon Sun

Personal Interviews

Major E. L. McCormick, Toronto, April 1977
Lieutenant Colonel Harwood E. Steele, Pulborough, England, March 1978

INDEX

INDEX

Hughes, Colonel John, 270
Hughes, Sam, 268–70, 273–74, 277, 279
Huot, Inspector, 185
Hutton, Major General Edward, 236–37

Indian Reserves, 105: Blood, 162, 183; Cree, 160; Lower Kootenay, 170; Piegan, 191; Saddle Lake, 149
Indian Treaties: Blackfoot, 52, 55; Carlton-Pitt, 69; Cree, 45, 46
Irvine, Commissioner A. G., 44, 63–64, 90, 92–93, 96, 105, 161–62, 164, 255
Isadore, Chief, 166–68, 171–78

Jarvis, Inspector W. O., 34–42
Johannesburg, 242–43, 245, 265
Johnston, George Hope, 117, 121, 123–24, 128, 154–55, 281
Joseph's Prairie, 166–67, 174–75

Kaffirs, 257–61, 264
Kaministiquia River, 11
Kapla, 171, 166, 168
Kelly, Bulldog, 114, 152–53
Kennedy, Dr., 68, 72, 101–3
Kerr, Constable, 123
Kerr, Jack, 16–17, 249
Kicking Horse Pass, 113
Kingston, 19–20, 23, 162, 165
Kipling, Rudyard, 15, 247
Kitchener, Lord, 247, 252, 256–58, 270, 272–74
Kittson, Dr., 68
Klondike, 197, 199–200, 209, 212, 226
Klondike Gold Rush, 196, 198.

See also Klondike
Klondike Nugget, 231
Knox, Major General Charles, 249
Komatipoort, 241
Kootenay District, 166–68, 170, 172, 176–78
Kootenays (Indian tribe), 166–67, 177–78
Kosi Bay, 241
Kruger, President Paul, 245, 257, 262

Labelle, Tom, 38
Ladysmith, 266
Laggan, 106, 111, 113
Laird, Lieutenant Governor David, 52–53
Lake, Sergeant Major Tom, 60, 168–69
Lake Bennett, 201, 204, 207, 209, 211, 213, 217, 227–28, 231
Lake Lebarge, 204
Lake Lindemann, 201
Lake Louise, 100, 106
Lansdowne Park, 239
La Roche Percée, 34–35
Lataba Hills, 259
Laurier, Sir Wilfrid, 230, 232, 248, 255
Laboma Mountains, 241
Leckie, Lieutenant, 246
Left Hand, 191
Legaré, Jean-Louis, 80
Little Big Horn, 44–45, 48, 51, 74
Little Fisher, 77
Little Isadore, 168
Liverpool, 253
Logan, Sergeant, 246
London, 5, 252, 274, 279
Loon Lake, 143, 146–48, 150, 267